HANDBOOK

OF

MODERN EQUITY

HANDBOOK

OF

MODERN EQUITY

SECOND EDITION

By

WILLIAM Q. DE FUNIAK

PROFESSOR OF LAW, UNIVERSITY OF SAN FRANCISCO

LITTLE, BROWN AND COMPANY
Boston   Toronto

PREFACE TO SECOND EDITION

When I undertook the publication of the original edition of this text, I did so because I believed that there was a place and a need for such a text. However, I did not foresee the flattering and somewhat overwhelming response from all parts of the country. This response not only necessitated three printings of the original edition but it has also imposed burdens on me in publishing and distributing the book which I have neither the time nor the capacity to shoulder. In this situation, I have been most fortunate in being able to turn to the aid of such an experienced publisher as Prentice-Hall, Inc., who will henceforth assume the publication of the book.

One of the advantages of this has been to allow revision of the book, by the addition and citation of new materials and the rearrangement of some of the existing material. But despite the opportunity to improve and add to the book, both the publisher and myself have recognized that the value and usefulness of the book have been its conciseness and simplicity. Accordingly, every effort has been made to retain and continue the former features. The spirit, language and arrangement are still largely the same as formerly. It is our sincere hope that the book will continue to be as useful and helpful as the original edition.

WILLIAM Q. DE FUNIAK

San Francisco, 1956

PREFACE TO FIRST EDITION

This handbook is designed as a concise presentation of the principles and rules of modern equity. The text is based, in the main, on modern cases plus some of the older cases that have stood the test of time. Such cases are the decisive and representative cases in the field and which appear in the standard present-day casebooks on the subject, in the selected case series and in the law reviews. Additional material of value is provided through the comprehensive citation of law review articles, comments and notes, and by citation of annotations and standard text works.

The law student will find the book a valuable accompaniment to his course in Equity as well as a concise means of review of the subject for the bar examination, while the practicing lawyer will find the present-day law of the subject stated with citation of valuable source material.

Although since revised and enlarged, many of the chapters appeared as articles in the law reviews, to whom I express my appreciation for their co-operation. Chapter I appeared in the Tulane Law Review, Chapters II–VIII appeared in the Kentucky Law Journal, and Chapter X in the Virginia Law Review.

I am particularly indebted to Professor Roy Moreland of the University of Kentucky College of Law for his encouragement, to my daughter for preparing the table of cases, and to the University of San Francisco.

WILLIAM QUINBY DE FUNIAK

San Francisco, 1950

TABLE OF CONTENTS

Chapter 1

ORIGIN AND NATURE OF EQUITY

Chapter 2

MEANS OF EQUITABLE RELIEF

Chapter 3

REQUISITES FOR PROTECTION AGAINST TORTS

ⳇChapter 4

PROTECTION AGAINST WASTE AND TRESPASS

ⳇChapter 5

PROTECTION AGAINST NUISANCE

ⳇChapter 6

PROTECTION OF PUBLIC OR SOCIAL WELFARE

Chapter 7

PROTECTION OF BUSINESS AND RIGHTS INCIDENT THERETO

Chapter 8

PROTECTION OF PERSONAL OR INDIVIDUAL RIGHTS

Chapter 9

POSSESSORY RELIEF

Chapter 10

SPECIFIC PERFORMANCE–CONTRACTS ENFORCEABLE

Chapter 11

REQUISITES AND CONDITIONS OF SPECIFIC PERFORMANCE

Chapter 12

THE VENDOR AND PURCHASER RELATIONSHIP

Chapter 13

DEFENSES TO SPECIFIC PERFORMANCE—DAMAGES

Chapter 14

RESCISSION AND REFORMATION

Chapter 15

OTHER EQUITABLE REMEDIES OR FORMS OF RELIEF

HANDBOOK

OF

MODERN EQUITY

CHAPTER 1.

ORIGIN AND NATURE OF EQUITY

Sec. 1. What is Equity?

All writers on the subject of equity seem to start their discussions in agreement that the term is difficult to define.   They then point out that equity in its popular sense signifies natural justice or whatever is right and just as between man and man, adding the cautionary statement that this, of course, is not the legal sense of the term.   They usually unite in offering as the technical or scientific legal meaning the definition that equity is that system of jurisprudence or justice originally administered by the High Court of Chancery of England and now administered in courts of this country which have such chancery jurisdiction, or *equity jurisdiction* as it is now generally called.[1]

To the reader approaching the subject for the first time, such a definition tells him exactly nothing.   He must proceed to learn what the High Court of Chancery was, how and why it came into being, just what this system was that it administered, and so on. I do not mean to imply that the writers who advance the fore-

---

[1] See, *e.g.*, Bispham, *Principles of Equity* (10th Ed.); Lawrence, *Equity Jurisprudence* (1929); Merwin, *Principles of Equity* (1895); Walsh, *Treatise on Equity* (1930); Maitland, *Equity* (2d Ed.) 1.   And see discussion by Glenn & Redden, *Equity: A Visit to the Founding Fathers*, 31 *Va. L. Rev.* 753 (1945).

going definition are unaware of the situation that surrounds it. The definition is, as one writer puts it, suggestive rather than precise and invites inquiry rather than answers it.[2]

I am in no better position than other writers to give a brief definition which will then permit me to embark on a presentation of modern equity, which is the purpose of this book. To understand modern equity and its application requires a knowledge of the origin and development of equity. These latter will be presented hereafter as concisely as possible, to the probable sacrifice of what may constitute scholarliness. In the meantime, the reader will have to be content with the statement, however inadequate, that equity is a system of jurisprudence which originated and developed outside the common law courts of England to supply to suitors remedial relief not obtainable in the common law courts.[3]

Sec. 2.   Jurisprudence in general.

Jurisprudence has been defined as the practical science of giving a wise interpretation to the laws and making a just application of them to all cases as they arise.[4] By "laws" is meant not merely statutory laws but also general customary laws developed from the customs of and common to the whole people or the entire country in domestic affairs, commercial practices, and the like.[5] Since laws are, briefly, rules of conduct for the people in their relation one to another, including a recognition of rights and responsibilities, the "just application" of the laws is the just enforcement of these rules of conduct by enforcing their performance or preventing their breach or by repairing or remedying so far as possible failure of performance or breach which has already occurred.

The arm of the government to which is delegated this duty of just enforcement is the judicial branch, or in other words the

---

[2] See Bispham, *Principles of Equity* (10th Ed.) Sec. 1. See also Maitland, *Equity* (2d Ed.) 1.

[3] See Blackstone's definition that equity exists for the correction of situations wherein the law, by reason of its universality, is deficient. 1 *Bl. Comm.* 62. See also Maitland, *Equity* (2d Ed.); McClintock, *Principles of Equity* (2d Ed.) 1 ff.

[4] Moore, *Cyc. Law Dict.* (3d Ed.).

[5] The term "common law" is used in England and the United States to designate this type of law. See Maitland, *Equity* (2d Ed.) 2.

courts. The courts, then, are to be looked to as the source of jurisprudence, that is for the wise interpretation of the law and a just application of it to all cases as they arise. This should, with reason, include the application of such methods of remedial relief, not repugnant to the good sense of the people, which will effectively accomplish a just application. It was the failure, in this regard, of the courts of law of England which led to the development of another system of courts, the courts of chancery, and the system of jurisprudence which they administered, designed to afford the remedial relief not available in the courts of law.[6]

Sec. 3. Origin of equity jurisprudence.

The courts of law of England, established on a national scale in the time of Henry II,[7] existed at a time when ways of life were patently not of the complexity of modern times and when justice was of a crude sort, from our standpoint.[8] Since all power rested in the king, the power of the courts of law was the power delegated by the king. The right to resort to the courts was obtained by purchasing a so-called writ from the king through the person of his secretary, the Chancellor, whose position originally corresponded more or less to that of the Prime Minister today. The writ so obtained was presented to the court, which then had the duty of hearing the cause so brought before it and granting the appropriate relief. Where a new situation arose upon the facts existent, a new writ was provided, thus allowing for flexibility.[9]

---

[6] Generally, as to origin and development of equity in England, see 1 Holdsworth, *History of English Law* (6th Ed., 1938) 395–476; Walsh, *Treatise on Equity* (1930) Chaps. I and II; Radin, *Handbook of Anglo-American Legal History* (1936) Secs. 232–37; Maitland, *Equity* (2d Ed.) Lectures I and II; Keigwin, "The Origin of Equity," 18 *Geo. L.J.* 15, 92, 215, 299 (1929–30), 19 *Geo. L.J.* 48, 165 (1930–31).

[7] See Walsh, *Treatise on Equity* (1930) Sec. 2.

[8] In this regard, see Pound, "The End of Law as Developed in Legal Rules and Doctrines," 27 *Harv. L. Rev.* 195 (1913).

That the complexities of the present social order bring about conditions unknown when the English courts of equity were established was remarked on in De Garmo v. Goldman, 19 Cal.2d 755, 123 P.2d 1 (1942), in regard to looking to the historical basis of a plaintiff's rights to determine whether they are classifiable as equitable or legal in nature.

[9] See Walsh, *Treatise on Equity* (1930) Sec. 2; Adams, "The Origin of English Equity," 16 *Col. L. Rev.* 87 (1916); Maitland, *Equity* (2d Ed.) 3.

However, it must be borne in mind that personal rights, political rights, civil rights and the like, as we understand them, were not recognized in those days. Property and rights and interests therein were paramount and litigation chiefly revolved around such matters.[10] But to the extent of the subject matter of the litigation, and the comparative simplicities of the questions involved, the relief given was that designed to do justice and frequently involved the prevention of wrong or injury, or the specific enforcement of rights, as well as the award of compensation for wrong or injury already committed.[11]

For reasons which are not always clearly discernible, because the period of change seems to have extended over some 200 years, a hardening process took place in the administration of justice in the courts of law. This is partly traceable to the Provisions of Oxford, in 1258, which expressly forbade the Chancellor to frame new writs to meet new situations, except with the consent of the king and his council.[12] But as England changed from an agricultural to a commercial nation, undoubtedly the complexities thereby brought about introduced new situations involving rights and interferences therewith not previously contemplated and for which no writs and thus no remedial action existed.

Where such situations arose, with no writ or form of action to supply relief, it became common to resort to the king, through the person of the Chancellor, for relief under the king's prerogative of grace, that arbitrary power of the king to do good and dispense justice. Moreover, frequently where a writ lay in the courts of law, it was not possible to obtain justice because of the power and influence of the adverse party who was able to overawe the court. In such instances, direct resort through the Chancellor to the king's prerogative of grace provided the only means of relief.[13]

The result of the foregoing was the gradual development and

---

10 See especially, *infra*, Chapter 8.

11 See Barbour, "Some Aspects of Fifteenth Century Chancery," 31 *Harv. L. Rev.* 834 (1918); Adams, "The Origin of English Equity," 16 *Col. L. Rev.* 87 (1916).

12 See Walsh, *Treatise on Equity* (1930) Sec. 2; Adams, "The Origin of English Equity," 16 *Col. L. Rev.* 87 (1916).

13 As to this royal prerogative, see Adams, *op. cit.*, 87.

establishment of the Chancellor as a judicial officer and of his department, the Chancery, as a court, for the purpose of affording relief which was not obtainable in the courts of law. During this period, also, the courts of law seem to have gradually diminished the relief awarded (except for ejectment of one from land of which he had dispossessed the owner, or a limited recovery of personal property) to pecuniary compensation in the nature of damages. A growing worship of formalism and technicality also began to obsess the courts of law. Even though the Chancellor might, to the extent that the Provisions of Oxford permitted, invent new writs, the conservatism of the courts of law led them to quash writs materially different from those generally used.[14]

The effect of this gradual change, over the years, was to produce the following startling results as to the courts of law and the remedies at common law available in such courts. No suit would lie to prevent an injury to property; the only relief available was money damages for an injury already done. The common law, *i.e.*, as administered by the court of law, could not compel the performance of a duty, whether arising from a contract or imposed by law; the only relief available was money damages for the injury resulting from the failure to perform the duty. In all suits at common law, *i.e.*, in the courts of law, upon written contracts or other written instruments, the instrument had to stand or fall as written. No correction or alteration of any of its terms was permissible, however clear the proof of mistake in writing it. We thus are faced with the startling view of a system of so-called jurisprudence that can interpose only after a wrong has been done and is impotent to stay the hand of the wrongdoer; which is powerless to compel men to perform their obligations and can only give damages for their non-performance; and which cannot take notice of or repair the mistakes and omissions that so frequently arise in business affairs. In short, a system of jurisprudence grossly imperfect and deficient.[15]

As the courts of law gradually decreased the scope of the relief available therein, Chancery, ultimately established as the High Court of Chancery, was more frequently resorted to and developed

---

[14] See Maitland, *Equity* (2d Ed.) 5.
[15] See Merwin, *Principles of Equity* (1895) 17.

forms of preventive or specific relief to meet the new situations presented to it. That this court was attempting to do equity, that is to accomplish justice, has brought about the use of the term equity to designate the system of jurisprudence involved and, certainly in this country, to cause the court possessing such power to be commonly termed a court of equity. This is not to say that such a term as court of chancery is not used at all in this country. This designation is still to be found in jurisdictions where equity is still administered in separate courts. But in those jurisdictions which have merged legal and equitable procedure into one form of civil action in one court possessing both legal and equitable powers, the terms equity court or court of equity will be found in common use. Whereby is really meant the one court while acting in the exercise of its equity powers.

Only in England, and with concomitant results in this country, do we find the peculiarity of two separate systems of jurisprudence, with separate courts and separate systems of procedure, one highly developed to make a just application of the law because of the deficiencies of the other system.[16]

Sec. 4. Equity jurisprudence in the United States.

English law, with its two separate systems of jurisprudence, common law and equity, was brought to this country by the English settlers and constitutes the basis of the law of all of our states except Louisiana, where the civil law prevails.[17] It is quite true that the extent to which the English common law was adopted as the basis or as the rule of decision may vary from state to state, but this does not alter the fact that English law generally is the foundation of our law and legal concepts.[18] It is also quite

---

16 Modification of this result in the United States, see the section following. In England the Judicature Acts of 1873 and 1875 have resulted in merging legal and equitable procedure into one form of action in one court. Those Acts did not have the effect of fusing the substantive law of the two systems but only fused the courts which administered law and equity, as pointed out by 1 Holdsworth, *History of English Law* (3d Ed.) 449.

17 As to Louisiana, see Haas, "Does Equity as it Prevails in Common-Law Jurisdictions Obtain in the Civil Law State of Louisiana?" 62 *Am. L. Rev.* 430 (1928); Morse, "Federal Equity Jurisdiction in Louisiana," 7 *Loyola L. Rev.* 1 (1953).

18 Exception in some states as to law of marital property, see de Funiak, *Principles of Community Property* (1943) Ch. 4.

true that the English equity jurisprudence did not find equal footholds or equal acceptance in the various jurisdictions in this country either during colonial times or during the early period of the republic. Nevertheless, it did either originally or eventually obtain recognition as a necessary concomitant of the common law to supply the gaps in the latter in the way of remedial relief.[19]

Upon the realization, sooner or later, that courts of law administering an English-derived common law could frequently supply no relief or at most an inadequate or incomplete relief, it was recognized as necessary that the other part of the bifurcated system of English jurisprudence be used. Since this required a separate system administered in separate courts, considerable financial strain was placed on many of the young states which could ill afford to maintain two sets of courts. While some states did institute and maintain a double set of courts, others escaped this by having the same judge perform a double function, that is, sit at one time as a court of law and at another time as a court of equity.[20]

Even this was a clumsy and inefficient method of procedure, from the standpoint of American enterprise. Beginning with New York, in 1848, the states began to merge legal and equitable powers in one court with provision for one form of civil action.[21] One form of pleading and procedure was provided, whether the relief

---

[19] As to the origin and early development of equity in the United States, see Walsh, "The Growing Function of Equity in the Development of the Law," *N.Y.U. L. Rev.*, Centennial Number (1936) 137; also set out in Walsh, *Cases on Equity* (1937) 34–42.
"In this State, where we have no Court of Chancery to compel the execution of a trust, or the performance of a contract, from necessity our Courts of Common Law have assumed chancery powers . . ." Peebles v. Reading, 8 S. & R. (Pa.) 484 (1822).

[20] See Walsh, "The Growing Function of Equity in the Development of the Law," *N.Y.U. L. Rev.*, Centennial Number (1936) 137; Chafee & Simpson, *Equity in the United States, Cases on Equity* (2d Ed. 1946) 9; Radin, *Handbook of Anglo-American Legal History* (1936).

[21] This merger exists in all but a few states: Alabama, Arkansas, Delaware, Mississippi and Tennessee. In New Jersey, existence of separate courts of law and equity has been modified by constitutional reorganization of the judicial system. There is provision for one system of courts, although the chief trial court, the Superior Court, has a Chancery Division and a Law Division. See Conover, "New Jersey Reorganizes its Judicial System," 34 *A.B.A. Jour.* 11 (1948). Effect of merger of law and equity upon procedural aspects of trial by jury in New Jersey, see 6 *Intra. L. Rev.* (N.Y.U.) 64. Merger in the federal courts was instituted on Sept. 1, 1938, by the Federal Rules of Civil Procedure.

sought be legal or equitable in nature. Such pleading and procedure was taken over almost entirely from equity since that system was more flexible and fair and not given to the technicalities and formalism that bound the pleading and procedure at common law.

But it must be kept in mind that this does not merge common law and equity into one homogeneous system of jurisprudence. The respective substantive rules of the two systems still remain, as do the respective types of relief given under each system. What is merged is the procedural sides of the two systems, with the two systems enforceable in one action in one court as two co-ordinated branches of the whole law of the state.[22] One result of this is that with the development of codal or statutory law and the development of statutory remedies, the statutory law and statutory remedies on any subject must be classified as legal or equitable to determine under which of the co-ordinate branches the subject falls.[23]

The bar in the way of complete merger of law and equity into one homogeneous system is the fact that the federal and state constitutions have made provision for the continuance of the two systems. Tremendous difficulty results from the constitutional continuance of the right of trial by jury in all cases where it had previously existed, which was, of course, in the courts of law. In courts of chancery or equity, trial was by the judge without a jury. Right of trial by jury, in any homogeneous system of jurisprudence, would have to be given in all cases or abandoned in all cases or else the necessity would still exist of distinguishing between the nature of actions and the type of relief sought, to determine whether or not the action was in fact one originally at law in which a trial by jury is assured.[24]

---

[22] See Walsh, *Treatise on Equity* (1930) 37, 38; Rose, "Equitable defenses to actions at law," 34 *Ore. L. Rev.* 55 (1954).

In the federal courts, the Federal Rules of Civil Procedure have not obliterated the historic differences between law and equity except procedurally. See Ettelson v. Metropolitan Life Ins. Co., 317 U.S. 188, 63 S.Ct. 163, 87 L. Ed. 176 (1943).

[23] See Philpott v. Superior Court, 1 Cal.2d 512, 36 P.2d 635, 95 A.L.R. 990 (1934).

[24] See Reubens v. Joel, 13 N.Y. 488 (1856). And see Clark, "The Union of Law and Equity, 25 *Col. L. Rev.* 1 (1925); and note, "Effect of Merger of Law and Equity on Right of Jury Trial in Federal Courts," 36 *Geo. L.J.* 666 (1948).

That law and equity are still effectively unmerged in New York, see comment, 55 *Yale L.J.* 826 (1946).

Even in states, such as California, which have never had separate courts of law and equity and in which there has always been a merger of law and equity in one form of civil action in one court, the substantive distinction between the two systems continues to exist. The California Supreme Court has expressed regret that the state constitution places jurisdiction upon such a theoretical basis as a differentiation between law and equity, remarking that with the growth of statutory remedies it becomes difficult to define and to distinguish between actions at law and proceedings in equity. The doctrine, it continues, that when classification is necessary a court should look to the historical basis of the plaintiff's rights under the English law in the light of such modifications as have taken place in this country is not always an accurate one, in view of the complexities of the present social order which bring about conditions unknown when the English courts of equity were established.[25] In such a situation, in determining what remedy to grant, whether legal or equitable, it has been said that the court must be controlled by the pleadings and evidence, independent of any technical considerations formerly applicable.[26]

Sec. 5. Requisites of equity jurisdiction.

One of the difficulties brought about by the state of affairs already described is that chancery or equity, in order not to infringe upon or interfere with the established courts of law, has always refused to take jurisdiction of a cause and award relief except upon a showing that there is no remedy or no adequate remedy at law. By adequate remedy at law is meant one which is as speedy, efficient, and complete as that which equity can afford, or in other words, as practical and efficient to the ends of justice

---

See Merwin, *Principles of Equity* (1895) 8, that "the standard to which we are to refer is the jurisdiction of the English court of chancery as it existed at the time when our Constituion was adopted. If the subject was then within the jurisdiction of a court of chancery, the right of trial by jury does not now exist in regard to it. But where the equity jurisdiction has, since that time, been created by statute in this country, as regards such cases the right of trial by jury still obtains. [Mississippi Mills v. Cohn, 150 U.S. 202.] This was decided in Massachusetts in the recent case of Powers v. Raymond [137 Mass. 483]."

[25] De Garmo v. Goldman, 19 Cal.2d 755, 123 P.2d 1 (1942).

[26] McKenzie v. Crook, 110 Colo. 29, 129 P.2d 906 (1942).

and its prompt administration as the remedy in equity.[27]   Thus, equity is generally reluctant to grant a mere recovery of money since available remedies at law are usually sufficient for that. However, if the remedy at law is not certain, complete, and sufficient, as where an accounting is necessary to determine the amount due or a constructive trust or equitable lien must be sought to bring about pecuniary relief, the case may be one peculiarly within the jurisdiction of equity.[28]

The foregoing, then, is one of the two chief prerequisites for equity jurisdiction.   The other, resulting from the condition of affairs at the time equity originated and developed, is that some property right, element, or interest must be involved.[29]   The rule is usually stated that equity protects only property rights or rights of substance in the nature of property rights and does not protect personal or individual rights.   But as we shall see subsequently, there have begun to be departures from this second prerequisite to equity taking jurisdiction.[30]

Both of these matters are considered more at length in the chapters following.

---

[27] Boyce v. Grundy, 3 Pet. (U.S.) 210, 7 L. Ed. 655 (1830). See also *infra*, Sec. 18.

[28] See, *e.g.*, Filson v. Fountain, 171 F.2d 999 (1948).

[29] For the importance of property rights in a period of development of equity, see Sec. 3 *supra* and Chapter 8 *infra*.

[30] See Chapters 6 and 8. See note, "Requirement of a 'Property Right' as Basis for Equitable Jurisdiction," 20 *Rocky Mt. Law Rev.* 304 (1948).

CHAPTER 2.

MEANS OF EQUITABLE RELIEF

Sec. 6.   Equity acts upon the person.

It has always been an important characteristic of equity juris-prudence that "equity acts upon the person" or, in the Latin phrase, in personam. It deals with the individual by acting upon his conscience and compelling him to do his duty in the specific case.[1] In other words, where equity has jurisdiction over the person of the defendant, i.e., where he has been properly served with process so as to subject him to the authority, power and control of the court, the court lays its command upon him personally and thus brings about the relief sought by the plaintiff.[2] The failure or refusal of the defendant to obey this command or order laid personally upon him constitutes a contempt of the court and

---

[1] See Maitland, *Equity* (2d Ed.); Merwin, *Principles of Equity* (1895); Langdell, *Summary of Equity Pleading* (2d Ed.) 35 ff.

[2] Practicability of enforcement of command, see *infra*, Sec. 14.

11

the court may resort to the contempt process to compel performance of its command or order.[3]

In this respect the decree or order in equity is radically different from the judgment or order in an action at law. In the action at law, there is no personal command laid upon the defendant and if he does not obey the judgment it is enforced by execution in rem through the aid of the sheriff. Where the action at law is in ejectment or in the nature of ejectment, the sheriff puts the plaintiff in possession of the land; where the action at law is one for damages, the sheriff levies on and sells property of the defendant to pay the damages.[4]

However, the principle that equity acts upon the person should not be allowed to confuse the reader into thinking that this is a limitation upon equity's power and that equity cannot act in rem, that is, directly upon the res or subject matter of the suit. It is true that during the early days of equity, enforcement was accomplished by compulsion or coercion over the person of the party, but at the present time there is ability to act in personam or in rem.[5] While there has been dispute over whether equity has inherent power to act other than in personam,[6] the dispute has actually become academic or moot. Either recognition of an inherent power to act in rem exists or statutory authorization provides the power.[7] It will be noticed that in the so-called code state, where law and equity powers are merged in the same court, methods of enforcing judgments at law are usually available to the court to enforce its decrees of an equitable nature, if such in rem methods of enforcement are deemed appropriate.[8] Actually, it is probable that equitable means and aids will usually be more effec-

---

[3] See *infra*, Sec. 9.

[4] See Walsh, *Treatise on Equity* (1930) Sec. 9.

[5] See Lawrence, *Equity Jurisprudence* (1929) Ch. 6; Walsh, *Treatise on Equity* (1930) 45–50.

[6] Strong exponents of view that equity has only inherent power to act in personam, see Langdell, *Summary of Equity Pleading* (2d Ed.) 35 ff.; Glenn & Redden, *Cases on Equity* (2d Ed.) Ch. 2. Contra, see, *e.g.*, Lawrence and Walsh, *supra*, note 5. And see *infra*, Sec. 7.

[7] See discussion, Garfein v. McInnis, 248 N.Y. 261, 162 N.E. 73 (1938); also Lawrence and Walsh, *supra*, note 5.

[8] Enforcement of order or reimbursement by execution or by contempt proceedings provided cumulative and not mutually exclusive remedies for enforcement, see Ex parte Carboni, 46 Cal. App.2d 605, 116 P.2d 453 (1941).

tive and hence, in personam methods of enforcement will occur more frequently.

Sec. 7. Power in rem in contract and property cases.

It frequently happens in this country that the plaintiff and the res are within the court's jurisdiction but the defendant is not. In deciding rights of the plaintiff in the res and awarding him such rights, the court is in effect acting on the res or, in the Latin phrase, in rem. It is not acting on the person of the defendant since he is beyond the court's jurisdiction. It has been argued by some writers and considered by some courts that equity courts have inherent power so to act in rem.[9] Other writers and other courts insist with equal vigor that equity courts have no inherent power to act other than by acting upon the person and through such means controlling or affecting the res.[10] In most states, the matter is settled by virtue of statutes which authorize service by publication upon the absent defendant and action by the court upon the res.[11] However it is brought about, it is clear that nowadays in this country, equity frequently acts in rem as well as in personam.[12]

Because of our ever-present state boundary lines, it frequently happens that property which is the subject matter of the dispute

---

[9] See Walsh, *Treatise on Equity* (1930) 45–50, where it is pointed out that in Nevada and South Carolina, the courts have acted in rem without the aid of any statute. It also seems clear that the California Supreme Court, at a time prior to the existence of any statute authorizing it, considered that the court, in the exercise of its equity powers, could act in rem. See Rourke v. McLaughlin, 38 Cal. 196 (1869).

[10] See Glenn and Redden, "Equity: A Visit to the Founding Fathers," 31 *Va. L. Rev.* 753 (1945); Atlantic Seaboard Natural Gas Co. v. Whitten, 315 Pa. 529, 173 A. 305, 93 A.L.R. 615 (in effect overruled in Alpern v. Coe, 352 Pa. 208, 42 A.2d 542 [1945]).

[11] Garfein v. McInnis, 248 N.Y. 261, 162 N.E. 73 (1928); Bush v. Aldrich, 110 S.C. 491, 96 S.E. 922 (1918).

According to the United States Supreme Court, no power resides in an equity court to quiet title to property within its jurisdiction by acting in rem, unless the state statute expressly authorizes it to act in rem. Hart v. Sansom, 110 U.S. 151, 28 L. Ed. 101, 3 S.Ct. 586 (1884); Arndt v. Griggs, 134 U.S. 316, 10 S.Ct. 557 (1890). Contra, see Tenant's Heirs v. Fretts, 67 W.Va. 569, 68 S.E. 387 (1910).

[12] Consider Stevens v. Television, Inc., 111 N.J. Eq. 306, 162 A. 248 (1932).

Discussion of proceedings in rem, both at law and in equity, see Fraser, "Actions in Rem," 34 *Cornell L.Q.* 20 (1948).

Specific performance decree against vendor on constructive service, see comment, 32 *Cornell L.Q.* 103 (1946).

between the parties is outside the court's jurisdiction but the parties are within the court's jurisdiction. Some courts will not assume jurisdiction of such a case on the ground that the result of its decision may be to affect title to land outside of the jurisdiction of the court, and so not within its power to act.[13] Other courts refuse, not so much on the ground of lack of jurisdiction to act, but on the ground of not being the most convenient forum[14] or on the ground of impracticability of enforcement of its decree.[15] However, the majority of courts consider that so long as the parties are within its jurisdiction, the court may decide the equities between them and order the defendant to do some act with regard to the property.[16] In so far as the parties are concerned, the court is acting in personam. The difficulty comes about as to whether the court can actually affect the res through its control over the person of the defendant. If the defendant complies with the court's command, although such compliance may affect the title to property in another jurisdiction, courts of the latter jurisdiction uniformly give effect to this act as that of the defendant, despite the fact that it was done under coercion, so to speak.[17] But if the defendant fails to comply with the command, and the court by virtue of its decree or by act of one of its officers attempts to make some disposition of property interests in another jurisdiction, courts of the latter jurisdiction do not give effect to such attempt, as being in excess of or without jurisdiction.[18] But since the first court had jurisdiction of the persons of the parties and jurisdiction to decide the equities between them, the latter courts will accept the decree as record evidence of the equities of the parties

---

[13] See, West Point Min. & Mfr. Co. v. Allen, 143 Ala. 547, 39 So. —, 111 Am.St.Rep. 60, 5 Ann.Cas. 332 (1905).

[14] See Beal, "Equitable Interests in Foreign Property," 20 *Harv. L. Rev.* 382 (1907); Messner, "Jurisdiction of Court of Equity," 14 *Minn. L. Rev.* 494, 506 (1930).

[15] Practicability or impracticability of enforcement, see *infra*, Sec. 14.

[16] For discussion, see Messner, "Jurisdiction of Court of Equity over Persons to Compel Doing of Acts Outside Territorial Limits of State," 14 *Minn. L. Rev.* 494 (1930). Illustration of commands laid upon resident defendant, see Farnsworth v. Hubbard, 78 Ariz. 160, 277 P.2d 252 (1954).

[17] Deschenes v. Tallman, 248 N.Y. 33, 161 N.E. 321 (1928), noted in 27 *Mich. L. Rev.* 207.

[18] Bullock v. Bullock, 52 N.J. Eq. 561, 30 A. 676 (1894).

and will usually give it effect as a matter of comity, at least where breach of contract or trust or acts of fraud are concerned.[19]

Sec. 8. Injunctions.

Where equity prevents a threatened wrong or injury or proceeds to repair an injury, it accomplishes this by the writ of injunction.[20] Injunction is an order or process issuing from the court addressed to the defendant and commanding the defendant to abstain from doing, or commanding him to perform, a certain act. It may be, therefore, either preventive or remedial in its operation and, consequently, injunctions are divided into two great classes, prohibitory injunctions and mandatory injunctions.[21] Prohibitory injunctions are those requiring the defendant to abstain from doing a certain act or from pursuing a certain line of conduct. These constitute by far the larger part of injunctions granted by courts of equity. Mandatory injunctions are those which require the defendant to do some act.[22]

In this latter respect, mention may be made of suits for specific performance of contracts. While it seems customary to speak of "injunctions" in connection with suits to restrain torts and "orders of specific performance" in connection with suits for specific performance of contracts, it is obvious that the order to perform, in the latter type of case, is an injunction in mandatory form laid upon the person of the defendant.[23] But where the contract contains an agreement or covenant not to perform a cer-

---

[19] Redwood Inv. Co. v. Exley, 64 Cal. App. 455, 221 P. 973 (1923). See Bentley, "Equitable Decrees in Sister States," 8 *So.Cal. L. Rev.* 1 (1934).

Decision on rights and equities of parties considered conclusive, see Burnley v. Stevenson, 24 Ohio St. 474 (1873).

[20] Acknowledgement is made to Merwin, *Principles of Equity* (1895) 424–428, for much of the following discussion in this section.

[21] Statutes frequently define and make provisions for injunctions, at some length. However, the use of injunctions is inherent in equity jurisdiction and any court upon which general equity jurisdiction has been conferred has full power to issue injunctions. Certainly, where full equity jurisdiction is conferred by constitutional provision, no legislative act could limit the court with respect to this inherent power. Consider In re Shortridge, 99 Cal. 526, 34 P. 227, 21 L.R.A. 755, 37 Am.St.Rep. 78 (1893).

[22] Discussion, see Klein, "Mandatory Injunctions," 12 *Harv. L. Rev.* 95 (1898).

[23] Suits for specific performance of contracts, see *infra*, Chapter 10. See also *supra*, Sec. 7, in regard to power in rem in contract cases.

tain act, the term "injunction" is commonly used in connection
with the decree or order of the court which indirectly compels
performance of the contract by enjoining the defendant from
breaching this negative agreement or covenant. Here, the injunction, of course, is prohibitory in form.[24]

Injunctions are also subject to division pursuant to another
plan of classification. One kind is the preliminary or interlocutory injunction, the other is the final, permanent, or perpetual
injunction. This division has reference simply to the stage of the
case when the injunction is issued and to its duration, not to its
character otherwise.[25]

Injunctions are frequently issued upon the filing of the suit or
soon after, and before the case has been heard and decided upon the
merits. Such injunctions are the preliminary or interlocutory injunctions. They continue only until further order of the court.
They are always within the control and discretion of the court
and may, upon proper motion and proper cause shown at any
time during the progress of the cause, be modified or dissolved. If
the final decision upon the merits is in favor of the defendant,
then as a matter of course such injunctions are dissolved. If the
final decision on the merits is in favor of the plaintiff, then such
injunctions are usually made final or permanent.[26]

A strong prima facie case should be shown to justify interposition of the court by an injunction before the rights of the parties
have been determined by a full trial. The justice of the preliminary or interlocutory injunction lies in keeping everything
in statu quo until those rights can be determined. Where the act,
condition, or situation complained against by the plaintiff may
cause great damage if not halted or suspended pending the trial

---

[24] Negative contracts or covenants, see *infra*, Sec. 78.

[25] See *Rest. Torts*, Sec. 936, comment d.

[26] An outstanding illustration of the use of the interlocutory injunction appears
in United States v. United Mine Workers, 330 U.S. 258, 67 S.Ct. 677, 91 L. Ed.
554 (1947), commented on by Professor Simpson, "Equity," *1947 Annual Survey
of American Law.* The United States District Court was held to have the power
to issue a restraining order to preserve existing conditions pending a decision upon
its own jurisdiction. Injunctions erroneously entered or entered without jurisdiction, see *infra*, Sec. 9.

Temporary restraining order distinguished from interlocutory injunction, see
Wetzstein v. Boston, etc., Min. Co., 25 Mont. 135, 63 P. 1043 (1901).

on the merits, a final decision on the merits in the plaintiff's favor will be of little or doubtful value.[27] It may also be noticed that, although a conflict of opinion has existed, interlocutory injunctions which are mandatory in nature have been sustained, in order to restore the status quo.[28]

Final or permanent or perpetual injunctions are those which are ordered after a final hearing of the case upon its merits, when the decision is in favor of the plaintiff. Such an injunction constitutes a part of the final decree or judgment.[29] With the usual decree or judgment, unless the court reserves some right or power to modify it or set it aside, it passes from the control of the court and can be modified or set aside only upon a rehearing or review of the case. But a final injunction embodied within a decree or judgment presents a different situation. It is uniformly recognized that the court may dissolve or modify the final or permanent injunction where changes in circumstances or conditions warrant it.[30] Frequently, the injunctive decree provides an opportunity for the defendant to remove the cause of injury and its permanence may depend upon whether or not he accomplishes such removal.[31]

Sec. 9. Enforcement of injunction—Contempt.

As has been stated previously,[32] equity in accomplishing its purposes and affording relief to the complainant, ordinarily acts upon the person of the defendant. It lays its command upon the

---

[27] See, especially, Harriman v. Northern Securities Co., 132 F. 464, 475 (1904).
Effect on right to obtain preliminary injunction of long delay in seeking equitable relief, see Benton v. Kernan, 126 N.J. Eq. 343, 8 A.2d 719 (1939).
Contents of decree granting temporary injunction, see, e.g., Local 309, etc., C. I. O. v. Gates, 75 F. Supp. 620 (1948).
[28] See Keys v. Alligood, 178 N.C. 16, 100 S.E. 113 (1919).
Mandatory injunction prior to hearing of case, see annotation, 15 A.L.R.2d 213.
[29] Necessity of definiteness of terms of injunction, see Collins v. Wayne Iron Works, 227 Pa. 326, 76 A. 24, 19 Ann. Cas. 991 (1910).
[30] Santa Rita Oil Co. v. State Board of Equalization, 112 Mont. 359, 116 P.2d 1012, 136 A.L.R. 757 (1941); Ladner v. Siegel, 298 Pa. 487, 148 A. 699, 68 A.L.R. 1172 (1930).
See annotations, Power to modify permanent injunction, 68 A.L.R. 1180, 136 A.L.R. 765.
The situation is the same in the federal courts. See 13 Cyc. Fed. Proc. (2d Ed.) Sec. 6597.
[31] See, e.g., Payne v. Johnson, 20 Wash.2d 24, 145 P.2d 552 (1944).
[32] See supra, Sec. 6.

defendant personally to desist or to act.[33]   The injunction represents the formal expression of this demand and defines the extent or limits of what the defendant must or must not do.[34]   If the defendant fails or refuses to obey the injunctive order or process of the court, he is in contempt of court.[35]   The court may proceed against him to punish him for such contempt.   However, difficulty arises as to one not named in the injunction but who proceeds contrary to the command there laid down.   While one view proceeds on the basis that one who knows of the injunction is bound by its terms, the weight of authority is said to be clearly in favor of the view that a person not a party to an injunction suit may not be held guilty of contempt for violating the injunction unless he is shown to be identified with or is an aider or abetter of a party originally enjoined.[36]

Even though the restraining order or injunction is entered by the court erroneously or irregularly it must be obeyed until it is withdrawn or dissolved and the failure to obey is no less contempt because the order or injunction is subsequently found to have been irregularly or erroneously entered.   However, if the court has no jurisdiction over the subject matter involved or if it has exceeded its jurisdiction in granting an injunction in a matter beyond its jurisdiction, the injunction is absolutely void and there can be no contempt for its alleged violation.[37]   In this latter regard, it is interesting to notice that the United States Supreme Court has held that the United States District Court had power to issue a restraining order to preserve existing conditions pending a decision upon its own jurisdiction.[38]

---

[33] It is customary to direct the injunction not only to the person of the defendant but also to his agents, employees, assignees, etc.   Berger v. Superior Court, 175 Cal. 719, 167 P. 143, 15 A.L.R. 373 (1918).   See also Federal Rules of Civil Procedure, Rule 65 (d).

[34] Necessity of definiteness of terms of injunction, see Collins v. Wayne Iron Works, 227 Pa. 326, 76 A. 24, 19 Ann. Cas. 991 (1910).

[35] Sufficiency of notice or knowledge of order, see Cape May & S.L.R. Co. v. Johnson, 35 N.J. Eq. 422 (1882).

[36] Swetland v. Curry, 188 F.2d 841 (1951), disapproving view that court can bind world at large by its injunction or that one who merely knows of the decree is thereby bound by its terms.

[37] Ex parte Warfield, 40 Tex. Cr. Rep. 413, 50 S.W. 933, 76 Am.St.Rep. 724 (1899).   And see discussion by Cox, "The Void Order and the Duty to Obey," 16 U. Chi. L. Rev. 86 (1948).

[38] United States v. United Mine Workers, 330 U.S. 258, 67 S.Ct. 677, 91 L. Ed.

The contempt is that which is designated as civil contempt, as distinguished from criminal contempt.[39] While the proceeding to punish for civil contempt may involve some idea of retribution for defying the court and setting at naught the judicial processes of orderly government, its primary purpose is to compel the defendant to obey the order or decree of the court and thus obtain for the plaintiff the relief to which the court has adjudged him entitled.[40] Accordingly, it is not usually a separate proceeding but is merely part of the case in which it arose.[41]

The punishment imposed for contempt may be either by fine [42] or imprisonment [43] or both.[44] The defendant can remove himself from further contempt of court by obeying the court's order. In fact, the court may give him this opportunity to repent before passing sentence of fine or imprisonment.[45] It may be mentioned, incidentally, that the defendant can purge himself of contempt by showing that it is impossible for him to carry out the order, where this inability has not resulted from his own fault and where his conduct has not been wilful or contumacious.[46]

It is incumbent upon the plaintiff to call to the court's attention the fact that the defendant has failed or refused to obey, where-

---

884 (1947), commented on by Professor Simpson, "Equity," 1947 Annual Survey of American Law.

[39] Discussion of civil and criminal contempt, see Parker v. United States, 153 F.2d 66, 163 A.L.R. 379 (1946); In re Nevitt, 117 F. 448, 458 (1902).

[40] "Civil as distinguished from criminal contempt is a sanction to enforce compliance with an order of the court or to compensate for losses or damages sustained by reason of noncompliance. . . . Since the purpose is remedial, it matters not with what intent the defendant did the prohibited act." McComb v. Jacksonville Paper Co., 336 U.S. 187, 69 S.Ct. 497 (1949).

[41] No right of trial by jury, see Walton Lunch Co. v. Kearney, 236 Mass. 310, 128 N.E. 429 (1920).

[42] Fine as for benefit of injured plaintiff, see Montgomery, "Fines for Contempt as Indemnity to Party to Action," 16 Minn. L. Rev. 791 (1932).
Proof of damages by plaintiff to enable court to determine amount of fine, see Root v. MacDonald, 260 Mass. 344, 157 N.E. 684, 54 A.L.R. 1422 (1927).

[43] Legislation limiting extent of imprisonment for contempt conformed with by court as furnishing useful yardstick, and so long as such legislation does not infringe upon constitutional power of courts to punish by contempt. In re Shortridge, 99 Cal. 526, 34 P. 227, 21 L.R.A. 755, 37 Am.St.Rep. 78 (1893). See also Nelles, "The Summary Power to Punish for Contempt," 31 Col. L. Rev. 956 (1931).

[44] Violation of injunction and punishment therefor in federal courts, see Cyc. Fed. Proc. (3d Ed.) Chaps. 73, 87.

[45] Keys v. Alligood, 178 N.C. 16, 100 S.E. 113 (1919).

[46] Andrews v. McMahan, 43 N.M. 87, 85 P.2d 743, 120 A.L.R. 697 (1938), and annotation at p. 703.

upon notice or process is served upon him as in other legal proceedings. If he is not so served, there is no jurisdiction in the
court to proceed against him for contempt.[47] Is it possible, then,
for the defendant to escape carrying out the court's command
and the punishment therefor, by removing himself from the court's
jurisdiction so as not to be reached by service of such notice or
process? If he is a nonresident of the state, he may successfully
accomplish this design, if one discounts the practical aspects which
may involve the necessity of leaving business or property interests
unattended. These practical aspects are even more apparent in
the case of a foreign corporation doing business in the state. But
if he is a domiciliary of the state, by the usual conflict of laws rule,
he may be served with notice or process by publication or the like,
since a domiciliary, even though temporarily absent from the state,
remains subject to the jurisdiction of the courts of his state.[48]
Contempt proceedings could accordingly be instituted and an
adjudication of guilt be entered and fine imposed which could be
enforced by seizure of property of the domiciliary in the state.[49]

Sec. 10. —Means generally other than contempt.

In addition to the contempt process, already referred to, the
equity courts developed and still frequently use other aids or means
of making effective their commands and decrees. The appointment and use of officers has been common, to supervise and check
on the conduct and obedience of the parties on whom commands
have been laid or to take charge of and preserve property, and
the like.[50] The better known of these officers are probably the

---

[47] See Parker v. United States, 153 F.2d 66, 163 A.L.R. 379 (1946).

[48] While domicile serves as a basis for jurisdiction so that personal service within
the state may be dispensed with, the substitute that is most likely to reach the
defendant is required in order to accomplish substantial justice. McDonald v.
Mabee, 243 U.S. 90, 37 S.Ct. 343, 61 L. Ed. 608, L.R.A. 1917 F. 458 (1917).

[49] Blackmer v. United States, 284 U.S. 421, 52 S.Ct. 252, 76 L. Ed. 375 (1932),
where District of Columbia court issued order to show cause why United States
citizen then in France should not be adjudged guilty of contempt in refusing to
obey subpoena of the court and there was held to be suitable notice of such order
and adequate opportunity to appear and be heard. The imposition of a fine to be
satisfied by seizure and sale of his property was valid and proper.

[50] See, e.g., Amey v. Colebrook Guaranty Sav. Bank, 92 F.2d 62 (1937) (supervision and gathering of information in another state); Madden v. Rosseter, 114
Misc. Rep. 416, 187 N.Y.S. 462 (1921), aff'd 196 App. Div. 891, 187 N.Y.S. 943,
also 117 Misc. 244, 192 N.Y.S. 113 (obtaining possession of property in another

masters in chancery,[51] and the receivers,[52] and the trustees as well.

Likewise, the equity courts, or courts in the exercise of equitable powers, have developed and used so-called writs, such as the writ of assistance,[53] the writ of ne exeat,[54] the writ of sequestration,[55] most of which enlist the services of the sheriff. Frequently, these aids may amount to in rem enforcement of the court's orders.[56]

Some of the matters mentioned are dealt with at more length in the sections following, but any greatly detailed treatment is not possible in a work of this length.

Sec. 11. —Ne exeat or statutory equivalent.

One of the means, although of perhaps limited application, in aid of the jurisdiction in equity and to secure the giving of relief has been the so-called writ of ne exeat (in the Latin—"that he depart not").[57] Such a writ might be issued upon the commencement of the suit for equitable relief, during the pendency of the suit, or upon issuance of the final decree to secure its enforcement. But such writ related primarily to the person of the defendant and issued only upon satisfactory proof that he planned or intended to remove himself, beyond the court's jurisdiction so that he might escape obedience to such command as might be or had been laid upon him. The writ has been frequently termed an equitable bail. It involves taking and keeping the defendant in custody until he gives bail or bond in a designated amount, conditioned upon his keeping himself amenable to the enforcive processes of the court. Its use seems to have been confined to equitable suits relating to a demand based upon an equitable debt or pecuniary claim and to suits to preserve property and jurisdiction over it.[58]

---

state). Notice as to lack of official capacity of officer in state other than that of appointment.

[51] Defined, see Moore, *Cyc. Law Dict.* (3d Ed.). Discussion, see Judge Bryant, "The Office of Master in Chancery—Development and Use in Illinois," 49 *N.W. Law Rev.* 458 (1954).

[52] Defined, see Moore, *Cyc. Law Dict.* (3d Ed.). Receivership, see *infra*, Sec. 12.

[53] Briefly, a writ to aid in obtaining possession of property. It is now frequently superseded by statutory writs or proceedings.

[54] See *infra*, Sec. 11.

[55] See *infra*, Sec. 12.

[56] For another matter of dispute in the argument whether equity has inherent power to act other than in personam. See *supra*, Secs. 6, 7.

[57] See Moore, *Cyc. Law Dict.* (3d Ed.) "Ne Exeat" and "Ne Exeat Regno."

[58] See note, 51 *Col. L. Rev.* 394 (1951).

In the first-named use, the result has been that in many jurisdictions it has been termed a form of imprisonment for debt so as to fall within the general abolition of imprisonment for debt.[59]   But other jurisdictions have considered it not an imprisonment for debt and so not within any abolition of imprisonment for debt.[60] Whether or not it has been abolished in a particular jurisdiction, statutory equivalents are frequently found which authorize the court to require security from the defendant that he will carry out the order or decree of the court.[61]

While the writ is directed at the person of the defendant as a means of preventing him removing himself from the court's jurisdiction and control, it has also been used by the control over the person as a means of preventing the removal of property.   It will be seen that the removal of his property by the defendant would permit him to prevent its application to payment of the equitable debt or pecuniary claim, where that is the subject of the suit, or to remove it from the court's control where its preservation is involved.[62]

The writ of ne exeat may frequently be a more effective means of seeing that the court's command is obeyed because it permits preventive measures to be taken before the disobedience actually occurs.   Otherwise, it is necessary to wait until the disobedience occurs and then proceed by way of contempt procedure.   To wait until a wrongful act is done is not consistent with customary principles of equity.[63]

Sec. 12.   —Sequestration; receivership.

One of the methods developed by the courts of equity to enforce their commands has been the writ of sequestration, a writ or order

---

[59] See de Funiak, "Is Writ of Ne Exeat No Longer Available in California?" 18 *Calif. S.B.J.* 110 (1943).

[60] See Ne Exeat, 38 Am. Jur. 617; annotation, 118 Am.St.Rep. 988. In Wisconsin, see de Funiak and Williams, *Wisconsin Pleading and Practice* (3d Ed.) Sec. 75.01.

[61] See Ne Exeat, 38 Am. Jur. 619.
Statutory equivalent in New York discussed, see note, 51 *Col. L. Rev.* 394 (1951).
Requiring applicant for injunction to give security is frequently provided for by statute and should, of course, be distinguished.

[62] See Caughron v. Stinespring, 132 Tenn. 636, 179 S.W. 152, L.R.A. 1916C 403 (1915), and annotation thereto at 407.

[63] See de Funiak, 18 *Calif. S.B.J.* 110 (1943).

for the sequestering or taking over of property and the rents and profits thereof, in order to enforce a decree or command or to preserve the subject matter of a suit.[64] In other words, property of the defendant is sequestered so as to prevent him enjoying the property until he carries out the command of the court, or sequestered so as to use the income of the property or to sell the property and apply the proceeds either to pay money called for by the decree or to pay fines imposed for contempt. (Whether the use of this writ constitutes acting in rem rather than in personam has been a matter of dispute.[65])

It has been said that there are no principles of equity to support the sequestration or impounding of assets or property of the defendant to secure obedience to such future commands as may be laid upon him.[66] Nevertheless, the writ of sequestration has been issued, not only to preserve property pending hearing, but also to secure obedience to future commands of the court although no specific interest in, right to, or lien upon the property was asserted and no question was involved of the defendant being in contempt.[67]

A modern application of sequestration of property, no doubt familiar to the reader, is the receivership proceeding whereby the court takes over property, placing it in the care of its appointed officer, the receiver, in order to preserve the property for the purposes in hand. No effort is made here to consider receivership in any further detail, since it is dealt with more specifically in courses and treatises dealing with corporations, the rights of creditors, or insolvency.[68]

Sec. 13. —Anticipatory measures.

May the court, at the outset or during the pendency of the suit, seek to anticipate and prevent the possibility of disobedience of any commands it may lay upon the defendant? To the extent

---

[64] See Moore, *Cyc. Law Dict.* (3d Ed.) "Sequestration."

[65] See Langdell, *Summary of Equity Pleading* (2d Ed.) 35; Walsh, *Treatise on Equity* (1930) 48.

[66] See note, 31 *Va. L. Rev.* 946 (1945), to De Beers Consol. Mines v. United States, 324, U.S. 212, 65 S.Ct. 1130, 89 L. Ed. (1945).

[67] Ippolito v. Ippolito, 3 N.J. 561, 71 A.2d 196, noted and criticised, 38 *Geo.L.J.* 683 (1950).

[68] As provisional or auxiliary remedy, see Vila v. Grand Island, etc., Co., 68 Nebr. 222, 94 N.W. 136, 97 N.W. 613, 63 L.R.A. 791, 4 Ann. Cas. 59, 110 Am.St.Rep. 400 (1903).

that it is practicable for the court to act and to the extent that the
means developed to aid and enforce its jurisdiction permit, <u>it is
clear that it has been the policy of equity to prevent a disobedience
which appears reasonably probable</u>.   In some of the preceding
sections of this chapter, examples have already been seen of the
use of ne exeat [69] and even of sequestration [70] as anticipation measures.   A more detailed study of equity than the scope of this work
permits will make evident such policy.

Sec. 14.   —Practicability of enforcement.

<u>It may well happen that an equity court has jurisdiction of the
defendant to enter an injunction against him, but the circumstances are such as to make it impracticable for the court to see
to its enforcement.</u>   This may result from the fact that the defendant may easily remove himself from the control of the court
or that the acts necessary to be done by him must be done beyond
or without the court's jurisdiction, where it cannot enforce or
supervise a proper performance.[71]   Or it may be that the nature
of the acts necessary to be done is such that the court has not the
capacity or means of supervising them or determining that they
are properly performed, even though performance would be carried out within the court's jurisdiction.[72]   Where the court has the
theoretical power to grant an injunction but enforcement is impracticable or impossible, the court will not grant the injunction.
<u>It would be derogatory of the dignity of the court to enter orders
it could not enforce.</u>[73]

The question is frequently raised here, particularly by the law
student, as to why the injunctive decree cannot be entered, leaving it to the plaintiff to seek out the defendant in whatever other
jurisdiction he is and there bring action on this decree; that, as a
decree or judgment by a court having jurisdiction over the defendant, it must be given full faith and credit in the other jurisdiction

---

[69] See *supra*, Sec. 11.

[70] See *supra*, Sec. 12.

[71] Power to act in rem in contract and property cases, see *supra*, Sec. 7.

[72] Difficulties of supervision and the conflicting views as to the court's ability
to supervise performance of an act or acts are more specifically illustrated in later
chapters.   See, *e.g.*, Ch. 10.

[73] See also Walsh, *Treatise on Equity* (1930) Sec. 18.

and a similar decree entered.   For one thing, it must be considered that the court is not primarily concerned with the issuance of a decree to be enforced in another jurisdiction, but rather with the issuance of a decree which it can itself enforce.   But more importantly, the conflict of laws principle is that a valid judgment that the defendant do or refrain from doing an act other than the payment of money will not be enforced in another jurisdiction by an action on such judgment.   An action on the original claim may be brought and the effect of res judicata given to the findings of fact in the prior suit.   It rests in the discretion of the second court, as it did in the discretion of the first court, to determine whether to leave the plaintiff to his ordinary remedy of recovering compensatory damages or to award him equitable relief.   The decision by the first court to give equitable relief is an exercise of discretion which is not binding on another court so as to preclude its exercise of discretion.[74]

Sec. 15.   —Act outside state causing injury within state.

Where the defendant is doing an act outside the state that is injuring or threatens to injure property of the plaintiff within the state, the court must necessarily order the defendant to do or refrain from doing acts outside the state where the court's jurisdiction does not reach.[75]   Where it is also clear that the defendant can easily remove himself from the court's control or will not

---

[74] See *Rest. Conflict of Laws*, Sec. 449.   See also Union Pac. R. Co. v. Rule, 155 Minn. 302, 193 N.W. 161 (1923), discussing application of federal constitution to matter of enforcing decree of another state enjoining defendant from suing in state where such decree now sought to be enforced.   Majority opinion holds no obligation to give decree full faith and credit under federal constitution, but note minority view.   Case approved, see note 37 *Harv. L. Rev.* 157 (1923); disapproved, see note 33 *Yale L.J.* 95 (1923).

See annotation, Decree granting or refusing injunction as res judicata in action for damages in relation to matter concerning which injunction was asked in first suit, 26 A.L.R.2d 446.

[75] The situation should be distinguished in which not only is the injurious act being done outside the state but the property injured is also outside the state. In this situation, some courts have not hesitated to act, on the ground that the parties were before it and amenable to its process, as in Alexander v. Tolleston Club, 110 Ill. 65 (1884).   Other courts have declined to act in such situation on the ground that the cause of action was local in nature and could be brought only where the property was, as in Ophir Silver Min., etc. Co. v. Superior Court, 147 Cal. 467, 82 P. 70, 3 Ann. Cas. 340 (1905).

remain subject to the court's control, enjoining him would probably be a useless act.[76] But if, as usually is the case, the defendant will continue to be subject to the court's control, the court is thereby in a position to see that he gives obedience to its command, even though the acts of obedience must be performed beyond the confines of the court's jurisdiction.[77] The act, for example, may be performed through an agent. If the defendant is a citizen of the state or is a nonresident or a foreign corporation doing business in the state, it may safely be assumed that the defendant is not in a position to remove himself from the court's control without loss, probably severe loss.

A situation similar to the foregoing is that in which a domiciliary of the state is ordered to discontinue prosecution of litigation which he has commenced in another state, because it imposes undue hardship and pecuniary loss to the defendant in such litigation to be sued there instead of in the state where the injunction is now sought by him. The expediency of granting such injunction rests largely in the court's ability to control the defendant and coerce him.[78]

---

[76] See *supra*, Sec. 14.

[77] See The Salton Sea Cases, 172 F. 792 (1909), noted 23 *Harv. L. Rev.* 390 (1910); Vineyard Land & Stock Co. v. Twin Falls, etc. Co., 245 F. 9 (1917), noted 31 *Harv. L. Rev.* 646 (1918), 27 *Yale L.J.* 946 (1918).
【A case frequently cited to the contrary is Port Royal R. Co. v. Hammond, 58 Ga. 523 (1877). There the defendant who would have to be ordered to do acts in another state was a corporation incorporated in Georgia and under the view of corporations at that time had no legal existence beyond the state of its incorporation so as to be able to do an act in another state. *And it is true that some courts make a distinction, in that they will enjoin the commission of an act outside the state but will not order the performance of a positive act) See, *e.g.*, Gunter v. Arlington Mills, 271 Mass. 314, 171 N.E. 486, 71 A.L.R. 1348 (1930).

[78] See, *e.g.*, Reed's Adm'x v. Illinois Cent. R. Co., 182 Ky. 455, 206 S.W. 794 (1918); Kempson v. Kempson, 58 N.J. Eq. 94, 43 A. 97 (1899), ibid., 63 N.J. Eq. 783, 53 A. 625 (1902).

Chapter 3

REQUISITES FOR PROTECTION AGAINST TORTS

Sec. 16.   In general.

It may be stated as a general rule that whenever a person threatens or undertakes to perform any act affecting property, contrary to the legal right of another, the consequences of which will be permanent or irreparable injury to the property, equity will give relief by way of injunctive decree.[1]   To justify a suit for injunctive relief, it is not necessary that any injurious act shall actually have been done by the defendant.   When there is reasonable probability of injury, when the intention to do the wrong has clearly been manifested, equity at once interferes.   However, mere idle words or mere possibility of injury do not suffice, although one is not in a position to complain that equity has taken him at his word.[2]

---

[1] See Merwin, *Principles of Equity* (1895) 18.
Injunctions, see *supra*, Sec. 8.
[2] Reasonable probability is important, since mere possibility or anything short

Nor is it any sufficient answer to the suit for the defendant to come in and say that he no longer harbors his wrongful purpose but has abandoned it. The court will not leave the plaintiff to the good will of a defendant who has once shown an intention to disregard his rights, but will by its decree take care that the defendant's good professions are carried out. Of course, if the court is satisfied that there is no likelihood of the occurrence or repetition, as the case may be, of the wrong complained of, and evidence of abandonment or repentance is convincing, the court may deny the application for injunction.[3]

Relief can be accomplished, if necessary, by requiring the taking of any affirmative or positive steps to remove or render harmless the source or cause of the threatened injury.[4] If the act has already been committed and, with reasonable probability, will be continued or repeated, equity can compel the wrongdoer to desist in future from repetition of the wrong and, as well, compel him to repair the injury which he has already done, to the extent that this is possible.[5] Repairing the injury may consist of payment of pecuniary compensation, since it has long been established in equity that pecuniary compensation may be granted as an incident of the injunctive relief,[6] or it may consist of the performance of

---

of reasonable probability of injury is said to be insufficient to warrant equitable relief. See, *e.g.*, Lorenz v. Waldron, 96 Cal. 243, 249, 31 P. 54 (1892). Compare Edison v. Edison Polyform Mfg. Co., 73 N.J. Eq. 136, 67 A. 392 (1907), as to "possibility of injury."

For anticipated nuisance, see *infra*, Sec. 34.

[3] Snyder v. Gurnsey, 43 F. Supp. 204 (1942).

The court should, nevertheless, proceed to allow substitutional redress by way of money damages. Lewis v. North Kingstown, 16 R.I. 15, 11 A. 173, 27 Am.St.Rep. 724 (1887). That this should not include prospective damages, see Cox v. City of New York, 265 N.Y. 411, 193 N.E. 251, 105 A.L.R. 1378 (1934).

[4] Consistent, of course, with the ability or practicability on the part of the court of supervising and making effective its order or decree. See Sec. 14.

[5] See later chapters, on specific torts.

[6] Originally, in the separate courts of chancery or equity this was frequently done by exacting an accounting of the profits of a wrong or sometimes by the allowance of damages as an incident to the granting of equitable relief, as the circumstances warranted. In the so-called code states, where there is only one form of civil action in one court, damages may be obtained in the same proceeding as an injunction. These, as formerly, may usually be assessed by the court as an incident of the equitable relief, without the necessity of a jury. See Judson v. Los Angeles Suburban Gas Co., 157 Cal. 168, 106 P. 581, 26 L.R.A.N.S. 183, 21 Ann. Cas. 1247 (1910). That this should not include prospective damages, see Cox v. City of New York, 265 N.Y. 411, 193 N.E. 251, 105 A.L.R. 1378 (1934).

positive or affirmative acts to remove or to discontinue the cause or source of injury,[7] or both.[8]

From the foregoing, it is necessary to branch off on discussions of several interrelated matters. For one, what is property? [9] For another, what is permanent or irreparable injury? [10] Both of these matters are of importance in view of the principle that equity does not assume jurisdiction where there is an adequate remedy at law [11] and the principle, although subject nowadays to exception,[12] that equity does not assume jurisdiction except to protect property and property rights. And conceding that a sufficient so-called property right or interest is present, does the threat of permanent or irreparable injury present the only situation in which the remedy at law will be inadequate? Or do other situations instanced by the courts as those in which the remedy at law is inadequate constitute, in effect, situations of irreparable injury? [13]

Conduct of the complainant which may affect his ability to obtain equitable relief must also be considered.[14]

Sec. 17. Property and other rights of substance.

The development of equity during a period when property rights rather than personal or individual rights were paramount has already been referred to.[15] Its result has been the repeated statement of the principle that equity intervenes or interposes only

---

[7] Where continuing injury was being done to plaintiff by abuse of license to pile rocks on plaintiff's land, defendant was ordered to remove the rocks. Wheelock v. Noonan, 108 N.Y. 179, 15 N.E. 67, 2 Am.St.Rep. 405 (1888). At law the plaintiff would have had to assume what would have amounted to an unconscionable burden of removing the rocks himself and suing for the cost thereof; or else he would have to allow the rocks to remain and recover damages based on the rental value of the land, meanwhile losing the use, etc., of the land.

[8] See The Salton Sea Cases, 172 F. 792 (1909), cert. denied, 215 U.S. 603, 30 S.Ct. 405, 45 L. Ed. 345 (1909).
"Injunctions under both English and American law are not confined to the prevention of future wrongs, but may require restoration of the status quo and payment of damages." McComb v. Frank Scerbo & Sons, Inc., 80 F. Supp. 457 (1948).

[9] See infra, Sec. 17.
[10] See infra, Sec. 19.
[11] See infra, Sec. 18.
[12] See infra, Chapter 8.
[13] See infra, Secs. 18, 19.
[14] See infra, Sec. 24.
[15] See supra, Chapter 1; infra, Sec. 56.

to protect property and rights and interests therein. So, as equitable relief was extended to the field of torts, its protection was confined to the protection of property and rights therein. It must be kept in mind, then, that though there have been departures from this prerequisite to equity jurisdiction in the past and though there is a growing tendency to depart from it, the rule is still followed rigidly in many jurisdictions and is given at least lip service in many others.[16]

Since real property and rights therein were, in early England, the chief sources of wealth, power, and influence, equitable relief against torts developed in relation to real property, as against the torts of waste, trespass, and nuisance. Gradually, by reason of the national growth and the consequent complexities of the modern social and economic order, the concept of property was extended to include intangibles as well as tangibles, in other words, incorporeal things of value. So, the term "property" thus came to include the right to carry on a lawful business, with all the incidents thereof which gave or added value to a business. Whether the right to carry on a lawful business, or for that matter the power to earn a living, is strictly a property right or a personal right is now an academic question. The fact is that equity has termed business and similar rights of substance to be property rights in order to justify its interference on the ground of protecting property and property rights. Thus the idea of property has been extended to include what are sometimes termed rights of substance, in the nature of property rights, having a pecuniary value.[17]

There is no reason why equity should not extend its relief to all cases of substantial rights conferred by law, whether such rights of substance are termed personal rights or property rights. In this country we recognize many rights of substance other than so-called property rights, and neither the common law nor statutory remedies may provide the complete and adequate protection of such rights and the prevention of injury to them which equity can afford. Certainly, so far as property rights or rights in the

---

[16] For modifications of or departures from the rule, see *infra*, Chapter 8.

[17] Protection of the right to carry on a lawful business or the power to earn a living, see *infra*, Chapter 7.

nature thereof have been concerned, equity looks to their importance to the complainant and may consider them substantial as to him, without requiring a great pecuniary value.[18]

Sec. 18.   Adequacy or inadequacy of the remedy at law.

The development of equity as a system of jurisprudence to supply the deficiencies or inadequacies of the relief available at common law in the courts of law and the unwillingness of equity to infringe on or invade the province of the courts of law [19] have resulted in the question of the adequacy or inadequacy of the remedy at law in a given case becoming one of importance. It is considered as prerequisite to equity jurisdiction that there be no remedy at law available or that it be inadequate.[20] By inadequate is meant that the remedy at law is not so speedy, practical, and efficient to the ends of justice and its prompt administration as the remedy in equity.[21]

Where law and equity are administered in separate courts, the decision of the equity court in a given case that there is an adequate remedy at law results in the dismissal of the suit in equity. Delay and expense are thus imposed on the complainant who must begin all over again in another court. It is true that in more recent periods there have developed frequent situations in which the

---

[18] See Felsenthal v. Warring, 40 Cal. App. 119, 180 P. 57 (1919), where defendant had prescriptive right to maintain a certain irrigation ditch on plaintiff's land. When a large part of the ditch was washed away by a flood, defendant began construction of a new ditch at a different point, claiming the right to maintain a ditch anywhere on plaintiff's land. The value of the land so taken was only $12. It was held that the easement included no right to change the mode of use or enjoyment by shifting it and that so long as a substantial right of plaintiff was involved, whatever its small pecuniary value, he was entitled to have such right protected.
As to balancing equities, see *infra*, Sec. 25.
[19] See *supra*, Chapter 1.
[20] See Lawrence, *Equity Jurisprudence* (1929) Chap. VII; McClintock, *Handbook of Equity* (2d Ed.) Sec. 43; Walsh, *Treatise on Equity* (1930) Sec. 25.
It should be borne in mind that a term such as "remedy at law" must be given a broader interpretation than it originally had. Modern jurisprudence has expanded the relief available to a litigant by the development of such things as declaratory judgments and administrative remedies. See *Rest. Torts*, Sec. 938, comment c.
[21] Boyce v. Grundy, 3 Pet. (U.S.) 210, 7 L. Ed. 655 (1830). See also *Rest. Torts*, Sec. 933, Special Note.

equity court has awarded some form of temporary relief while the action in the court of law is being tried,[22] as well as the fact that statutes have frequently been enacted to soften the difficulties brought about by two sets of courts.[23]

The situation is much less harsh in jurisdictions where code or statutory provisions have merged legal and equitable powers in one court. The substantive differences between the two systems of jurisprudence, law and equity, still remain, in that the complainant seeking equitable relief may still have to show that there is no adequate legal remedy available.[24] But if it develops that there is an adequate legal remedy, no dismissal of the proceeding follows, since the court under its merged powers may proceed to give the relief called for by the issues.[25] At most, the complainant is required only to amend his complaint to ask for the legal relief which has been determined to be available and adequate.[26]

Sec. 19. —Irreparable injury.

Irreparable injury has been defined as that which cannot be repaired, restored, or adequately compensated in money or where the compensation cannot be safely measured.[27] On the other hand it has been said that irreparable injury does not mean that the injury is beyond the possibility of repair or beyond the possibility of compensation in damages, but rather that the injury is of such constant and frequent recurrence that no fair or reasonable redress can be had therefor in an action at law.[28] It will be noticed

---

[22] Temporary restraining order or injunction against trespass while legal title determined in an action at law, see *infra*, Sec. 31.

[23] As by providing that where a legal issue arises in an equity case the chancellor may impanel a jury to make a finding thereon, or by providing for sending the legal issue to a court of law for a jury finding thereon and its certification back to the court of equity. See *infra*, Sec. 28.

[24] Effect of absence of objection by defendant that there is no equity jurisdiction, see section following.

[25] See, *e.g.*, Cal. Code of Civ. Proc., Sec. 580; N. Y. Civ. Prac. Act, Sec. 275. See also Clark, "The Union of Law and Equity," 25 *Col. L. Rev.* 1 (1925); Clark, *Code Pleading* (1928) 44 ff., discussing the frequent inconsistencies and hostility of the courts in dealing with this problem.

[26] Nevertheless, some courts in code states have insisted on dismissal. See Clark, *op. cit.*, footnote 25, *supra*.

[27] Bettman v. Harness, 42 W.Va. 433, 26 S.E. 271, 36 L.R.A. 566 (1896).

[28] Donovan v. Pennsylvania Co., 199 U.S. 279, 26 S.Ct. 91, 50 L. Ed. 192 (1905).

that the latter statement seems more directly addressed to a wrong of a continuing or repeated nature rather than to one threatened initially.[29]

In short, then, it would seem that the standard is that some or all of the very substance of the estate or property or right, if destroyed, will be destroyed to the extent that no pecuniary compensation can provide replacement of the original or restore exactly the status quo,[30] or that no fair or reasonable redress is available at law. Money will only provide the injured person with some substitute for the right of substance that was previously legally his and to the destruction of which he has had to submit. There is no reason, from the standpoint of equity, why a person should have to submit to the destruction or loss of a substantial right which is legally his and accept something else in its place.[31] Nor is there any reason why he should have to submit to restriction to a remedy that cannot offer a fair and reasonable redress.[32]

Indeed, if equitable principles were followed to a logical conclusion, there would seem to be no reason why a person should

[29] "The term 'irreparable injury,' however, is not to be taken in its strict literal sense. The rule does not require that the threatened injury should be one not physically capable of being repaired. If the threatened injury would be substantial and serious—one not easily to be estimated, or repaired by money—and if the loss or inconvenience to the plaintiff if the injunction should be refused (his title proving good) would be much greater than any which can be suffered by the defendant through the granting of the injunction, although his title ultimately prevails, the case is one of such probable great or 'irreparable' damage as will justify a preliminary injunction." Merwin, *Principles of Equity* (1895) 426.

[30] Although destruction of some or all of the substance of the estate or property or right originally seems to have meant injury to the freehold by cutting of timber, quarrying rock or removal of ore, injury to the substance of the estate which causes irreparable injury is now exceedingly broad in its meaning. Kellogg v. King, 114 Cal. 378, 46 P. 166, 55 Am.St.Rep. 54 (1896), holding that acts impairing or destroying a hunting privilege impaired or destroyed the substance of the right or estate or interest held so as to cause irreparable injury.

[31] A court of equity will not license a wrong and compel the owner of the property to exchange what is his by right for some substitute. Gregory v. Nelson, 41 Cal. 278 (1871).

"The plea that a remedy for money damages exists is made in defense of every application for an injunction. In some ways, under the law at least, any injury may be compensated by an award for money damages. Under the law even the taking of a human life may be so compensated." Fox v. Krug, 70 F. Supp. 721 (1947), to the effect that regardless of existence of such remedy for money damages, irreparable injury will warrant injunction.

[32] That the modern rule, in this regard, is less strict than the earlier view of equity, see, *e.g.*, Colliton v. Oxborough, 86 Minn. 361, 90 N.W. 793 (1902).

have to submit to any wrong even though he can thereafter recover money damages sufficient to replace in kind and quality the very thing lost or destroyed, without appreciable change in his status. In no civilized country should the jurisprudence insist that a wrong be allowed to happen and compensation be sought thereafter rather than preventing the occurrence of the wrong.[33] One may, of course, distinguish merely trivial matter [34] or matters for which other adequate remedies than equitable exist to prevent the occurrence or the repetition of the wrong.[35]

Sec. 20. —Multiplicity of actions at law.

One of the grounds frequently advanced as rendering the remedy at law inadequate is that a multiplicity of actions will be required.[36] It is apparent that where the injury is recurring, one action after another at law is required to recover for the damages as each act is done. This is expensive, time-consuming and vexatious. Moreover, the continuous or repeated injuries may eventually result in permanent or irreparable injury. And too great a delay or failure to bring actions may result in the wrongdoer acquiring an easement or adverse right.[37] Of course, the mere necessity of bringing a multiplicity of actions at law as a ground for equitable relief would not, at first glance, seem to meet the

---

[33] Professor Walsh points out that the growth of modern equity has been in the direction of granting specific relief more freely where definitely superior to damages and that the code merger of law and equity has contributed to this. Walsh, *Treatise on Equity* (1930) Sec. 25.

[34] An illustrative maxim is that "Equity does not stoop to pick up pins." Formerly, at least, in England and in some American jurisdictions arbitrary amounts ' have been imposed either by the courts or by statute as requisite to equity jurisdiction. See Lawrence, *Equity Jurisprudence* (1929) Sec. 43, who warns against application of this principle of triviality where the relief sought is not properly measurable by the pecuniary damage immediately imminent, as where the grievance is a recurring one or one which may lead to acquisition of a prescriptive right. Certainly, distinction must be made between the merely trivial where some other remedy is available and the situation where a substantial right, although of small value in dollars, is threatened, as in Felsenthal v. Warring, 40 Cal. App. 119, 180 P. 57 (1919).

[35] As where a policeman may well be called. See Randall v. Freed, 154 Cal. 299, 97 P. 669 (1908); Mechanics' Foundry v. Ryall, 75 Cal. 601, 17 P. 703 (1888).

[36] See also *infra*, Sec. 107, as to bills of peace.

[37] Although the term "multiplicity of actions at law" originally, and still occasionally, seems to have been applied only to causes of action against a plurality of persons, it is now also applied to the situation of a succession of actions between the same parties. See Lawrence, *Equity Jurisprudence* (1929) Sec. 872.

express requirement of many jurisdictions that it is prerequisite to the obtaining of equitable relief that irreparable injury be threatened with reasonable probability. However, it will usually be found, as already indicated, that the continued recurrence of the injurious act may result in irreparable injury or in the acquisition of an easement or other adverse right which by reducing the substance of the estate results in irreparable injury.[38] It may also be noticed that irreparable injury is sometimes defined as one for which no fair and reasonable redress is afforded.[39]

Sec. 21.   —Damages at law speculative or conjectural.

Another ground frequently advanced as rendering the remedy at law inadequate is that damages are too speculative or conjectural to provide a basis for seeking relief in an action at law. However, such a ground usually exists in connection with other grounds,[40] or results particularly from the probable irreparable injury.[41]   And, indeed, irreparable injury is sometimes defined, as already remarked, as an injury for which no safe measure of recovery is provided.[42]

Sec. 22.   —Insolvency.

From a practical standpoint it might well be said that the remedy at law by way of damages is more or less meaningless if the defendant is insolvent. This consideration has led to the view in many jurisdictions that the insolvency of the defendant renders the remedy at law inadequate and is sufficient ground alone for granting equitable relief.[43]   It should be pointed out, however,

---

[38] See *infra*, Sec. 29.

[39] See *supra*, Sec. 19.

[40] See, *e.g.*, Baker v. Howard County Hunt, 171 Md. 159, 188 A. 223 (1936), involving impossibility of measuring damages, repetition of trespass, and interference with peaceful enjoyment of property.

[41] See particularly *infra*, Sec. 30, as to matter of trespass.

[42] See *supra*, Sec. 19.

[43] Martin v. Davis, 96 Iowa 718, 65 N.W. 1001 (1896); Clark v. Flint, 22 Pick. (Mass.) 231, 33 Am.Dec. 733 (1839); Milan Steam Mills v. Hickey, 59 N.H. 241 (1879); Wilson v. Hill, 46 N.J.Eq. 267, 19 A. 1097 (1890).

See McClintock, "Adequacy of Ineffective Remedy at Law," 16 *Minn. L. Rev.* 233 (1932); Moreland, "Insolvency of the Defendant as a Basis of Equity Jurisdiction in Tort Cases," 22 *Ky. L.J.* 1 (1933).

Conversely, mere fact that defendant is solvent does not defeat equity jurisdic-

that in many of the cases so holding the injury or threatened injury is of such a nature that in any event the remedy at law would not be adequate.[44]   In fact, some of the cases remark on the immateriality of the circumstance whether the defendant is solvent or insolvent, in view of the nature of the threatened injury.[45]   Nevertheless, there are definitely situations in which, but for the insolvency, the remedy at law would be adequate and, hence, the fact of insolvency is the determinative factor in construing the remedy at law as inadequate.[46]   In those jurisdictions which specify that "irreparable injury" must appear in order to render the remedy at law inadequate, it is explained that leaving a plaintiff to a remedy at law against an insolvent defendant would cause him to suffer irreparable injury.[47]

---

tion since recovery of damages may not, of course, constitute as adequate and efficacious a remedy as that available in equity.   See Edwards Mfg. Co. v. Hood, 167 Ga. 144, 145 S.E. 87 (1928).

Statutory requirement that injunction shall not be denied on ground of adequacy of remedy at law unless defendant shall show to court's satisfaction that he has property from which damages can be made or shall give bond to answer all damages and costs, see Universal Realty Corp. v. Felser, 179 Md. 635, 22 A.2d 448 (1941).

[44] See, *e.g.*, Slater v. Gunn, 170 Mass. 509, 49 N.E. 1017, 41 L.R.A. 268 (1898).

[45] See, *e.g.*, Richards v. Dower, 64 Cal. 62, 28 P. 113 (1883).

As Professor Moreland points out, where waste or trespass in the nature of waste is threatened there is no adequate remedy at law in any event.   See Moreland, *op. cit.*, Footnote 43, *supra*.

[46] "These situations are: (1) Where a repeated trespass or a continuing trespass is likely to be committed by an insolvent defendant over a short period of time, the remedy at law is adequate in the absence of the element of insolvency.   (2) Where the asportation of non-unique personal property is threatened, the insolvency of the defendant becomes a material factor in giving equity jurisdiction to grant preventive relief for in its absence there is an adequate remedy at law." Moreland, *op. cit.*, Footnote 43, *supra*.

[47] See, *e.g.*, Milan Steam Mills v. Hickey, 59 N.H. 241 (1879).

In California, where it is uniformly held that irreparable injury must be alleged and proved in order to obtain equitable relief against torts, several cases have held that insolvency of the defendant was sufficient to render the remedy at law inadequate and warrant equitable relief, on the ground that leaving the injured person to pursuit of a legal remedy against one who was insolvent would cause him to suffer irreparable injury.   Rohrer v. Babcock, 114 Cal. 124, 45 P. 1054 (1896); Paige v. Akins, 112 Cal. 401, 44 P. 666 (1896).   In the first case, the insolvent defendant was taking plaintiff's hay and feeding it to his own cattle.

In the second case the insolvent defendant was harvesting and removing crops from the plaintiff's land under a claim of right.   Cf. Mechanics' Foundry v. Ryall, 75 Cal. 601, 17 P. 703 (1888), where defendant's insolvency is not considered irreparable injury because of the availability of self help.   It has also been stated that if irreparable injury on some other ground is stated, insolvency need not be pleaded.   Crescent City Wharf & Lighter Co. v. Simpson, 77 Cal. 286, 19 P. 426

On the other hand, in many jurisdictions it is considered that the proper test continues to be whether the threatened injury will be irreparable so that no relief at law would be adequate, and that if the situation is ordinarily one in which a remedy at law is adequate, it is not determinative of the matter that the judgment at law in the immediate case might not procure any pecuniary compensation.[48]   However, in these jurisdictions the concession is frequently made that insolvency of the defendant is a factor which may be considered in connection with other matters in determining whether there is an adequate or inadequate remedy at law.[49]

Which of the opposing views is the majority view is a matter of dispute, with the judges and legal writers usually declaring for the view which they happen to favor.[50]

Sec. 23.   Objection to equity jurisdiction; waiver.

Objection to the existence or exercise of equity jurisdiction is usually made on the ground that there is an adequate remedy at law,[51] although it may also, in many jurisdictions, be made on the ground that no property or property rights or rights in the nature thereof are involved or threatened.[52]   According to the practice of the particular jurisdiction, it is made by demurrer or by motion or in the answer to the merits.[53]

(1888). The situation in California is confused by cases for relief by way of specific performance which hold, without citation of any of the tort cases, that insolvency alone is not ground for equitable relief but only a factor which may be considered with other matters in.determining the adequacy or inadequacy of the remedy at law. McLaughlin v. Piatti, 27 Cal. 452 (1865); Emerzian v. Asato, 23 Cal. App. 251, 137 P. 1072 (1913).

[48] Thompson v. Allen County, 115 U.S. 550, 6 S.Ct. 140, 29 L. Ed. 472 (1885); Tampa, etc. R. Co. v. Mulhern, 73 Fla. 146, 74 So. 297 (1917); Moore v. Halliday, 43 Or. 243, 72 P. 801, 99 Am.St.Rep. 724 (1903).

[49] Analysis may show, however, that the situation is one in which equity would in any event grant relief on other grounds of inadequacy of legal remedy. See Moreland, "Insolvency as Basis of Equity Jurisdiction in Tort Cases," 22 Ky. L.J. 1 (1933).

[50] Conflicting opinions of writers are shown by McClintock, *Handbook of Equity* (2d Ed.) Sec. 47, who favors the view that insolvency alone is ground for equitable relief, and Walsh, *Treatise on Equity* (1930) Sec. 63, who argues that it should not be. Consider the *Rest. Torts*, Sec. 944, comment i, which seems to favor the inadequacy of legal remedy view.

[51] That a remedy at law by way of money damages exists is pleaded in defense of every application for injunction is pointed out, with some truth, in Fox v. Krug, 70 F. Supp. 721 (1947).

[52] See *infra*, Chapter 8.

[53] As to modes of objecting in various jurisdictions, see Equity, 30 C.J.S. 449 ff.

If the objection is not raised in any form in the pleadings, is the objection waived or must the court take notice, of its own motion, of the absence of equity jurisdiction?   The answer to this requires recognition of the fact that the term equity jurisdiction does not refer to jurisdiction in the sense of the power conferred by the sovereign on the court over specified subject-matters or to jurisdiction over the res or the persons of the parties in a particular proceeding but refers rather to the merits.   The want of equity jurisdiction does not mean that the court has no power to act but that it should not act, as on the ground, for example, that there is an adequate remedy at law.[54]

Undoubtedly, in jurisdictions where law and equity are administered in separate courts, the courts of equity, being loath to invade the province of the courts of law, will take notice, of their own motion, of the absence of equity jurisdiction.   Indeed, they may even be inclined to state that the availability of adequate remedies at law goes to the very power of the courts of equity to act.[55]   The usual view, however, as already indicated, is that want of equity jurisdiction, as because of the existence of an adequate remedy at law, goes not to the power of the court but to the merits.[56]

In this country, the widespread code merger of legal and equity powers in the same court has resulted in the tendency of the courts to proceed to hear the petition for equitable relief in the absence of an objection on the ground of lack of equity jurisdiction.   In some jurisdictions, so long as there is a waiver by reason of failure of the defendant to object that there is a lack of equity jurisdiction, the court does not take notice, on its own motion, of any such lack and proceeds to render equitable relief if the merits in favor of the plaintiff warrant it.[57]   The failure to object means the failure to raise the objection by such motion or pleading as is required in the jurisdiction.   Ordinarily, objection comes too late during the course of the hearing.[58]   In other jurisdictions, as in

---

[54] See McClintock, *Handbook of Equity* (2d Ed.) Sec. 40.
[55] See Merwin, *Principles of Equity* (1895) 56.
[56] Viles v. Prudential Ins. Co., 124 F.2d 78 (1941).
[57] See, *e.g.*, Bangs v. Duckinfield, 18 N.Y. 592 (1859).
As to this view in Massachusetts, see Merwin, *Principles of Equity* (1895) 57.
[58] See, *e.g.*, Lehigh Zinc Co. v. Trotter, 43 N.J. Eq. 185, 110 A. 607 (1887); Town of Mentz v. Cook, 108 N.Y. 504, 15 N.E. 541 (1888).

the federal courts, the failure to object is a waiver only if the want of equity jurisdiction is not obvious. If such want is obvious, the court may and should notice it of its own motion.[59]

Sec. 24. Equitable conduct of complainant.

Pursuant to the equitable maxim that "He who comes into equity must come with clean hands," the so-called "clean hands" doctrine, the complainant seeking equitable relief must not himself have been guilty of any inequitable or wrongful conduct with respect to the transaction or subject matter sued on. Equity will not give relief to one seeking to restrain or enjoin a tortious act where he has himself been guilty of fraud, illegality, tortious conduct or the like in respect of the same matter in litigation.[60] Not only must the complainant come into equity with clean hands but he must keep them clean throughout the course of the litigation.[61] The principle is a matter of public policy and not a matter of defense.[62] The inequitable conduct need not even be pleaded but may come to the attention of the court in any way; the court will act of its own accord.[63]

But the rule or doctrine applies only to the particular matter under consideration, for the court will not go outside of the case for the purpose of examining the conduct of the complainant in other matters or for the purpose of questioning his general character for fair dealing.[64] Even though the conduct of the complain-

---

[59] Viles v. Prudential Ins. Co., 124 F.2d 78 (1941). See also Pusey & Jones Co. v. Hanssen, 261 U.S. 491, 43 S.Ct. 454, 67 L. Ed. 763 (1923).

[60] Mas v. Coca-Cola Co., 163 F.2d 505 (1947); Western Lithograph Co. v. W. H. Brady Co., 71 F. Supp. 383 (1947) (unclean hands in matter of business competition).

Unethical conduct of plaintiff in inducing baseball player to breach his contract of employment with another, see Weeghman v. Killifer, 215 F. 168 (1914).

Other illustrations of unclean hands will be found in the chapters dealing with specific torts.

[61] Hall v. Wright, 125 F. Supp. 269 (1954).

[62] White v. Baugher, 82 Colo. 75, 256 P. 1092 (1927).

[63] Hall v. Wright, 125 F. Supp. 269 (1954).

[64] Lyman v. Lyman, 90 Conn. 399, 97 A. 312 (1916); Mills v. Susanka, 394 Ill. 439, 68 N.E.2d 904 (1946), noted 33 Va. L. Rev. 207 (1947); Tami v. Pikowitz, 148 N.J. Eq. 410, 48 A.2d 221 (1946).

That this was the original application of the maxim, see the interesting discussion by Chafee, "Coming Into Equity with Clean Hands," 47 Mich. L. Rev. 877, 1065 (1949).

"But a court of equity is not an avenger of wrongs committed at large by those who resort to it for relief, however careful it may be to withhold its approval from

ant is similar to that of the defendant or in respect of similar matters, it is not ground for denial of equitable relief where it is not connected with the matter in dispute between the immediate parties, according to the usual rule.[65]   It is true that one finds statements to the contrary, to the effect that similar but disconnected acts by the complainant constitute unclean hands barring him from relief.[66]   However, the cases cited to these statements usually turn out, upon analysis, to be cases in which the similar but disconnected acts of the plaintiff constituted a fraud upon the public, or involve the commission of illegal acts injurious to the public or contrary to public policy, or involving conduct verging on connection with, if not actually connected with, the matter in litigation.   It is also necessary to keep in mind that the acts or conduct of the plaintiff not connected with the matter sued upon, if causing injury to the defendant himself, may place the plaintiff in equal guilt with the defendant so far as inequitable conduct is concerned and thus bar his right to relief.

An exception to the clean hands doctrine, as indicated in the preceding paragraph, exists where the conduct of the complainant, although not connected with the matter in litigation, amounts to a fraud on or deceit of the public.   In such cases, the conduct of the complainant bars him from obtaining equitable relief.[67]   Although there is less certainty as to the situation where the complainant's conduct does not fall exactly within the realm of fraud on or deceit of the public but constitutes conduct violative of

---

those which are involved in the subject-matter of the suit, and which prejudicially affect the rights of one against whom relief is sought." Kinner v. Lake Shore, etc., R. Co., 69 Ohio St. 339, 69 N.E. 614 (1903).

[65] Miller v. Enterprise Canal Co., 142 Cal. 208, 75 P. 770, 100 Am.St.Rep. 115 (1904), wherein plaintiff canal company sought to enjoin defendants from obstructing a river and diverting water, in violation of rights of plaintiff which was itself obstructing another stream so as to constitute a public nuisance.

[66] See, e.g., Equity, 30 C.J.S. 483, text and notes, 40, 41.

[67] Worden v. California Fig Syrup Co., 187 U.S. 516, 23 S.Ct. 161, 47 L. Ed. 282 (1903); American University v. Wood, 294 Ill. 186, 128 N.E. 330 (1920); A. N. Chamberlain Medicine Co. v. H. A. Chamberlain Medicine Co., 43 Ind. App. 213, 86 N.E. 1025 (1904).

Indeed, the explanation has been given that the conduct of the plaintiff is connected with the transaction sued on, where a business, the very thing which is sought to be protected by the court, is unclean, where it is of a nature to defraud the public.   See Memphis Keeley Institute v. Keeley Co., 155 F. 964, 16 L.R.A.N.S. 921 (1907).

public policy,[68] it logically appears that the latter conduct is as injurious to the public welfare and should constitute a bar to equitable relief.

Another somewhat similar maxim or principle is the one that "He who seeks equity must do equity." This requires that the one seeking the equitable relief must himself, as a prerequisite to obtaining such relief, have done whatever is in his power to restore the status quo. He must not seek to bring about the cessation of the wrong to him and at the same time retain any benefits, at the defendant's expense, that may have accrued to him from the defendant's acts. This maxim, however, will be found more applicable to equitable suits involving contracts than to those involving torts.[69]

The plaintiff must also not be guilty of laches, that is, he must not be presenting or attempting to enforce a so-called stale demand. According to the governing maxim, "Equity aids the vigilant, not those who slumber on their rights." Incidentally, this manner of stating the principle is somewhat misleading, since it disregards the element of the effect of the delay. For laches does not result from a mere lapse of time but from the fact that, during the lapse of time, changed circumstances inequitably work to the disadvantage or prejudice of another if the claim is now allowed to be enforced. By his negligent delay, the plaintiff may have misled the defendant or others into acting on the assumption that the plaintiff has abandoned his claim, or that he acquiesces in the situation, or changed circumstances may make it more difficult to defend against the claim.[70]

Laches, therefore, does not depend upon any fixed or arbitrary time limit as does a statute of limitations since it is not mere lapse of time which constitutes laches. And statutes of limitation, unless expressly so providing, do not relate to suits of an equitable nature

---

68 See Kinner v. Lake Shore, etc., R. Co., *supra*, wherein complainant railroad's conduct of being party to an illegal combination in restraint of trade did not bar its relief.

69 The similarity of the two maxims is discussed in Kinner v. Lake Shore & M. S. R. Co., 69 Ohio St. 339, 69 N.E. 614 (1903).

70 See *Merwin, Principles of Equity* (1895) 512, 513.

"Lapse of time alone does not constitute laches. Delay will not bar relief where it has not worked injury, prejudice, or disadvantage to the defendant or others adversely interested." Shell v. Strong, 151 F.2d 909 (1945).

but only to actions at law.[71]   Accordingly, a court of equity may refuse relief on the ground of laches although the pursuit of a legal remedy on the same cause would not be barred by the applicable statute of limitations, or it may grant relief after the bar of the statute of limitations has been raised against the legal remedy.[72] The discretion of the court, in view of the circumstances of the case, is freely exercised.[73]   Sometimes, the equity court does apply the analogous statute of limitations on the presumption that the lapse of time fixed by the statute carries with it injurious consequences,[74] although usually with the qualification that a lapse of time for a lesser period than that provided in actions at law may nevertheless constitute laches under the particular circumstances of the case.[75]

Since laches implies fault, lapse of time due to ignorance of one's rights will not serve to constitute laches, if the ignorance does not, of course, result from lack of diligence.[76]   This is also true where disability operates to prevent bringing of suit.[77]

Sec. 25.   Balancing of equities or conveniences.

A matter which may be highly determinative of whether or not equitable relief should be granted is the doctrine variously described as the balancing of equities or the balancing of conveniences or hardships.[78]   The rule commonly owes its existence to its development by courts in the exercise of equitable powers,[79] but its appli-

---

[71] In McClintock, *Handbook of Equity* (2d Ed.) Sec. 28, it is advanced that, although statutes of limitation did not originally apply to suits in equity, latter-day statutes do. Their application, however, must be determined from their language. Walsh, in his *Treatise on Equity* (1930) 474, 475, notes the existence in the code states of statutes of limitations governing certain of the important equitable suits. Chafee and Simpson, in their *Cases on Equity* (2d Ed., 1946) 654, n. 75, state that statutes of limitation in more than half the states apply to suits in equity either expressly or by necessary implication.

[72] Stevenson v. Boyd, 153 Cal. 630, 96 P. 284, 19 L.R.A.N.S. 525 (1908).

[73] See Ide v. Trorlicht, 115 F. 137 (1902).

[74] See note, 79 *U. Pa. L. Rev.* 341 (1931), alleging a growing tendency in this regard.

[75] See Castner v. Walrod, 83 Ill. 171, 25 Am. Rep. 369 (1876).

[76] Citizens Nat. Bank v. Blizzard, 80 W.Va. 511, 93 S.E. 338, L.R.A. 1918 A. 129 (1917).

[77] Scheel v. Jacobson, 112 N.J. Eq. 265, 164 A. 270 (1933).

[78] See discussion, *Rest. Torts*, Sec. 941, comment a, which remarks on the complexity of the problem and suggests the phrase "relative hardship."

[79] Doctrine of balancing the equities in trespass cases has no place in Louisiana

cation is authorized by statute in some states.[80]   Its application will be found most frequently in trespass and nuisance cases.[81]

The doctrine or rule is sometimes stated to be that the court will weigh the loss, injury, or hardship resulting to the respective parties from granting or withholding equitable relief; that if the loss resulting to the plaintiff from denying the equitable relief will be slight as compared to the loss or hardship caused to the defendant if the injunction is granted, the equitable relief will be denied. The plaintiff is left to pursuit of damages as his remedy.[82]

Too strict an application of the doctrine or rule, as the rule was just stated, may lead too often to placing the plaintiff's right to relief upon a dollars and cents basis, whereby what to the plaintiff is a substantial right is lost or irreparably injured simply because it does not approach in pecuniary amount the loss or hardship that the defendant will suffer if relief is granted.   Accordingly, many courts refuse to follow or give weight to the doctrine or rule as laid down above.   They insist that if a substantial right of the plaintiff is endangered by the defendant's wrongful act or threatened wrongful act, the latter will be enjoined even though the loss or hardship therefrom to the defendant exceeds the pecuniary value of the plaintiff's right.[83]   If, however, the right of the plaintiff is describable as trifling or insubstantial, the loss or hardship to the defendant will be considered and the plaintiff left to a remedy by

---

jurisprudence, see Esnard v. Cangelosi, 200 La. 703, 8 So.2d 673 (1942), noted 5 *La. L. Rev.* 41 (1942).

80 In Obermiller, "The Balance of Convenience Doctrine," 19 *Notre Dame Law.* 360 (1944), the author cites Colorado, Georgia, and Tennessee statutes to this effect.   Application of statute in Colorado with respect to mining, see Whiles v. Grand Junction Mining & Fuel Co., 86 Colo. 418, 218 P. 260 (1920).

81 Discussions, see McClintock, "Discretion to Deny Injunction against Trespass and Nuisance," 12 *Minn. L. Rev.* 565 (1928); Morris, "Balancing the Equities," 18 *Tex. L. Rev.* 412 (1940).

82 See Madison v. Ducktown Sulphur, Copper & Iron Co., 113 Tenn. 331, 83 S.W. 658 (1904).

Or to put it another way, will the benefit to the plaintiff from granting the equitable relief be slight as compared with the loss or hardship thereby caused to the defendant?

83 Wright v. Best, 19 Cal.2d 368, 121 P.2d 702 (1942); Felsenthal v. Warring, 40 Cal. App. 119, 180 P. 57 (1919) (where value of plaintiff's land threatened to be taken was only $12 but the plaintiff's right was as to him a substantial right); Goldstein v. Beal, 317 Mass. 750, 59 N.E.2d 712 (1945); Whalen v. Union Bag Co., 208 N.Y. 1, 191 N.E. 805 (1913).

way of damages.[84]   The doctrine or rule may also properly include giving the defendant an opportunity to remove the cause of injury, instead of arbitrarily throwing a severe loss upon him by flatly enjoining from all further activities,[85] or may include the taking of steps to determine whether the cause of injury may reasonably be reduced or eliminated, instead of compelling the plaintiff to submit to the condition and accept damages.[86]   The appointment of experts to determine whether reduction or elimination is possible is often resorted to by the courts.[87]   In short, of course, the court is trying to reach an equitable solution so far as both parties are concerned and frequently exercises its discretion in order to accomplish an equitable solution.[88]   If this is kept in mind, some of the cases may not be so irreconcilable as appears at first view.[89]

In either of the two approaches to the doctrine or rule, it will be found that if the defendant's act is wilfully tortious or is committed with knowledge of the plaintiff's right, the courts will refuse to balance the equities or conveniences and will grant the equitable relief sought.   It will be observed that the defendant's conduct has been such as not to entitle him to consideration on the part of the court.[90]

---

[84] In Tramonte v. Calarusso, 256 Mass. 299, 152 N.E. 90 (1926), not only was the injury to plaintiff's land trifling in nature, but plaintiff refused defendant access to accomplish removal of offending obstruction.

[85] Payne v. Johnson, 20 Wash.2d 24, 145 P.2d 552 (1944).

[86] See Godard v. Babson-Dow Mfg. Co., 313 Mass. 280, 47 N.E.2d 303, 145 A.L.R. 603 (1943).

[87] See Hannum v. Gruber, 346 Pa. 417, 31 A.2d 99 (1943).

[88] See Lynch v. Union Institution for Savings, 159 Mass. 306, 34 N.E. 364, 20 L.R.A. 842 (1893); Rest. Torts, Sec. 941, comment b.

Attempt to balance rights of both parties to the use of their respective properties, see Smith v. Staso Milling Co., 18 F.2d 736 (1927).

Effect of delay in seeking equitable relief and injury to defendant as affecting right to preliminary injunction, see Benton v. Kern, 126 N.J. Eq. 343, 8 A.2d 719 (1939).

[89] In fact, in many of the cases in which the application of the doctrine is under consideration, the concern is immediately with an application for issuance of a temporary or interlocutory injunction, where the viewpoint of the court may be entirely different from its viewpoint where the plaintiff's right and the injury thereto are clearly established.   See discussion, Hennessy v. Carmony, 50 N.J. Eq. 616, 25 A. 374 (1892).

[90] Tucker v. Howard, 128 Mass. 361 (1880) (encroachment in the nature of a trespass); Evangelical Lutheran Church v. Sahlem, 254 N.Y. 161, 172 N.E. 455 (1930) (where church with knowledge of restrictive covenants against other than private dwellings nevertheless bought lots for the purpose of erecting church building).

What may be described as another exception or qualification occurs where the grant of equitable relief by restraint of the defendant will affect the public convenience or rights of the public. In such a situation the hardship upon or great inconvenience to the public outweighs any right, however substantial, of the plaintiff to relief, and he is left to his remedy in damages.[91] There is some difference of opinion among the courts as to when the rights or conveniences of the public are involved. Some courts have confined the balancing of equities or conveniences to situations where the defendant is a political subdivision or in the nature of a public service corporation, curtailment or prevention of whose activities will definitely affect the public interest.[92] It has been said that to apply any balancing of equities in favor of a corporation essentially private in nature, for instance because it pays large taxes and employs a great number of people locally, would permit such a corporation in effect to condemn property of the plaintiff for private purposes.[93] In other jurisdictions, though, in such a situation the interest of the public has been considered to outweigh the right of the plaintiff.[94] In conclusion, however, it may be remarked that there would seem to be no reason why an unqualifiedly free hand should be given a defendant just because the public interest is involved. In appropriate circumstances, an equity court might well be warranted in

"The master finds that the permanent damage to the plaintiff's estate, if the defendant's building is allowed to remain as it is, is $200, and that the building can be altered in the manner directed by the decree appealed from at an expense of $530. . . . The defendant having, by the service of process, full knowledge of the plaintiff's claim, went on to build at his own risk; and the injury caused to the plaintiff's estate by the defendant's wrongful act being substantial, a court of equity will not allow the wrongdoer to compel innocent persons to sell their right at a valuation, but will compel him to restore the premises, as nearly as may be, to their original condition." Tucker v. Howard, 128 Mass. 361 (1880).

[91] See City of Harrisonville, Mo. v. W. S. Dickey Clay Mfg. Co., 289 U.S. 334, 53 S.Ct. 602, 77 L. Ed. 1208 (1933).

[92] See Ukhtomski v. Tioga Mut. Water Co., 12 Cal.App.2d 726, 55 P.2d 1251 (1936); Barger v. City of Tekamah, 128 Neb. 805, 260 N.W. 366 (1935).

[93] Hulbert v. California Portland Cement Co., 161 Cal. 239, 118 P. 928, 38 L.R.A.N.S. 436 (1911); Whalen v. Union Bag Co., 208 N.Y. 1, 101 N.E. 805 (1913).

[94] Madison v. Ducktown Sulphur, Copper & Iron Co., 113 Tenn. 331, 83 S.W. 658 (1904). See also Harris-Stanley Coal & Land Co. v. Chesapeake & O. R. Co., 154 F.2d 450 (1946), cert. denied 329 U.S. 761, 67 S.Ct. 111, 91 L. Ed. 656 (1947).
Trivial nature of plaintiff's injury and serious interference with essential war work by injunction, see Haack v. Lindsay Light & Chemical Co., 393 Ill. 367, 66 N.E.2d 391 (1946).

refusing to balance the relative hardships if it reasonably appears that the defendant can reduce or remove the cause of injury to the plaintiff.[95]

---

[95] Consider City of Lakeland v. State, 143 Fla. 761, 197 So. 470 (1940).

Chapter 4.

PROTECTION AGAINST WASTE AND TRESPASS

Sec. 26. Waste generally.

Waste is a permanent injury to real property committed by one having some title less than the whole in derogation of the rights of those having the remaining interest. There must be privity of estate. If the injury is done by a stranger, one not in privity of estate, then it is a trespass or nuisance, as distinguished from waste.[1] Waste may be described as permissive or voluntary. Permissive waste is that arising from neglect or omission of care while voluntary waste is that which is active or wilful, as by commission of destructive acts.[2] The conflict of opinion as to pre-

---

[1] See Merwin, *Principles of Equity* (1895) 428.

"Waste may be defined as injury to the inheritance by one rightfully in possession, but having an estate less than a fee, — as, for example, a tenant for life or for years. . . . Waste, because of its nature (injury to the inheritance, permanent damage to the land), necessarily results, if permitted to occur, in irreparable injury." Moreland, "Insolvency as Basis of Equity Jurisdiction," 22 *Ky. L.J.* 1 (1933).

[2] Moore, *Cyc. Law Dict.* (3d Ed.); Bispham, *Principles of Equity* (10th Ed.) 680; Tiffany, *Real Property* (3d Ed.) Secs. 630, 640. See also Grafell v. Honeysuckle, 30 Wash.2d 390, 191 P.2d 858 (1948).

ventability of permissive waste by equity is discussed in the following section.

At the early common law there was provision for a writ of waste whereby, in limited situations, recovery of damages could be had for waste. The writ lay only against tenants of estates created by the law as distinguished from those which came into being through act of the owner of realty.[3] Subsequently, by statute the class liable for waste was enlarged to include tenants for life and tenants for terms of years, and thus to include estates created by the owner, and by additional statute the punishment for waste was fixed at forfeiture of the thing or place wasted and treble damages.[4] To the extent that waste is thus recognized at common law it is termed legal waste. However, technicalities of the common law prevented resort to the action in several instances.[5]

In such instances, where no remedy was available at law, resort began to be had to equity for relief. Thus, we have the situation developed where conduct was not recognized as waste at law or at least was not recognized as giving rise to any cause of action at law but was recognized by equity as a ground for relief, because of the permanent injury threatened. We thus have the development of the so-called equitable waste. In addition, it seems to have become common in England for one creating estates to place in the instrument creating the estate the provision that the estate or interest was to be held without being subject to "impeachment of waste," under which there was no liability at law. Despite this provision, unconscionable acts of destruction by a tenant might

---

[3] Camden Trust Co. v. Handle, 132 N.J. Eq. 97, 26 A.2d 865, 154 A.L.R. 602 (1942), noted 27 *Minn. L. Rev.* 407 (1943).

[4] Camden Trust Co. v. Handle, 132 N.J. Eq. 97, 26 A.2d 865, 154 A.L.R. 602 (1942), noted 27 *Minn. L. Rev.* 407 (1943).
Several of our states have statutes providing for treble damages and a few have provisions for double damages. See Tiffany, *Real Property* (3d Ed.) Sec. 646; *Rest. Prop.*, Sec. 198, note. Illustration of recovery of statutory treble damages, see Grafell v. Honeysuckle, 30 Wash.2d 390, 191 P.2d 858 (1948).

[5] "For purely technical reasons the remainderman or reversioner in fee could not maintain this writ against the tenant in possession if a second life estate intervened, and the second life tenant had no remedy at law in such cases because the action of waste could be brought only by the owner of the immediate estate of inheritance." Walsh, *Treatise on Equity* (1930) 135.

"No person shall have an action of waste unless he hath the immediate estate of inheritance." Coke, Littleton, 53, b.

still be grounds for relief, in the eyes of equity, as being equitable waste.[6]

It will be noticed that resort to equity is in any event much more advisable since the prevention of the permanent injury is naturally a more adequate remedy. Although this reason for resorting to equity seems to have developed at a later period, it is now the primary reason for doing so. The result is that the distinctions between legal waste and equitable waste now have very little importance since the great majority of proceedings for relief are in equity.[7] And equity applies its own standards in determining whether equitable relief is warranted, whether the waste be called legal or equitable. Moreover, it is the consequences, not so much the nature of injury, with which equity is concerned.[8] From the standpoint of equity, waste may be committed, among others, by a tenant for life or for years as against the reversioner or remainderman,[9] by one joint tenant or tenant in common against his

---

[6] See Walsh, *Equity* (1930) 142.

It has not been customary in the United States to include such a provision. For an illustration, however, see Clement v. Wheeler, 25 N.H. 361 (1852).

[7] See Bispham, *Principles of Equity* (10th Ed.) 679.

"The remedy by a bill in equity is so much more easy, expeditious and complete, that it is almost invariably resorted to. By such a bill not only may future waste be prevented, but, as we have already seen, an account may be decreed and compensation given for past waste." Story, *Equity Jurisprudence*, Sec. 917, quoted in Poertner v. Russell, 33 Wis. 193 (1873). Or, in view of the code merger of law and equity in one court, in most states an injunction plus damages for the waste so far committed may be obtained in the same action.

[8] "Chancery goes greater lengths than the courts of law in staying waste. It is a wholesome jurisdiction, to be liberally exercised in the prevention of irreparable injury, and depends on much latitude of discretion in the court." Kane v. Vanderburgh, 1 Johns. Ch. (N. Y.) 11 (1814).

The solicitude of equity in cases of alleged waste and the reasons therefor is discussed by Lawrence, *Equity Jurisprudence* (1929) Sec. 878. See also Biggs v. Bank of Marshfield, 90 Ind. App. 467, 169 N.E. 71 (1929).

The usual requisites of equity jurisdiction should be present, such as inadequacy of the remedy at law, reasonable probability of irreparable injury, practicability of enforcement of injunctive decrees, etc. Generally, see *supra*, chapter 2.

[9] "The weight of authority in the United States holds both classes of tenants (liable)." Chafee, *Cases on Equitable Relief against Torts* (1933) 16, note.

Tenant for one year enjoined, see Poertner v. Russell, 33 Wis. 193 (1873).

Tenants from year to year of tenant for life enjoined by latter, see Kane v. Vanderburgh, 1 Johns. Ch. (N. Y.) 11 (1814).

cotenant,[10] and generally by one in possession of realty which is security for a right or claim held by another.[11]

Originally the typical illustrations of waste were permanent injury to the estate by the cutting of timber or by removing stone, coal, or ore which it will be remarked constitute acts of voluntary waste,[12] but waste, from the standpoint of equity would now extend to any injury which impairs or destroys the substance of the estate so as to cause permanent injury.[13]

Sec. 27.   —Permissive waste.

As already remarked in the preceding section, permissive waste is that arising from neglect or omission of care.   It will be apparent that to prevent this type of waste will ordinarily require an order that certain positive acts be done.

While the English statutes were early construed to include permissive as well as voluntary waste, it seems now to be the view in

---

[10] Although the Statute of Westminster II provided for an action of waste between cotenants, it did not define waste. Since cotenants have equal rights in the use and enjoyment of the estate, to warrant equitable relief the conduct of one would have to be malicious or unconscionable enough to constitute waste in the eyes of equity, i.e., constitute equitable waste. See McCord v. Oakland, etc., Mining Co., 64 Cal. 134, 27 P. 863, 49 Am. Rep. 686 (1883), that only equitable waste may be restrained by cotenant. Although some cases had declared that the cotenant can restrain legal waste, as in Williamson v. Jones, 43 W.Va. 562, 27 S.E. 411, 38 L.R.A. 694, 64 Am.St.Rep. 891 (1897), the test to determine what is legal waste will be found to be exactly that used to determine equitable waste. See Walsh, Equity (1930) 146.

[11] Thus, waste may be enjoinable by a mortgagee against his mortgagor, or for that matter by the mortgagor against the mortgagee in possession, by a contract purchaser against his vendor in possession or by the vendor against the contract purchaser in possession. For cases illustrative of these and other situations, see Chafee, Cases on Equitable Relief against Torts (1933) 29, 30, note. See also Glenn, Mortgages (1943) Sec. 194 ff.; annotation, Right of mortgagee to maintain suit to stay waste, 48 A.L.R. 1156; annotation, Exploitation of oil or gas resources by mortgagor, or purchaser or lessee subsequently to mortgage, as waste against mortgagee, 95 A.L.R. 957.

[12] Notice that in the United States, particularly in the earlier days of this country, a different view might be taken from that in England as to a tenant cutting timber. The necessity of clearing the land for purposes of habitation and agriculture might be involved, necessitating cutting at least a reasonable amount of timber. See Bispham, Principles of Equity (10th Ed.) 680; note 15 Cornell L.Q. 501, 503 (1930).

[13] "Waste is an unreasonable or improper use, abuse, mismanagement or omission of duty touching real estate by one rightfully in possession, which results in its substantial injury." Thayer v. Shorey, 287 Mass. 76, 191 N.E. 435, 94 A.L.R. 307 (1934).

England that equity will not restrain permissive waste necessarily involving mandatory orders to perform positive acts.[14]   While the same view has sometimes been taken in the American cases, on the ground that it is too difficult, or not practicable, for the court to supervise the performance of positive acts,[15] the contrary view has frequently been taken,[16] and the modern cases generally can be expected to take the present more liberal view of the ability of equity to supervise performance of positive acts and to grant equitable relief against permissive waste.[17]

Sec. 28.   —Meliorating or technical waste.

Even acts which increase the value of the estate may technically be waste because they change the character of the estate.   This type of waste is called meliorating waste.   Whether equity should prevent the commission of this type of waste should depend on what is ascertained to have been the intent of the one creating the estates or interests or what was his reasonably presumed intent.   Such intent or reasonably presumed intent should control.   Despite the fact that the value of the estate may be increased, it may have

---

[14] Camden Trust Co. v. Handle, 132 N.J. Eq. 97, 26 A.2d 865, 154 A.L.R. 602 (1942), noted 27 *Minn. L. Rev.* 407 (1943); Kirchwey, "Liability for Waste," 8 *Col. L. Rev.* 425, 624 (1908).

[15] See Camden Trust Co. v. Handle, 132 N.J. Eq. 97, 26 A.2d 865, 154 A.L.R. 602 (1942), noted 27 *Minn. L. Rev.* 407 (1943).

Tiffany, *Real Property* (3d Ed.) Sec. 642, declares that "it has usually been decided" that courts of equity will not take jurisdiction of a proceeding to restrain permissive waste. It is to be noticed that several of the authorities cited are English or Canadian.   American authorities to the contrary are disregarded.

[16] Prevalence of American cases granting equitable relief, see Walsh, *Treatise on Equity* (1930), 140, 141; Kirchwey, "Liability for Waste," 8 *Col. L. Rev.* 624, 634 (1908).

". . . in equity an injunction will be granted to restrain permissive as well as voluntary waste."   Poertner v. Russell, 33 Wis. 193 (1873), citing 2 *Story's Equity Jurisprudence* (Sec. 917).

In the case of voluntary waste, courts have not only enjoined further acts of waste, but ordered restoration of what has already been wasted or injured, thus definitely requiring a positive or affirmative act.   The classic example of this is Vane v. Lord Barnard, 2 Vern. 738, 23 Eng. Rep. 1082 (1716).

[17] But see Camden Trust Co. v. Handle, 132 N.J. Eq. 97, 26 A.2d 865, 154 A.L.R. 602 (1942), noted 27 *Minn. L. Rev.* 407 (1943).

Failure of a life tenant to pay taxes, with possibility of a resulting tax sale, has been treated as permissive waste.   See Thayer v. Shorey, 287 Mass. 76, 191 N.E. 435, 94 A.L.R. 307 (1934), and annotation thereto.   The expediency of extending the term waste to such a default is subject to doubt, as remarked by Tiffany, *Real Property* (3d Ed.) Sec. 630.

been the intent that it should be preserved in its original condition.[18] The reasonable wishes of those having the remaining interests should also be given consideration by the equity court.[19] Of course, consideration may be and is frequently given to the nature of the estate and the necessity of adapting it to the uses for which it was created.[20]

Sec. 29.   Trespass generally.

Trespass, as distinguished from waste, is some direct injury to real property committed by a stranger, in other words by one not in any privity of estate or title with the plaintiff.[21] By direct injury to real property is usually meant injury resulting from actual physical or tangible contact or invasion on or below the surface of the property. This physical invasion may be by the defendant in person or by some force projected by him.[22] Actual invasion above the surface, even if physically touching some building or other improvement on the property, while sometimes

---

[18] See Tiffany, *Real Property* (3d Ed.) Sec. 630; note, 15 *Cornell L.Q.* 501 (1930).

[19] See Brokaw v. Fairchild, 135 Misc. 70, 237 N.Y.S. 6 (1929), noted 15 *Cornell L.Q.* 501, 43 *Harv. L. Rev.* 506 (1930), aff'd 237 App. Div. 704, 245 N.Y.S. 420 (1930), 256 N.Y. 670, 177 N.E. 186 (without opinion) (1931); *Rest. Property*, Sec. 140.

[20] See J. H. Bellows Co. v. Covell, 28 Ohio App. 277, 162 N.E. 621 (1927).

[21] See Merwin, *Principles of Equity* (1895) 429.

At an early date it became established that the English courts of chancery, although enjoining waste, did not enjoin trespass. Eventually, it was recognized that trespass constituting a permanent injury to the freehold, as in the case of waste, was logically ground for equitable relief, hence the origin of the term "trespass in the nature of waste." As in the case of waste, equitable relief has been extended to any injury from trespass which impairs or destroys the substance of the estate. See Kellogg v. King, 114 Cal. 378, 46 P. 166, 55 Am.St.Rep. 54 (1896); McClintock, *Handbook of Equity* (2d Ed.) Sec. 133; Walsh, *Treatise on Equity* (1930) Sec. 28.

[22] Where blasting on neighboring property causes rocks or the like to be hurled on plaintiff's land, there is certainly a sufficient physical invasion to constitute trespass. See East v. Saks, 214 Ala. 58, 106 So. 185 (1925). Where the injury results from the shock or force of the blast of the explosion, there may be some conflict of opinion but it would seem more correct to term the situation a nuisance.

Some disagreement appears to exist as to whether allowing impounded waters to escape or percolate to the plaintiff's property to his injury or discharging water on his property is a nuisance or a trespass. Classified as a nuisance, see Nelson v. Robinson, 47 Cal.App.2d 520, 118 P.2d 350 (1941); classified as a trespass, see Rueckert v. Sicking, 20 Ohio App. 162, 153 N.E. 129 (1923).

classed as a trespass,[23] is frequently distinguished by courts of equity from a trespass and classified as a nuisance.[24]   The trespass may be committed under no claim or color of right, in which event it involves no dispute as to title, or it may be committed under some claim or color of right or title which is in conflict with or hostile to the plaintiff's claimed ownership and thus involve an issue of fact at law as to title.   In the latter situation a difficulty is presented in non-code states which is discussed subsequently.[25]

Sec. 30.   —Inadequacy of legal remedy.

Equitable relief, by way of injunction, is warranted where the remedy at law is inadequate.   The remedy at law is considered inadequate where the injury being caused or which is threatened with reasonable probability will be substantial and permanent or, to phrase it otherwise, will be irreparable.[26]   The situation is one in which no pecuniary recovery, no matter how large, can repair the injury or restore the status quo.   However, if the injury so described is to be interpreted as meaning one essentially destructive of the freehold, it must be recognized that the modern rule is less strict.[27]   This can be seen from consideration of the paragraphs following.

In many jurisdictions, the remedy at law is also considered inade-

---

[23] Conflict of opinion as to whether this is an adverse user or a dispossession, with reference to availability of legal action of ejectment, see Walsh, *Treatise on Equity* (1930) Sec. 31.

Where airplanes are involved, as in low-level flights over property of plaintiff, the act to the extent that it is wrongful is usually termed a trespass and enjoinable as such.   See Causby v. United States, 60 F. Supp. 751 (1945), noted 58 *Harv. L. Rev.* 1252 (1945); Burnham v. Beverly Airways, Inc., 311 Mass. 628, 42 N.E.2d 575 (1942), noted 22 *B. U. L. Rev.* 625 (1942), 28 *Cornell L.Q.* 200 (1943); *Rest. Torts*, Sec. 159, Comment e, Sec. 194.   Discussion, see Mace, "Ownership of Airspace," 17 *U. Cin. L. Rev.* 343 (1948).

[24] "The wrong here complained of was an encroachment, not upon plaintiff's land, but upon the space above the land, and therefore was not a trespass but a nuisance."   Kafka v. Bozio, 191 Cal. 746, 218 P. 753, 29 A.L.R. 833 (1923), citing Wood, *Nuisances* (3d Ed.) 33, noted 33 *Yale L.J.* 557 (1924).

[25] See *infra*, Sec. 31.

Notice that in waste, although both parties have or claim a right or title, their rights or titles are in privity; are parts of one whole.

[26] "Before a court of equity will interfere to restrain a trespass, it must appear that the injury to result from the trespass will be irreparable."   Mechanics' Foundry v. Ryall, 75 Cal. 601, 17 P. 703 (1888).

[27] See, *e.g.*, Colliton v. Oxborough, 86 Minn. 361, 90 N.W. 793 (1902).

quate where the trespass is repeated or continuous, involving recourse to a multiplicity of actions at law for damages and thus resulting in serious vexation or oppression.[28]   In jurisdictions which specifically require that irreparable injury be alleged and proven to be threatened, as a prerequisite to equitable relief, it would not appear that mere necessity of recourse to a multiplicity of actions at law for damages would constitute irreparable injury.[29]   These latter jurisdictions, however, quite frequently advance the ground that the repeated or continuous acts of trespass might give rise to an easement or adverse right or title in the property which would constitute irreparable injury since it would reduce the substance of the plaintiff's estate.[30]   And there is also the probability that the cumulative effect of recurring acts of trespass will be permanent or irreparable injury.[31]   It may also be noticed that repeated or continuous acts of trespass may interfere with the plaintiff's reasonable enjoyment and use of the property and thus in that way reduce or destroy the substance of his estate.[32]

Another ground for equitable relief advanced in the case of trespass has been that damages are so speculative or conjectural that compensation cannot be adequately measured or determined at law.[33]   However, this ground will usually be found to exist in connection with others, such as the probability of permanent or irreparable injury or necessity of multiplicity of actions at law.[34]

---

[28] Baker v. Howard County Hunt, 171 Md. 159, 188 A. 223 (1936).

Although the term "multiplicity of actions at law" originally meant causes of action against a plurality of persons, the term now is also applied to a succession of actions between the same parties, in the case of repeated or continuing trespasses. See Lawrence, *Equity Jurisprudence* (1929) Sec. 872.

[29] As in California. See Footnote 26, *supra*.

[30] Union Oil Co. v. Domengaux, 30 Cal.App.2d 266, 86 P.2d 127 (1939).

[31] As where repeated trespasses to cut down timber will result in converting timber land into waste and pasture land. See Shipley v. Ritter, 7 Md. 408, 61 Am. Dec. 371 (1855).

[32] Kellogg v. King, 114 Cal. 378, 46 P. 166, 55 Am.St.Rep. 54 (1896) (wherein plaintiff had leased hunting privileges on certain land and repeated acts of trespass by numerous individuals interfered with or impaired his privilege; it was stated by the court that the impairment or destruction of his privilege impaired or destroyed the very substance of his estate or right or interest to his irreparable injury); Baker v. Howard County Hunt, 171 Md. 159, 188 A. 233 (1936); Colliton v. Oxborough, 86 Minn. 361, 90 N.W. 793 (1902); Ashinsky v. Levenson, 256 Pa. 14, 100 A. 491, L.R.A. 1917 D 994 (1917).

[33] Baker v. Howard County Hunt, 171 Md. 159, 188 A. 223 (1936).

[34] *Ibid.*

Whether insolvency of the defendant renders the remedy at law inadequate has been previously discussed.[35]

In the case of trespasses in the nature of encroachments, if the encroachments are removable by the plaintiff himself with little trouble and expense, the remedy at law by way of damages is considered adequate.[36] On the other hand, if the removal of the encroachment imposes heavy burden and hardship on the plaintiff, it is not equitable to leave him subject to such burden and hardship by reason of the wrongful conduct of another. Accordingly, adequate relief is not supplied by an action for damages. The defendant should be required by act of the court of equity to remove the encroachment himself.[37] Particularly, where the nature of the encroachment is a structure, such as a wall or the side of a building, the remedy in equity has been considered more efficacious than ejectment at law. Equity can lay its command on the defendant that he remove the encroachment, thus placing the burden directly upon him. In ejectment, removal depends upon execution issued to the sheriff, who finds himself under difficulty and subject to considerable risk. If he requires bond from the plaintiff to protect himself, the plaintiff is subjected to burden and expense.[38]

In the case of an occasional trespass, temporary in its results, threatening no permanent or irreparable injury or not vexatious or oppressive in nature, the plaintiff is left to his remedy at law. Indeed, resort to the calling of a policeman may be sufficient in some cases.[39]

Sec. 31. —Trespass under claim or color of title.

Where the plaintiff alleges trespass by the defendant and the latter justifies himself under some claim of legal right or title hostile to or in conflict with the plaintiff's legal right or title, the plaintiff's legal right must first be established before it can be determined

---

[35] See *supra*, Sec. 22.

[36] Boyden v. Bragraw, 53 N.J. Eq. 26, 30 A. 330 (1894).

[37] Wheelock v. Noonan, 108 N.Y. 179, 15 N.E. 67, 2 Am.St.Rep. 405 (1888), followed in Eno v. Christ, 25 Misc. 24, 54 N.Y.S. 400 (1898); Denhart v. Valicenti, 157 Pa. Super. 143, 41 A.2d 884 (1945).

[38] See note, 28 *Cornell L.Q.* 110 (1942); *Rest. Torts*, Sec. 945.

[39] Randall v. Freed, 154 Cal. 299, 97 P. 669 (1908); Mechanics' Foundry v. Ryall, 75 Cal. 601, 17 P. 703 (1888).

whether he is entitled to equitable relief. The determination of the legal right is not within the jurisdiction of equity. Where law and equity are administered in separate courts, the view has originally been that the equity court will refuse to assume jurisdiction until the plaintiff's legal right has been determined in his favor in an action at law.[40]   Even then it must appear, to warrant equity jurisdiction and relief, that the determination in favor of the plaintiff's legal right or title in the court of law has proved inadequate to provide the means of terminating the defendant's trespass.[41]

However, gradual modification of this situation has come about in this country even where law and equity have been administered in separate courts. For example, on occasion the equity courts have retained the suit in equity, with the issuance of a temporary injunction, while the matter of the legal title was determined in a court of law.[42]   Or statutes may authorize the retention of the suit in the equity court and the sending of the issue at law to the law court for determination and the certification of such determination back to the court of equity which then proceeds from that point, dismissing the suit if the legal title had been determined favorably to the defendant or proceeding to consider the need of equitable relief if the determination has been favorable to the plaintiff.[43]   Or it may be provided that the equity court itself may determine the question of legal title, without a jury, upon consent of the parties, or else be authorized to impanel a jury for determination of the question.[44]

---

[40] See McRaven v. Culley, 324 Ill. 451, 155 N.E. 282 (1927); Kavanaugh v. Rabior, 215 Mich. 231, 183 N.W. 715 (1921).

[41] See Hirschberg v. Flusser, 87 N.J. Eq. 588, 101 A. 191 (1917), where means of enforcement of the judgment in plaintiff's favor in an action at law were inadequate to remove an encroachment by defendant on plaintiff's land.

[42] Erhardt v. Boaro, 113 U.S. 537, 5 S.Ct. 565, 28 L. Ed. 1116 (1885).
Use of temporary injunction in action of ejectment, see Snyder v. Hopkins, 31 Kan. 557, 3 P. 367 (1884) (wherein injunctive order of trial court was modified).

[43] See Lake Lenore v. Delaware, L. & W. R. Co., 113 N.J. Eq. 533, 168 A. 178 (1933).

[44] "The Chancellor may himself determine the question, if there be no objection; or he may order the legal title settled by a judgment at law or by a jury upon a feigned issue, at the election of the defendant." Lake Lenore v. Delaware, L. & W. R. Co., 113 N.J. Eq. 533, 168 A. 178 (1933).
Apparently even without statutory authorization, many cases in the past have held that, if the parties waive the question of a jury trial, the equity court could settle the disputed question of title. See Walsh, Treatise on Equity (1930) 165.

The merger of law and equity powers in one court, in one form of civil action, under the codes, has resulted in removing any difficulties by permitting the same courts in which the request for equitable relief is filed to determine the matter of the legal title and then proceed from there to the equitable issue; [45] or to grant equitable relief as ancillary to and pending the action for legal relief, in order to preserve the status quo or to prevent irreparable injury resulting during the pendency of the legal action.[46] Some question may arise, of course, as to whether an action of ejectment may not be proper as affording adequate relief, rendering it unnecessary if not actually improper to seek to resort to the equitable powers of the court. This condition may be especially applicable where recovery of the possession of realty is the real basis, rather than the prevention of repeated or continuous trespasses not involving a continued dispossession of the plaintiff.[47] This distinction may become a matter of prime importance to the defendant who is entitled to a jury trial in the action of ejectment but who will be deprived of a jury trial if the action is phrased as one for equitable relief.[48] Certainly, where the plaintiff is required to pursue ejectment he should be entitled, in a code state where legal and equitable

---

[45] Colliton v. Oxborough, 86 Minn. 361, 90 N.W. 793 (1902); Corning v. Troy Iron & Nail Factory, 40 N.Y. 191 (1869).

[46] "This blending of an action at law, with a petition for ancillary relief to the equity side of the court, is admissible under our system of practice. But to prevent confusion, and preserve the simplicity and directness requisite in the averments of a complaint in an action at law, the grounds of equity interposition should be stated subsequently to, and distinct from, those upon which the judgment at law is sought. It would be better practice, in such case, to commence that portion of the complaint which seeks the equitable relief, with the form: 'and for equitable relief, pending the above action, the plaintiff further represents;' or, 'and, for a further cause of action, the plaintiff represents.'" Natoma Water & Min. Co. v. Clarkin, 14 Cal. 544 (1860), an action of ejectment and to enjoin trespass in the nature of waste pending the action. See also Snyder v. Hopkins, 31 Kan. 557, 3 P. 367 (1884).

[47] See Walsh, *Treatise on Equity* (1930) 165.

[48] In Campbell v. Rustigian, 60 Cal.App.2d 500, 140 P.2d 998 (1943), it was stated that the right to trial by jury must be determined from the pleadings; even though the plaintiff is not in possession, if the pleadings do not raise the issue of the right to possession but merely seek to quiet title to realty, no issue of law is raised which requires a trial by jury and the proceeding is equitable in nature. But compare Newman v. Duane, 89 Cal. 597, 27 P. 66 (1891); Syracuse v. Hogan, 234 N.Y. 457, 138 N.E. 406 (1923); to effect that even though equitable relief alone was sought, the recovery of possession was the main question and thus presented an action of ejectment requiring a jury trial.

powers are merged in the same court, to obtain a temporary injunction during the pendency of the action of ejectment where circumstances warrant it.[49]   However, if the trespass is accomplished by an encroachment in the nature of a building or the like, it becomes apparent that equitable relief is much more adequate to effect its removal.[50]

---

[49] See Natoma Water & Min. Co. v. Clarkin, 14 Cal. 544 (1860); Snyder v. Hopkins, 31 Kan. 557, 3 P. 367 (1884). In the Snyder case the temporary injunction was held to be too broad as denying defendant the use of the property in the ordinary way while title was being decided; it was remarked that acts in the nature of waste might be enjoined but not use in the ordinary way.

[50] This is illustrated by Hahl v. Sugo, 169 N.Y. 109, 62 N.E. 135 (1901). And see *supra*, Sec. 18.

Chapter 5.

PROTECTION AGAINST NUISANCE

Sec. 32. Nuisance defined.
Sec. 33. —When existent; specific acts of nuisance.
Sec. 34. Anticipated nuisance.
Sec. 35. Prescription—Coming to a nuisance.
Sec. 36. Relief available.

Sec. 32. Nuisance defined.

A nuisance is to be distinguished from a trespass which, as has been seen, is some direct injury to or upon real property. A nuisance has been defined as an unlawful act which causes injury to a person in the enjoyment of his estate, unaccompanied by an actual invasion of the property itself.[1] But further expansion of this definition is desirable, for, as it has been said, nuisance is used to designate two distinct groups of wrongs. One, the use of his land by the defendants so as wrongfully to interfere with the plaintiff's reasonable use and enjoyment of his land, as by the creation of unpleasant, or unhealthful, or dangerous conditions. Two, the interference with some easement or other incorporeal right of the plaintiff upon or appurtenant to land.[2]

The definitions so far given are applicable to the so-called private nuisance, as distinguished from a public nuisance. The former is an injury to one or more particular individuals in distinction from

[1] Merwin, *Principles of Equity* (1895) 431.
Some disagreements as to designation of particular torts as trespasses or nuisances have been noted in the discussion of trespasses. See *supra*, Sec. 29.
[2] See McClintock, *Handbook of Equity* (2d Ed.) Sec. 134; Walsh, *Treatise on Equity* (1930) 170.

men in general. The latter is an injury to the public generally, or
to a community or neighborhood or even to some considerable
number of persons.[3] To the extent that the public nuisance is
especially injurious to one member of the public or of the community or of the neighborhood, as causing him special damage, it
is as to him a private nuisance.[4] The public nuisance encompasses
a wide field and involves such matters as the protection of public
rights of way and navigation, public welfare, public health, public
safety, and public morals. Hence, many writers and courts prefer
to refer to the subject as the protection of the public or social welfare or the like rather than as public nuisances. Whatever designation is applied, it deserves separate consideration.[5] Accordingly,
the present chapter is confined to the so-called private nuisance.

Sec. 33. —When existent; specific acts of nuisance.

What is a use of land so as wrongfully to interfere with a neigh-
bor's reasonable use and enjoyment of his property is not subject
to precise definition. What is wrongful interference in one locality may not be in another. Creation of a condition or manner of
using property in a manufacturing or industrial district may not
there constitute a nuisance but if done in a residential district may
be a nuisance. What is done in a residential district may there
constitute a nuisance but would not constitute one if done in a
rural area. The most that can be said, perhaps, is that to constitute
a nuisance the use must be such as to produce a tangible and
appreciable injury to neighboring property or such as to render
its enjoyment especially uncomfortable or inconvenient.[6]

Nuisances of the type constituting an interference with the plain-

---

[3] See Merwin, *Principles of Equity* (1895) 432, 433.

[4] Just in what way this one member of the public or of the community must
suffer injury is not always clear from the cases. May the damage differ merely
in degree or must it differ in kind? That it should in its nature be special and
peculiar to the plaintiff, see Wesson v. Washburn, 95 Mass. 95 (1866). Difference
in degree, see Gulf States Steel Co. v. Beveridge, 209 Ala. 473, 96 So. 587 (1923).
See also McClintock, *Handbook of Equity* (2d Ed.) Sec. 165; Walsh, *Treatise on
Equity* (1930) 210, 211; Lawrence, *Equity Jurisprudence* (1929) 954.

[5] See *infra*, Chapter 6.

[6] See Hurlburt v. McKone, 55 Conn. 31, 10 A. 164 (1886); Campbell v. Seaman,
63 N.Y. 568, 20 Am. Rep. 567 (1876).

As to sufficiency of allegations of bill or complaint in this regard, consider
Hart v. Wagner, 184 Md. 40, 40 A.2d 47 (1944).

The mortuary or undertaking establishment provides an illustration. It may

tiff's reasonable use and enjoyment of his property are of many and varied kinds.[7]   Some illustrations are the generation of noxious, unpleasant, or unhealthful odors,[8] or causing smoke and dust,[9] noise,[10] vibration,[11] obstructions or encroachments on neighboring property above the surface,[12] permitting the escape or percolation or seepage of impounded waters, or of sewage, or the like, onto neighboring property,[13] or by storage of explosives or maintenance of other dangerous conditions.[14]

Illustrations of the nuisance involving interference with an easement or other incorporeal right are such matters as interfering with a right of way,[15] interference with ingress or egress,[16] interference

---

constitute a perfectly proper business in one locality but constitute a nuisance if maintained and operated in a strictly residential neighborhood. See annotations, 87 A.L.R. 1061, 39 A.L.R.2d 1000; note, 36 *Iowa L. Rev.* 710 (1951). Effect of zoning ordinances on the law of nuisance, see Fiske, 54 *Mich. L. Rev.* 266 (1955); Beuscher & Morrison, [1955] *Wis. L. Rev.* 440.

[7] Besides the illustrations immediately following, others are cited or referred to throughout this chapter.

Numerous annotations will be found in A.L.R. relating to specific matters or conditions as nuisances. As to airports and airplanes, see discussion by Mace, "Ownership of Airspace," 17 *U. Cin. L. Rev.* 343 (1948). Drive-in theater as nuisance, see note, 5 *Wyo. L.J.* 207 (1951).

[8] Pollution of air in residential district by gas reservoir. Romano v. Birmingham Ry., L. & P. Co., 182 Ala. 335, 62 So. 677, 46 L.R.A.N.S. 642, Ann. Cas. 1915D 776 (1913).

Sulphuric acid gas from brick kiln injurious to trees and shrubbery. Campbell v. Seaman, 63 N.Y. 568, 20 Am. Rep. 567 (1876).

[9] Hulbert v. California Portland Cement Co., 161 Cal. 239, 118 P. 928, 38 L.R.A.N.S. 436 (1911).

[10] Assembly of God Church v. Bradley, (1946; Tex. Civ. App.) 196 S.W.2d 696; Payne v. Johnson, 20 Wash.2d 24, 145 P.2d 552 (1944).

Conditions under which noise is a nuisance, see Smilie v. Taft Stadium Bd. of Control, 201 Okla. 303, 205 P.2d 301 (1949).

[11] Hennessy v. Carmony, 50 N.J. Eq. 616, 25 A. 374 (1892).

[12] Kafka v. Bozio, 191 Cal. 746, 218 P. 753, 29 A.L.R. 833 (1923), noted 33 *Yale L.J.* 557 (1924).

As to distinction between encroachments above or upon the surface as nuisances or trespasses, see also *supra*, Chapter 3.

[13] Percolation from artificial canal. Nelson v. Robinson, 47 Cal.App.2d 520, 118 P.2d 350 (1941).

Absolute nuisance theory in Pennsylvania, see comment, 95 *U. Pa. L. Rev.* 781 (1947).

[14] People's Gas Co. v. Tyner, 131 Ind. 277, 31 N.E. 59, 16 L.R.A. 443, 31 Am.St.Rep. 433 (stored explosives) (1891).

See annotation, Pesthouse or contagious disease hospital as nuisance, 48 A.L.R. 518.

[15] Stallard v. Cushing, 76 Cal. 472, 18 P. 427 (1888); Tucker v. Howard, 128 Mass. 361 (1880).

[16] Shamhart v. Morrison Cafeteria Co., 159 Fla. 629, 32 So.2d 727 (1948); Tushbant v. Greenfield's, Inc., 308 Mich. 626, 14 N.W.2d 520 (1944). See also Sec. 59, Footnote 49.

with right of lateral support,[17] and interference with riparian easements in streams as by pollution [18] or by diversion of the water.[19] The easement interfered with may be an easement of right, of necessity, or acquired by grant or agreement.

Easements of light and windows, so-called, as of right are not generally recognized in this country,[20] although they are acquirable by grant or agreement and when so acquired are entitled to equitable protection.[21]   There is, however, some recognition of easements of light as a matter of right in favor of those whose property fronts on public streets.[22]   It is frequently customary to couple with the term "light" that of "air" so that statements of the rule read that easements of light and air do not exist as of right.   But while technically there may be no protectible easement of air as of right, it is clear that the matter is reached in another way.   As already indicated, pollution of the air by obnoxious odors, smoke, dust, etc., is enjoinable where it interferes with the reasonable use and enjoyment of the plaintiff's property.   So, though the matter is not reachable as interference with an easement it is reachable under the type of nuisance constituting interference with the reasonable use and enjoyment of property.

Sec. 34.   Anticipated nuisance.

While generally the nuisance is already existent at the time the plaintiff seeks equitable relief, the nuisance need not actually exist in order to warrant injunction.   The reasonable probability of

---

[17] Trowbridge v. True, 52 Conn. 190, 52 Am. Rep. 579 (1884).

There is very little equitable authority on this question, according to Walsh, *Treatise on Equity* (1930) 183.   Compare Merwin, *Principles of Equity* (1895) 434, 435.   And see Universal Realty Corp. v. Felser, 179 Md. 635, 22 A.2d 448 (1941), as to right of support from party wall.

[18] Lockwood Co. v. Lawrence, 77 Me. 297, 52 Am. Rep. 763 (1885); Farley v. Crystal Coal & Coke Co., 85 W.Va. 595, 102 S.E. 265, 9 A.L.R. 933 (1920).

[19] Harding v. Stamford Water Co., 41 Conn. 87 (1874); Amsterdam Knitting Co. v. Dean, 162 N.Y. 278, 56 N.E. 757 (1900).

[20] This was remarked upon over 50 years ago by Merwin, *Principles of Equity* (1895) 435, pointing out that the rule is otherwise in England and formerly in Massachusetts.

[21] Hennen v. Deveny, 71 W.Va. 629, 77 S.E. 142, L.R.A. 1917 A. 524 (1913).
[22] See Lahr v. Metropolitan Ry., 104 N.Y. 268, 10 N.E. 528 (1887).

The use of light itself so as to constitute a nuisance was considered in Amphitheatres, Inc. v. Portland Meadows, 47 Ore. 77, 198 P.2d 847 (1948), noted 24 *Notre Dame Law.* 254 (1949), 62 *Harv. L. Rev.* 704 (1949).

injury from an anticipated nuisance will warrant injunction in a proper case against the creation or establishment of the condition or matter from which the nuisance is to be anticipated.[23] The condition, matter, or thing may in itself be a nuisance, what is termed a nuisance per se,[24] or may result in a nuisance from the manner in which it will be maintained or operated[25] or because of the place at which it is to be maintained.[26] Anticipation of a nuisance from conduct or manner of maintenance or operation may be more easily determined where there has been past conduct to judge by. For example, the construction of a church has been enjoined on the ground that its manner of use would constitute a nuisance where past conduct of the congregation in holding revival meetings at night in a tent on the premises had consisted of singing and shouting in loud voices heard as far as half a mile away.[27]

However, relief is not warranted if it does not appear that the danger to the plaintiff is real and immediate and that the injury will be material.[28] Where a thing or condition is not in itself a nuisance, that is, is not what is describable as a nuisance per se, but will result in a nuisance only from its manner of maintenance or operation, its establishment or construction should not be enjoined

---

23 McPherson v. First Presbyterian Church, 120 Okla. 40, 248 P. 561, 51 A.L.R. 1251 (1926).

Although, in Adams v. Michael, 38 Md. 123, 17 Am. Rep. 516 (1873), referred to approvingly as a leading case in Hart v. Wagner, 184 Md. 40, 40 A.2d 47 (1944), the court declared that "the general rule is that an injunction will only be granted to restrain an actually existing nuisance," in reality injunction was denied because the court was unable to determine from the facts alleged whether the nuisance would have been of the nature and character supposed so as to subject the plaintiff to substantial injury.

24 Generally, a condition or thing which from its very nature will work serious annoyance or injury in any circumstances. Even so, the term must be considered to be relative. Definition, see Denney v. United States, 185 F.2d 108 (1950).

25 Assembly of God Church v. Bradley, (1946; Tex. Civ. App.) 196 S.W.2d 696.

26 For example, it is now generally considered that the maintenance and operation of a mortuary or undertaking business in a residential district constitutes a nuisance and hence injunction will issue to restrain its establishment in such a neighborhood. Brown v. Arbuckle, 88 Cal.App.2d 258, 198 P.2d 550 (1948). See also annotation, 87 A.L.R. 1061.

27 Assembly of God Church v. Bradley, (1946; Tex. Civ. App.) 196 S.W.2d 696.

28 Vaszil v. Molnar, 133 N.J. Eq. 577, 33 A.2d 743 (1943), where the apparent intention of the defendant to keep chickens in his back yard, adjoining the plaintiff's premises, was held not to create an apprehension of a nuisance.

merely upon the possibility that its management or operation could be such as to make it a nuisance.[29]   In the case previously referred to, the church was not a nuisance per se but its manner of use, reasonably to be foretold in advance, would constitute a nuisance.

Sec. 35.   Prescription—Coming to a nuisance.

Whether a right may be acquired by prescription to maintain a nuisance is a question upon which the authorities are confused. Upon analysis, the logical view develops that no such right is acquirable.[30]   Where one maintains a certain condition upon his land, such condition cannot constitute a nuisance to someone else until someone is affected by the condition.   Suppose that the defendant maintains a certain condition upon his land and has done so for many years.   The plaintiff now acquires land in the vicinity and moves upon it.   He then discovers that his reasonable use and full enjoyment of his property is seriously affected by the condition maintained by the defendant and will continue to be so affected.   The condition may not previously have been injurious to anyone, but as to the plaintiff it constitutes a freshly instituted injury.   As to him it has not been maintained long enough to give any so-called prescriptive right to the defendant.[31]   If it be maintained that the prescriptive right of the defendant has been acquired against the land of the plaintiff before he obtained it or entered upon it, this would permit the defendant virtually to condemn to his own private purposes and uses all the property surrounding him and allow the defendant to limit the uses to which the surrounding

---

[29] Collins v. Lanier, 201 Ga. 527, 40 S.E.2d 424 (1946), noted 9 *Ga. B. J.* 325 (1947); Essick v. Shillam, 347 Pa. 373, 32 A.2d 416, 146 A.L.R. 1399 (1943).

Construction of airport not enjoined since airport was not a nuisance per se and would become one only if improperly managed. Warren Tp. v. City of Detroit, 308 Mich. 460, 14 N.W.2d 134 (1944), noted 29 *Minn. L. Rev.* 38 (1944), 20 *Notre Dame Law.* 441 (1945).

[30] See Hall v. Budde, 293 Ky. 436, 169 S.W.2d 33, 167 A.L.R. 1361 (1943).
[31] *Ibid.*

Voluntarily coming to a nuisance does not prevent enjoining its maintenance, especially where the nuisance has since become greater. Dolata v. Berthelet Fuel & Supply Co., 254 Wis. 194, 36 N.W.2d 97 (1948).

See annotation, "Coming to a nuisance" as a defense or operating as an estoppel, 167 A.L.R. 1364; comment, "Defense of unoccupied property against nuisance," 21 *Notre Dame Law.* 358 (1946).

property could be put.[32]   Even in the case of vacant land already owned but not yet occupied by the plaintiff, injunctive relief has been allowed the plaintiff on the ground that future enjoyment and benefit of his land would be interfered with when it came to be occupied.[33]

If the plaintiff at the time of acquiring his property is aware of the condition maintained by the defendant, is he estopped or in any way equitably barred from seeking relief?   The mere fact that he knew of the condition is in itself no indication that he knew or realized the effect it would have upon him in the ownership or occupancy of his property.   Even if the plaintiff knew of the effect it would have upon his use and enjoyment of his property, he is not thereby estopped from seeking equitable relief, if his use of his property rather than the defendant's use of the defendant's property is in conformity with the general use of property in the locality.   It must always be borne in mind that the general nature or use of the neighborhood may affect right to relief.   One could not move into what is a manufacturing neighborhood for a residential purpose only and insist on the prevalence of the same conditions obtaining in a residential neighborhood.[34]

But has a defendant acquired a prescriptive right against a plaintiff who has actually occupied nearby property for, say, 20 years and not within that time objected to the condition maintained by the defendant?   No, for what actually is the case is that the plaintiff is estopped or barred by laches from obtaining equitable relief.[35] If the defendant is described as having acquired a prescriptive right, it is against the plaintiff only and personally.   If the latter now sold to a third person, the third person would be faced with a condition that was a nuisance as to him as being freshly instituted,

---

[32] See especially, Hulbert v. California Portland Cement Co., 161 Cal. 239, 118 P. 928, 38 L.R.A.N.S. 436 (1911); Campbell v. Seaman, 63 N.Y. 568, 20 Am. Rep. 567 (1876).

[33] Romano v. Birmingham Ry. L. & P. Co., 182 Ala. 335, 62 So. 667, 46 L.R.A.N.S. 642, Ann. Cas. 1915 D 776 (1913).

[34] Effect of location of property, see annotation, 167 A.L.R. 1364, at 1378 ff.

[35] Effect of delay in seeking equitable relief as defeating obtaining of preliminary injunction, see Benton v. Kern, 126 N.J. Eq. 343, 8 A.2d 719 (1939), although permanent injunction was granted, 127 N.J. Eq. 434, 13 A.2d 825 (1940), aff'd with modifications in 130 N.J. Eq. 193, 21 A.2d 755 (1941).

which is the situation just previously discussed. In regard to the foregoing, it is to be noticed that even though the plaintiff has occupied his property for years in the vicinity of the defendant, during which period the defendant has maintained a certain condition, the condition so maintained may not during that period have constituted any nuisance to the plaintiff. But upon the plaintiff making another but reasonable use of his property, the condition now interferes with him. If such is the case, it may then for the first time become a nuisance as to him and be enjoinable and no so-called prescriptive right exists in favor of the defendant.[36]

So far the discussion has concerned the type of nuisance that is an interference with the reasonable use and enjoyment of property. Where the nuisance results from interference with an easement, it appears common to declare that a prescriptive right to interfere may be acquired, or that the easement may be lost by prescription. In a situation, for instance, where riparian owners are entitled to use a certain amount of water from the stream and the upper owner takes more than he is entitled to, to the detriment of the lower owner, who does not object for many years, it might well be argued that the upper owner has acquired a prescriptive right to take the additional amount of water and that the lower owner has, correspondingly, lost his right to the former amount of water by reason of prescription. But, on the other hand, is this any more than a matter of estoppel or laches so far as concerns this particular lower riparian owner? If he now sells his riparian property to a third person, is this "prescription" effective against the third person? He has no notice from anything of record and may have no actual notice otherwise. There is no reason why the rule should be any different here from that in the case of interference with use and enjoyment of property.[37]

Sec. 36. Relief available.

If the circumstances justify it, the injured party may abate the nuisance himself, that is, resort to self help. This may be

---

[36] For example, the defendant for years maintained two mortars against a party wall for purposes of pounding loaf sugar, etc. Upon the plaintiff thereafter erecting his consulting room next to the party wall, the condition then became an enjoinable nuisance. Sturges v. Bridges, 11 Ch. Div. 852 (1879).

[37] Discussion of cases on prescriptive right to pollute stream, see annotation, 46 A.L.R. 8, at p. 68.

feasible in some instances and warranted by immediate necessity. For example, smashing a padlock on an occasion when a right of way is interfered with by the wrongful padlocking of a gate and immediate ingress and egress to a highway is necessary. This right to resort to self help is sometimes recognized and provided for by statute.[38] Whether or not it is recognized by statute, it has been uniformly recognized by courts of equity as a proper method of abating a nuisance where the circumstances warrant.[39] We sometimes find courts of equity denying the aid of equity on the ground that the remedy by way of self help provides an entirely adequate method of relief. Denial on such ground may well be confined to situations not productive of substantial injury.[40] There is no doubt, however, that any right of self help should be exercised with caution, for it may well lead to actual hostilities of some sort, with the resultant calling of a policeman, where one is available, who will most likely be totally ignorant of the injured party's right to use self help. Resort to the equity powers of a court, if permissible, may provide a more dignified method of procedure.

But, as in the case of trespass, the jurisdiction of equity depends upon whether the nuisance is continuous or repeated or merely casual and temporary. In the former case, continued or recurring nature of the nuisance threatening permanent or irreparable injury renders the remedy at law inadequate and warrants equitable relief. In the latter case, the injured party is left to his remedy at law. In addition to the award of equitable relief, the plaintiff may also recover damages. The amount of damages may be fixed by the

---

[38] As an illustration of statutory authorization of self help, see Cal. Civ. Code, secs. 3501–3503. It is specified that the abatement may be accomplished without subjecting the injured party to liability for breach of the peace. Where the nuisance results from mere omission by the wrongdoer, notice to him of the intention to abate it is required.

[39] Where the injured party has not encouraged the maintenance of the nuisance, he may act to remove it without giving notice of his intention, otherwise he should give notice of his intention to resort to self help, according to the view followed in many jurisdictions.

[40] See Smith v. Holt, 174 Va. 213, 5 S.E.2d 492, 128 A.L.R. 1217 (1939).

Availability of self help not preventing obtaining of equitable aid, see Gostina v. Ryland, 116 Wash. 228, 199 P. 298, 18 A.L.R. 650 (1921). Similarly, as to encroaching tree roots or overhanging boughs, see Mead v. Vincent, 199 Okla. 508, 187 P.2d 994 (1947), and note thereto in 46 *Mich. L. Rev.* 997 (1948).

court where the exact extent of detriment is not susceptible of exact pecuniary computation.[41]

So far as concerns the requisite of property or a property right to warrant equitable jurisdiction, it will be seen that this requisite is definitely present in the case of a private nuisance.

Acts constituting nuisances are frequently described by statute as crimes but, as stated elsewhere,[42] this does not prevent resort to the aid of equity where the remedy obtainable through criminal proceedings is not so speedy, efficient, and adequate as that obtainable in equity to prevent irreparable or permanent injury.[43]

Where the question is raised as to whether the act or condition constitutes a nuisance or as to the right, title, or interest of the plaintiff as a warrant or basis for obtaining equitable relief, must this question be settled at law before he may proceed for equitable relief? [44] Where law and equity are administered in separate courts, it would seem that the plaintiff would first have to have the question of his right, title, or interest or the existence of a nuisance decided in his favor in a court of law, as in the case of trespass. But while this requirement may be found in some of those jurisdictions,[45] it appears to have been abandoned or ignored in others.[46] In code states, of course, the merger of law and equity has done away with any difficulty by permitting disposition of all questions arising, both legal and equitable, in the same proceeding. But even so, in the code states, the matter of having a jury determine the legal question raised seems generally to be ignored and the court, in the exercise of its equitable powers, determines all questions.[47]

---

[41] Judson v. Los Angeles Suburban Gas Co., 157 Cal. 168, 106 P. 581, 26 L.R.A.N.S. 183, 21 Ann. Cas. 1247 (1910).

In case of encroaching tree roots, see Mead v. Vincent, Footnote 40 *supra*.

[42] See *infra*, Secs. 39, 42.

[43] See Ingersoll v. Rousseau, 35 Wash. 92, 76 P. 513, 1 Ann. Cas. 35 (1904).

[44] See Lewis, "Injunctions Against Nuisances and Rule Requiring Plaintiff to Establish His Right at Law," 47 *U. Pa. L. Rev.* 289 (1908). See also McRae, "Development of Nuisance in Early Common Law," 1 *U. Fla. L. Rev.* 27 (1948).

As to this question in trespass, see *supra*, Sec. 31.

[45] See Parks v. Parks, 121 Me. 580, 119 A. 533 (1922).

[44] See Lewis, "Injunctions Against Nuisances and Rule Requiring Plaintiff to Laughlin, 208 Pa. 540, 57 A. 1065 (1904).

Waiver by not raising question in equity court, see Coast Co. v. Spring Lake, 56 N.J. Eq. 615, 36 A. 21 (1898).

[47] See discussion, Durfee, *Cases on Equity* (1928) 453, 454, notes. In Wisconsin, Nuisance abatement proceeding as legal or equitable in nature, see Comment note 39 *Marquette L. Rev.* 163 (1955).

Where maintenance of the particular condition alleged to be a nuisance has been authorized by law, as by legislative or other official license, is it nevertheless enjoinable? Where the authorization permits construction or maintenance or operation of something which does not necessarily produce an injurious result, but such result flows from a particular construction or maintenance or operation, the authorization is no defense to the application for equitable relief.[48] But where an act has been expressly authorized which must inevitably result in injury, what would otherwise be a nuisance is said to be legalized.[49]

Other matters constituting means of defense, such as laches, unclean hands, and balancing of equities or conveniences, have been previously discussed.[50]

---

[48] See Katencamp v. Union Realty Co., 6 Cal.2d 765, 59 P.2d 473 (1936).

[49] See Sayre v. Newark, 60 N.J. Eq. 361, 45 A. 985, 48 L.R.A. 722, 83 Am.St.Rep. 629 (1899); Dudding v. Automatic Gas Co., 145 Tex. 1, 193 S.W.2d 517 (1946), noted 25 *Tex. L. Rev.* 96 (1946).

Nuisance and legislative authorization, see 52 *Col. L. Rev.* 781 (1952). Effect of zoning ordinances on the law of nuisances, see Fiske, 54 *Mich. L. Rev.* 266 (1955).

[50] See *supra*, Chapter 3.

CHAPTER 6.

PROTECTION OF PUBLIC OR SOCIAL WELFARE

Sec. 37. Public nuisances.

A public nuisance is defined as such an inconvenience or troublesome offense as annoys, or infringes on the rights of, the whole community or some appreciable portion of it and not merely of some particular person.[1] The effectiveness of the interposition of equity and of its injunctive relief to prevent or to put a stop to such a situation is readily apparent.[2]

Somewhat briefly, it may be said that the first instances of protection of the public in early English equity jurisprudence involved the public health and purprestures.[3] That equitable jurisdiction and interposition is to be restricted to these matters has been indicated in some of the older American cases.[4] However, in most

---

[1] See Moore, *Cyc. Law Dict.* (3d Ed.)

[2] Discussion, see Leflar, "Equitable Protection of Public Wrongs," 14 *Tex L. Rev.* 427 (1936).

[3] Walsh, *Treatise on Equity* (1930) Sec. 37; Chafee, *Cases on Equitable Relief against Torts* (1924) 438–440.

Purprestures, see *infra*, Sec. 38.

[4] See, *e.g.*, State v. Uhrig, 14 Mo. App. 413 (1883), where the court lists three situations to which equitable jurisdiction has been confined in enjoining public nuisances: (1) Purprestures of public highways or navigations; (2) threatened nuisances dangerous to health of a whole community; (3) ultra vires acts of corporations injurious to public right. As a matter of fact, American courts are divided on the question of enjoining the third classification, since many consider the extraordinary remedy of quo warranto appropriate in that situation.

jurisdictions today the extent to which the jurisdiction and aid of equity may be invoked encompasses a wide range involving the public welfare generally. As well as protection of the public health,[5] equity protects such matters as the public safety,[6] property generally of the public,[7] public morals,[8] and the like.[9]

Because the protection of the rights of the public or a large part thereof is involved, it has seemed preferable to many courts and legal writers to term the matter the equitable protection of the public or social welfare rather than equitable protection against public nuisances. Since the extent of equitable protection of the public has, in most jurisdictions, gone far beyond the original consideration of what constituted a public nuisance, there may well be justification for the preferred terminology referred to.

Since the jurisdiction of equity has been so dependent upon the protection of property rights,[10] it is common to find the older cases expressing an unwillingness to enjoin as a public nuisance a situation which contravened public policy or threatened the general or social welfare rather than threatening property rights.[11] Even where the courts have inclined to protect the public welfare or morals or the like, it has frequently been pitched upon the property element by stating that the court is enjoining the use of his property by the defendant in a manner which would threaten the

---

[5] Village of Pine City v. Munch, 42 Minn. 342, 44 N.W. 197 (1890).

[6] See State ex rel. Hopkins v. Howat, 109 Kan. 376, 198 P. 686, 25 A.L.R. 1212 (1921), error dismissed 258 U.S. 181, 42 S.Ct. 277, 66 L. Ed. 550 (1921).

[7] Georgia v. Tennessee Copper Co., 206 U.S. 230, 51 L. Ed. 1038, 27 S.Ct. 618 (1906).

For an injunction to protect property interests of state in food fish in coastal waters on the ground that the remedy at law was inadequate, see People v. Monterey, etc., Co., 195 Cal. 548, 234 P. 398, 38 A.L.R. 1186 (1925).

[8] See subsequent discussion in this section.

[9] Enjoining usurious practices considered injurious to the public welfare. State ex rel. Smith v. McMahon, 128 Kan. 772, 280 P. 996, 66 A.L.R. 1072 (1929), noted 30 *Col. L. Rev.* 125 (1930), 15 *Cornell L.Q.* 472 (1930), 43 *Harv. L. Rev.* 499 (1930), 14 *Minn. L. Rev.* 690 (1930), 39 *Yale L.J.* 590; Commonwealth v. Continental Co., 275 Ky. 238, 121 S.W.2d 49 (1938), noted 1 *La. L. Rev.* 619 (1939); State ex rel. Goff v. O'Neil, 205 Minn. 366, 286 N.W. 316 (1939), noted 34 *Ill. L. Rev.* 497 (1939). *Contra*, see People ex rel. Stephens v. Seccombe, 103 Cal. App. 306, 284 P. 725 (1930), noted 18 *Cal. L. Rev.* 328 (1930).

[10] See *supra*, Sec. 17.

[11] See, *e.g.*, Attorney General v. Utica Ins. Co., 2 Johns. Ch. (N.Y.) 371 (1817). Even more recently, consider language of People v. Seccombe, 103 Cal. App. 306, 284 P. 725 (1929), noted 18 *Cal. L. Rev.* 328.

public welfare, morals, or the like.[12] Although this reasoning has frequently seemed to soothe the court and make it feel that it has not been forgetting the property element as a basis of equity jurisdiction, it will be noticed that the reasoning is somewhat twisted. If property is a necessary element of equity jurisdiction, it has been the fact that property or rights therein are being protected from irreparable injury. However, what may be termed the development of social consciousness in many courts has brought about their exercise of equity jurisdiction to protect the public or social welfare, without regard to the question of property,[13] and we thus find a situation in which definitely equity acts as a source of the only adequate relief without regard to the historic but sometimes crippling limitation upon its exercise of jurisdiction.

But leaving aside the property element, many courts display a great deal of caution about determining that acts or conduct constitute a public nuisance, especially as being injurious to public morals. Since standards of morality may change from one period to another or differ between one state and another, this cautious attitude is understandable.[14] Changing standards certainly tend to make decisions of another period or of another jurisdiction doubtful authority.

Sec. 38. Purprestures.

Reference has already been made to purprestures and, somewhat belatedly, we turn to a brief consideration of them. A purpresture is defined as an enclosure or appropriation to his own use by an individual of a part of a common or public domain. Usually, it involves enclosure or appropriation of a public right of way or

---

[12] Respass v. Commonwealth, 131 Ky. 807, 115 S.W. 1101 (1909).

[13] State ex rel. Smith v. McMahon, 128 Kan. 772, 280 P. 996, 66 A.L.R. 1072 (1929), noted 14 *Minn. L. Rev.* 690 (1930).

"No invasion of a property right need be shown in order to justify the use of an injunction to abate a public nuisance at the instance of the state. . . . The rule as to property rights applies only when the complainant is a private individual attempting to abate a public nuisance." State v. Phoenix Sav. Bank & Trust Co., 68 Ariz. 42, 198 P.2d 1018 (1948).

[14] Responsibility declared to rest upon the legislature to determine standards of public morality, violations of which shall constitute public nuisances, see People v. Lim, 18 Cal.2d 872, 118 P.2d 472 (1941), noted 15 *So. Calif. L. Rev.* 372 (1942), where operation of gambling house was sought to be enjoined as public nuisance.

public right of navigation.[15] Strictly, unless such enclosure or appropriation interferes with the public's use of the right of way or navigation, it is not a public nuisance.

Some American cases, particularly the earlier ones, influenced by English decisions, have taken the view that if the purpresture does not constitute a public nuisance or does not cause irreparable injury or does not interfere with legislative control, equitable relief is not available to the state and the legal remedy of ejectment must be pursued.[16] The better view is that a purpresture need not also be a public nuisance to warrant equitable relief where that is the most adequate means of relief to the state or the people of the state.[17] Where it is a public nuisance in that it interferes with the public in its use of public rights of way or navigation, injunctive relief is undoubtedly proper to prevent this interference.[18]

Sec. 39.   Act or conduct as a crime.

The mere fact that an act or conduct is in violation of a penal statute does not render such act or conduct a public nuisance. Equity does not enjoin an act merely because its commission will constitute a crime.[19] The act or conduct must be such as would constitute a public nuisance even in the absence of statute,[20] to warrant enjoining the act or conduct. If to allow the commission or continued commission of certain acts or conduct will result in irreparable injury to the public, equity will enjoin such commission even though the commission thereof is described by statute

---

15 See Moore, *Cyc. Law Dict.* (3d Ed.).

16 People v. Davidson, 30 Cal. 379 (1866).

17 See Story, *Equity Jurisprudence* (14th Ed., 1918) Sec. 1248 ff.

Injunction denied where purpresture did not constitute a public nuisance and defendant had easement as riparian owner to reach navigable portion of stream, see People v. Mould, 37 App. Div. 35, 55 N.Y.S. 453 (1899).

18 Hibbard & Co. v. Chicago, 173 Ill. 91, 50 N.E. 256 (1898).

Unusual illustration of purpresture, see Attorney General v. Williams, 174 Mass. 426, 55 N.E. 77, 47 L.R.A. 314 (1899).

19 People v. Steele, 4 Cal.App.2d 206, 40 P.2d 959, 41 P.2d 946 (1935); Commonwealth v. Smith, 266 Pa. 511, 109 A. 789, 9 A.L.R. 922 (1920).

20 It is apparent that it is often sought to prevent certain conduct by means of equitable remedies where resort to criminal prosecutions have proved unavailing because of unwillingness of juries to convict. Whether this resort to equity will prove successful will usually depend upon the attitude and beliefs and prejudices of the judges. Compare People v. Steele, 4 Cal.App.2d 206, 40 P.2d 959, 41 P.2d 946 (1935), with People v. Laman, 277 N.Y. 368, 14 N.E.2d 439 (1938).

as a crime.[21] However, it is not unusual for statutes to provide that an act is a crime and, as well, a public nuisance and enjoinable as such. Indeed, by statute an act may be declared to constitute a public nuisance although previously, in the absence of statute, it had not been considered to constitute a public nuisance.

Sec. 40. Procedure.

Suits to enjoin public nuisances ordinarily are provided by statute to be brought by the state attorney general or other designated officer, in the name of the state or of the people of state.[22] Usually the suit may not be brought by and in the name of individuals, although the suit is frequently brought in the name of the state on the information of (ex relatione) the party or parties immediately interested in or affected by the nuisance.[23] On occasion, by statute, the suit may be brought by and in the name of members of the public interested in or affected by the nuisance.[24]

---

[21] In re Debs, 158 U.S. 564, 15 S.Ct. 900, 39 L. Ed. 1092 (1895); People v. Laman, 277 N.Y. 368, 14 N.E.2d 439 (1938), noted 24 *Cornell L.Q.* 118 (1938), 17 *Tex. L. Rev.* 219 (1938), 25 *Va. L. Rev.* 99 (1938).

[22] See citations in preceding sections.

By the "Attorney General," see, *e.g.*, Attorney General v. Utica Ins. Co., 2 Johns Ch. (N.Y.) 371 (1817); Attorney General v. Williams, 174 Mass. 426, 55 N.E. 77, 47 L.R.A. 314 (1899).

[23] See citations in preceding sections.

[24] As in Carleton v. Rugg, 149 Mass. 550, 22 N.E. 55 (1889).

CHAPTER 7.

PROTECTION OF BUSINESS AND RIGHTS
INCIDENT THERETO

Sec. 41.   In general.

The right to carry on a lawful business is recognized in equity as a property right or as a substantial right having a pecuniary value which is in the nature of a property right.[1]   Indeed, since many of us cannot be fortunate enough to carry on an independent busi-

---

[1] See Walsh, *Treatise on Equity* (1930) Secs. 41, 44; Pound, "Equitable Relief against Defamation," *Harv. L. Rev.* 640 (1916).

"The rule that a court of equity concerns itself only in the protection of property rights treats any civil right of a pecuniary nature as a property right, . . . and the right to acquire property by honest labor or the conduct of a lawful business is as much entitled to protection as the right to guard property already acquired."   International News Service v. Associated Press, 248 U.S. 215, 39 S.Ct. 68, 63 L. Ed. 211, 2 A.L.R. 293 (1918).

ness or own a business with a physical plant of some kind but must depend upon our labor in employment in someone else's business, the power of an individual to earn a living or to exercise a trade, calling, or employment is equally a property right. It is a property right which has as much value and importance to the individual as the right to carry on a lawful business has to the one owning a business. This has also come to be recognized in equity.[2] Accordingly, a wrongful interference with the carrying on of a lawful business or with the exercise of a lawful trade, calling, or employment is an injury to property which may be enjoined in equity where the recovery of damages for the wrongful interference does not provide an adequate remedy.[3]

If the wrongful interference, as is usually the case, is continuing so as to require successive actions for damages, none of which will in itself serve to bring about a discontinuance of the wrong, or the extent of the pecuniary loss caused is impossible of ascertainment, and the injury may be described as irreparable, it is clear that the remedy at law, so-called, is inadequate and the case is one for the exercise of equitable restraints.[4] Not only can equity prevent the continuation of the wrong which will result in irreparable injury to or complete destruction of the business, it can also, to the extent that it is feasible in the particular case, award damages for the injury so far incurred or require an accounting for profits made by a competitor through his particular wrongful acts, according to the practice in the jurisdiction.[5] Although not within the

---

[2] Truax v. Raich, 239 U.S. 33, 36 S.Ct. 7, 60 L. Ed. 131, L.R.A. 1916 D 545, Ann. Cas. 1917 B 283 (1915); Standard Oil Co. v. Beretelsen, 186 Minn. 483, 243 N.W. 701 (1932); Erdman v. Mitchell, 207 Pa. 79, 56 A. 327, 63 L.R.A. 534, 99 Am.St.Rep. 783 (1905) (labor case); Gurtov v. Williams, (1937; Tex. Civ. App.) 105 S.W.2d 328 (labor case), writ of error denied by Texas Supreme Court.

Legislation designed to prevent discrimination in employment on racial or religious grounds, see note, "The Trend in State Fair Employment Practice Legislation," 23 Notre Dame Law. 107 (1947). Equitable aid may well become appropriate.

[3] Seniority rights given to employees by contract are cognizable in equity as property rights and protected as such. Ledford v. Chicago, etc., R. Co., 298 Ill. App. 298, 18 N.E.2d 568 (1939); Wagner v. Puget Sound Power & Light Co., 41 Wash.2d 306, 248 P.2d 1084 (1952).

[4] See Walsh, Treatise on Equity (1930) Sec. 44.

[5] See Nims, "Damages and Accounting Procedure in Unfair Competition Cases," 31 Cornell L.Q. 431, 32 Cornell L.Q. 24 (1946).

scope of this work, it may be noticed that under the Federal Trade Commission Act, resort may be had to the Federal Trade Commission to obtain restraint of unfair methods of competition by those engaged in interstate commerce. This restraint is accomplished by the Commission, after a hearing, issuing what is known as a "cease and desist" order.[6]

Injuries to the carrying on of a lawful business, to which most of the cases relate, may involve direct injuries committed by noncompetitors or direct or indirect injuries of various sorts committed by competitors. It is immaterial whether the wrong results from a desire to profit in a competing business or merely from a desire to injure the plaintiff.[7] The term "unfair competition" is used to designate under a general head the various sorts of wrongful interferences or acts by competitors. However, it is frequently extended to cover any acts, whether by a competitor or noncompetitor, which injure a business or business rights.[8] Since the successful operation of a lawful business or earning a living may depend upon the exclusive possession and use of trade secrets, patents, copyrights, trademarks, and other matters of similar nature, the unauthorized appropriation of or wrongful interference with any of these incidents or assets of the business to its detriment warrants equitable intervention. It becomes immaterial whether any one of these various things is describable as property in itself. The wrong in using, appropriating, or interfering with them is an injury to the right to carry on a lawful business or to earn a living and that right supplies the property interest or substantial right which is so frequently said to be a requisite of equity jurisdiction.[9]

---

[6] U.S. Code, Title 15, Sec. 45.

[7] While involving an action for damages rather than for equitable relief, the case of Tuttle v. Buck, 107 Minn. 145, 119 N.W. 946 (1909), is worthy of notice. In that case the defendant, a wealthy banker, set up a rival barber shop and ran it at a loss for the express purpose of destroying the business of the plaintiff.

Irreparable injury to carrying on business from discriminatory enforcement of ordinance, see Wade v. City and County of San Francisco, 82 Cal.App.2d 337, 186 P.2d 181 (1947).

[8] See Callman, "What is Unfair Competition," 28 *Geo. L.J.* 585 (1940); Chafee, "Unfair Competition," 53 *Harv. L. Rev.* 1289 (1940).

[9] See succeeding sections, this Chapter. See also Athearn, "The Federal Law of Unfair Competition," 28 *Rocky Mt. Law Rev.* 111 (1955).

Sec. 42. Criminal acts.

In several of the succeeding sections of this chapter are instances of acts which are crimes and also injuriously affect the carrying on of a business or the earning of a living.[10] Since these instances are not all inclusive, it is deemed advisable at this point to state the principles which govern in such situations.

It is well settled that equity does not interfere by injunction to prevent the commission of criminal acts, on the ground alone of their criminality. The enforcement of the criminal laws is ordinarily left to be effectuated by criminal procedure. But where the commission of a criminal act will cause irreparable injury to property or property rights or substantial rights having a pecuniary value which are considered in the nature of property, and the criminal proceeding will only be effective to impose punishment for the criminal act after its commission, equity will interpose to prevent its commission and the consequent irreparable injury.[11] Thus, acts which are crimes but which, if permitted to occur or to continue, will cause irreparable injury to the carrying on of a business or to the power to earn a living will be enjoined.[12] The criminal act may be one committed or about to be committed by a noncompetitor but nevertheless for the direct purpose of injuring the plaintiff's business or his power to earn a living.[13] If the criminal act is committed by a competitor it amounts to unfair competition.[14] The situation may be such that the plaintiff

---

[10] See, *e.g.,* Sec. 45, as to operating without a franchise or license in competition with a franchise or license holder; Sec. 54, publication of defamatory statements injurious to business which are also criminal libels.

[11] See Chapter 2.

Discussion, see Maloney, "Injunctive Law Enforcement: Leaven or Secret Weapon," 1 *Mercer L. Rev.* 1 (1949).

Enjoining criminal prosecutions in California despite wording of California code section, see comment, 37 *Cal. L. Rev.* 685 (1949).

[12] Bueneman v. City of Santa Barbara, 8 Cal.2d 405, 65 P.2d 884, 109 A.L.R. 895 (1937). See also cases cited in notes following.

That no special injury was suffered by plaintiff from competing automobile dealer keeping open on Sunday in violation of law, see Motor Car Dealers' Ass'n v. Fred S. Haines Co., 128 Wash. 267, 222 P. 611, 36 A.L.R. 493 (1924).

[13] Examples of this situation occur in labor disputes, as for instance where picketing of the plaintiff's business is accompanied by illegal acts injurious to his business.

[14] Farmers Co-operative Ass'n v. Quaker Oats Co., 233 Iowa 701, 7 N.W.2d 906

cannot successfully combat the competition except on the plane where it has been pitched by the defendant and this he cannot attempt without himself becoming a violator of the law.[15] Or the situation may be that the business of the plaintiff is being strangled by a criminal monopoly or combination or other acts in restraint of trade.[16] Where the delays and burdens inherent in the prosecution of the criminal acts threaten irreparable injury before the prosecutions can even be instituted, much less brought to a successful conclusion, equity affords the only speedy and effective relief. This may be particularly true where the number of offending competitors is so great as to render the institution of criminal proceedings exceedingly difficult and time consuming.[17]

Sec. 43. Copyrights and literary property.

Literary property is the interest or ownership which an author has in his original work and which gives him the sole right to the first printing and publishing of his work.[18] A copyright may be defined, somewhat generally, as the exclusive right one has to continue to print, publish, and sell a production of the mind, whether a writing, musical composition, drawing, design, or the like.[19]

While it was declared at one time in England that the right of one in his production or composition was a right of property at common law, independent of statute,[20] this was shortly thereafter

---

(1943); Seifert v. Buhl Optical Co., 276 Mich. 692, 268 N.W. 784 (1936), noted 35 *Mich. L. Rev.* 497 (1937); Glover v. Malloska, 238 Mich. 216, 213 N.W. 107, 52 A.L.R. 77 (1927) (lottery); Featherstone v. Independent Service Station Ass'n, (1928; Tex. Civ. App.) 10 S.W.2d 124 (lottery), noted 42 *Harv. L. Rev.* 693 (1929; 27 *Mich. L. Rev.* 833 (1929); Puget Sound, etc., Co. v. Grassmeyer, 102 Wash. 482, 173 P. 504, L.R.A. 1918 F 469 (competing without franchise or license, in violation of law) (1918).

See annotation, Right to enjoin rival or competitor from illegal acts or practices amounting to a crime, 52 A.L.R. 79.

[15] Featherstone v. Independent Service Station Ass'n, (1928; Tex. Civ. App.) 10 S.W.2d 124, noted 42 *Harv. L. Rev.* 693 (1929), 27 *Mich. L. Rev.* 833 (1929).

[16] Farmers Co-operative Ass'n v. Quaker Oats Co., 233 Iowa 74, 7 N.W.2d 906 (1943).

Restraints and monopolies as crimes under federal laws, see Sherman Anti-Trust Act and Clayton Act (U. S. Code, Title 15).

[17] Featherstone v. Independent Service Station Ass'n (1928; Tex. Civ. App.) 10 S.W.2d 124.

[18] See Moore, *Cyc. Law Dict.* (3d Ed.).

[19] Merwin, *Principles of Equity* (1895) 457; Moore, *Cyc. Law Dict.* (3d Ed.). As to copyright of musical composition, see *infra*.

[20] Millar v. Taylor, 4 Burr. 2303, 98 Eng. Rep. 201 (1769).

denied,[21] and this would seem to be consistent with the legal history of the subject which shows that it developed under statutory protection, insofar as there is a protectible right after general publication.[22]

In this country we recognize both a common law copyright and a copyright by statute. They are, however, fundamentally distinguishable and together make up one whole. At common law, an author is recognized as having a property right (which is transferable) [23] in his production until he dedicates it to the public by a general publication. He is entitled to the aid of equity to prevent the unauthorized use or publication of his literary property by another prior to his own dedication of it by a general publication. It will be seen that he is assured the exclusive right of first general publication.[24] The production of the mind must

---

[21] Donaldson v. Beckett, 4 Burr. 2408, 2 Bro. P. C. 129, 1 Eng. Rep. 837 (1774). It was again denied in a five to four decision, in Jeffreys v. Boosey, 4 H. L. C. 815, 10 Eng. Rep. 681 (1854). Walsh, in his *Treatise on Equity* (1930) 216, note, erroneously states that a majority favored the view of a common law property right.

[22] With the rise and development of printing in England, the printers and other allied crafts associated together in the Stationers Company which was incorporated in 1556 and which was entrusted by law with general supervision of publishing and dealing in books. With some exceptions, all publishers registered their books with the Company, which saw to it that no one else infringed on their exclusive right of publication and multiplication. Subsequent developments brought about enactment of the Copyright Act of 1709. See Holdsworth, "Press Control and Copyright in the 16th and 17th Centuries," 29 *Yale L.J.* 841 (1920). (In justice to Professor Holdsworth, it should be noted that he argues that in any event there was a common law property right.) See also articles by Rogers, 5 *Ill. L. Rev.* 551 (1911), 7 *Mich. L. Rev.* 101 (1908).

[23] Artist voluntarily divesting himself of title and ownership in publisher's favor, see Vargas v. Esquire, Inc., 164 F.2d 522 (1947).

[24] Bobbs-Merrill Co. v. Straus, 147 F. 15 (1906), noted 6 *Col. L. Rev.* 50 (1906), 19 *Harv. L. Rev.* 125 (1906), aff'd 210 U.S. 339, 28 S.Ct. 722, 52 L. Ed. 1086 (1907); Loew's, Inc. v. Superior Court, 18 Cal.2d 419, 115 P.2d 983 (1941); Frohman v. Ferris, 238 Ill. 430, 87 N.E. 327, 43 L.R.A.N.S. 639, 128 Am.St.Rep. 135 (1909), aff'd 223 U.S. 424, 32 S.Ct. 263, 56 L. Ed. 492 (1912).

See Kelley, "Rights of Authors and Artists Outside the Copyright Law," 5 *Cornell L.Q.* 48 (1919); Walsh, *Treatise on Equity* (1930) Sec. 42; Warner, "Protection of Radio and Television Programs by Common Law Copyright," 3 *Vand. L. Rev.* 209 (1950); note; "Literary Property: Common Law Protection of Dramatic Works," 38 *Cal. L. Rev.* 332 (1950); Berkowitz, "Common Law Copyright—Analysis of Some Recent Developments," 24 *So. Calif. L. Rev.* 65 (1950).

This common law copyright is incorporated into the statutes of some states. See Cal. Civ. Code, Sec. 980 ff.

Common law property right as extending to letters, see *supra*, Sec. 17.

be actually reduced to concrete form. Otherwise, it is a mere idea or abstract idea, which presents another question.[25]   Once he has dedicated it to the public by a general publication, the owner thereupon loses his common law property right and anyone may thereafter copy, publish and sell the production or composition, in the absence of further protection provided by statute.[26]

It is at this point of general publication that the statutory copyright becomes effective.   Under the federal laws governing copyright, the author upon compliance therewith obtains the exclusive right for a limited period to publish his production or, as it is sometimes expressed, the right to multiply copies to the exclusion of others.[27]   This exclusive right or monopoly granted by statute is

---

[25] Interests in ideas, see *infra*, Sec. 48.

When the common law copyright has been defined as an intangible incorporeal right existing separate and apart from the property in the paper on which it is written or the physical substance in which it is embodied, the incorporeal right is in the sense of the right to make copies or to make the first publication. See Local Trademarks, Inc. v. Price, 170 F.2d 715 (1948), and cases cited.

See Gershon, "Contractual Protection for Literary or Dramatic Material: When, Where and How Much?" 27 *So. Calif. L. Rev.* 290 (1954).

[26] Bobbs-Merrill Co. v. Straus, 147 F. 15 (1906); Loew's, Inc. v. Superior Court, 18 Cal.2d 419, 115 P.2d 983 (1941); Frohman v. Ferris, 238 Ill. 430, 87 N.E. 327, 43 L.R.A.N.S. 639, 128 Am.St.Rep. 135 (1909), aff'd 223 U.S. 424, 32 S.Ct. 263, 56 L. Ed. 492 (1912).

What constitutes a dedication to the public or a general publication is not always easily determinable.   It is settled that delivery or presentation of the product of the mind before a limited or selected group or class is not a dedication to the public.   If delivered or presented at a meeting open to the general public, there is a dedication or general publication.   Nevertheless, it is held in this country that presentation of an unpublished play to those who have paid to see it is not a general publication, although seemingly any members of the general public who are able to purchase admission may attend.   See Ferris v. Frohman, 223 U.S. 424, 32 S.Ct. 263, 56 L. Ed. 492 (1912); Tompkins v. Halleck, 133 Mass. 32 (1882). As to reading report before professional society, see New Jersey State Dental Society v. Dentacura Co., 57 N.J. Eq. 539, 41 A. 672 (1898); delivering lecture, Nutt v. National Institute, 31 F.2d 236 (1929); displaying dress design, Fashion Originators Guild v. Federal Trade Commission, 114 F.2d 80 (1940), aff'd 312 U.S. 457, 61 S.Ct. 703, 85 L. Ed. 949 (1941), noted 35 *Ill. L. Rev.* 546 (1941), 27 *Va. L. Rev.* 230 (1940); musical composition, Arnstein v. Edw. B. Marks Music Corp., 82 F.2d 275 (1936); reading script over radio, Uproar Co. v. National Broadcasting Co., 8 F. Supp. 358 (1934), modified and aff'd 81 F.2d 373 (1936); broadcasting news obtained by press agency for distribution to newspapers, see annotation, 104 A.L.R. 876.

See also Kaplan, "Publication in Copyright Law: The Question of Phonograph Records," 103 *U. Pa. L. Rev.* 469 (1955); Capitol Records, Inc. v. Mercury Records Corp., 221 F.2d 657 (1955), as to effect of general sale on property rights in phonograph records; Nimmer, "Copyright Publication," 56 *Col. L. Rev.* 185 (1956).

[27] Bobbs-Merrill Co. v. Straus, 147 F. 15 (1906); Loew's, Inc. v. Superior Court,

naturally a valuable asset in a commercial sense. It may be protected by equitable remedies against infringement or plagiarism where remedy by way of damages is inadequate. Since it is usually very difficult to determine at law to what extent there has been injury or loss from infringement or plagiarism, equitable relief may be particularly called for.[28] The relief may include restraint of further publication and sale of the infringing work and likewise an accounting of all profits made through the infringement and the surrender of infringing copies and the means of making them.[29] This relief must be sought in the federal courts since the state courts do not have jurisdiction of suits arising under the federal copyright laws.[30]

Even though an author avails himself of the protection of the federal copyright laws, his general publication remains a surrender of his common law property right. Upon the expiration of the statutory period of protection, his common law property right does not revive.[31] Even without a general publication, the copyrighting of one's literary property under the federal statute is said to constitute an election to protect one's right of property by means of

---

18 Cal.2d 419, 115 P.2d 983 (1941). See also Bricker, "Renewal and Extension of Copyright," 29 So. Calif. L. Rev. 23 (1955).

In the case of copyrighted musical compositions, it would seem that there are two distinct rights conferred on the copyright owner, the right to publish and sell copies of the work and the right to perform it publicly for profit. Selling the work to purchasers does not in itself confer on the purchasers the right to perform the work publicly for profit. Interstate Hotel Co. v. Remick Music Corp., 157 F.2d 744 (1946).

The federal act, U. S. Code, Title 32, does not annul or limit rights at common law or in equity in unpublished works. See Sec. 2 of that title.

[28] See Merwin, Principles of Equity (1895) 460.

Discussion of the various types of infringement of exclusive rights obtained under the federal copyright laws is not within the scope of this work. Reference may be had to general treatises on the subject. See also Callman, "Copyright and Unfair Competition," 2 La. L. Rev. 648 (1940); Driscoll, "Copyright Infringement," 11 Fordh. L. Rev. 63 (1942); Young, "Copyright Law," 28 Ky. L.J. 447 (1940); Linck, "Copyright Law Applied to Radio Broadcasting," 19 Notre Dame Law. 13 (1943); Borden, "Copyright of Advertising," 35 Ky. L.J. 205 (1947); Henn, "Magazine Rights—A Division of Indivisible Copyright," 40 Cornell L.Q. 411 (1955). Use of substantial portion of a copyrighted work for a burlesque or parody is not a fair use and is enjoinable. Loew's, Inc. v. Columbia Broadcasting System, 131 F. Supp. 165 (1955), noted 28 Rocky Mt. Law Rev. 134 (1955).

[29] U. S. Code, Title 17, Sec. 25.

[30] Generally, and as to suits "arising under" such laws, see Cyclopedia of Federal Procedure, 3d Ed., Chap. II. See also Loew's, Inc. v. Superior Court, 18 Cal.2d 419, 115 P.2d 983 (1941), noted 15 So. Calif. L. Rev. 104 (1941).

[31] Bobbs-Merrill Co. v. Straus, 147 F. 15 (1906), aff'd 210 U.S. 339, 28 S.Ct. 722, 52 L. Ed. 1086 (1907).

the remedies afforded by the statute and to be a surrender of one's common law property right and the protection afforded it.[32]

Sec. 44. Patents.

Although the word "patents" has other meanings, it is used here in its more usual meaning of those instruments by which the United States secures to inventors for a limited time the exclusive use of their own inventions.[33]

As in the case of literary property, the inventor who has reduced his idea to concrete form, as a design, diagram or the like, has a common law property right therein which is protectible in equity against unauthorized use prior to any general publication or marketing of the invention.[34]

The federal patent laws, as in the case of the federal copyright laws, afford him protection thereafter. Since the exclusive right or monopoly secured by the patenting under the federal statute is a substantial right having a definite pecuniary value, equitable relief may be resorted to for the purpose of restraining infringements of this right to the irreparable injury of the patentee or his assignees. Remedy by way of damages is inadequate where the infringement is continuing and successive actions for damages would be necessitated, none of which would be effective, of course, to bring the infringement to a close. Equitable relief may also include an accounting for the profits made by the infringer through his wrongful act.[35] The relief must be sought in the federal courts for the state courts are excluded from jurisdiction of cases arising under the patent laws.[36] If question arises as to the validity of the plaintiff's patent that question can be disposed

---

[32] Loew's, Inc. v. Superior Court, 18 Cal.2d 419, 115 P.2d 983 (1941), noted 15 *So. Calif. L. Rev.* 104(1941).

[33] Moore, *Cyc. Law Dict.* (3d Ed.).

[34] See Tabor v. Hoffman, 118 N.Y. 30, 23 N.E. 12, 16 Am.St.Rep. 740 (1889).

Rights and remedies independent of patent laws of one making invention, etc., against another utilizing it or disclosing it or threatening to do so, see annotation, 170 A.L.R. 449.

[35] Continental Paper Bag Co. v. Eastern Paper Bag Co., 210 U.S. 405, 28 S.Ct. 748, 52 L. Ed. 1122 (1906), noted 7 *Col. L. Rev.* 433 (1907), 20 *Harv. L. Rev.* 638 (1907), 18 *Yale L.J.* 52 (1907); Waterman v. Mackenzie, 138 U.S. 252, 11 S.Ct. 334, 34 L. Ed. 923 (1891) (distinguishing license from assignment).

Early history of patents in Chancery, see Chafee, *Cases on Equitable Relief Against Torts* (1924) 67.

[36] Generally, and as to actions "arising under" such laws, see Cyc. Fed. Proc., 3d Ed., Chap. II.

of by the court,[37] whatever may have been the rule in the past or in England requiring establishment of the validity of the patent in a prior action at law.[38] Upon final decree granting a permanent or perpetual injunction against infringement of the patent, permanent or perpetual means until the expiration of the patent.[39]

In this country it is immaterial that the owner of the patent right is not exercising his rights under the patent. Non-use by the patentee does not justify use of the patent by another,[40] even though he is willing to pay a reasonable value as fixed by a court for a license to use the patent.[41] On the other hand, if the patentee is using his patent to the detriment of the public interest, for example to create a monopoly or to restrain competition, equity will not afford him relief against an infringement.[42]

Sec. 45. Franchises or licenses.

In the sense that a franchise or license is a special privilege or grant by the government to a person or corporation to carry on some business, occupation, or profession, which is not a matter of common right,[43] it is usually considered by equity as a right of

---

37 Effect of procedural fusion of law and equity in federal courts, see Cyc. Fed. Proc., 3d Ed., Chap. IX.

38 As to former rule, see Walsh, *Treatise on Equity* (1930) Sec. 43, citing Chafee, *Cases on Equitable Relief Against Torts* (1924) 67; 1 Ames, *Cases on Equity* (1904) 629, n. 1.

For exceptions existing under former rule, see McCoy v. Nelson, 121 U.S. 484, 7 S.Ct. 1000, 30 L. Ed. 1017 (1887).

39 Merwin, *Principles of Equity* (1895) 444.

Effect of near approach time of expiration or expiration pending suit, see 40 Am. Jur., "Patents," Sec. 178.

40 Continental Paper Bag Co. v. Eastern Paper Bag Co., 210 U.S. 405, 28 S.Ct. 748, 52 L. Ed. 1122 (1906), noted 7 *Col. L. Rev.* 433 (1907), 20 *Harv. L. Rev.* 638 (1907).

Statutory rule in England, see 9 & 10 Geo. V, Sec. 27 (1919); note, 20 *Harv. L. Rev.* 638 (1907).

41 Campbell Printing Press & Mfg. Co. v. Manhattan Ry. Co., 49 F. 930 (1892).

42 Mercoid Corp. v. Mid-Continent Inv. Co., 320 U.S. 661, 64 S.Ct. 268, 88 L. Ed. 376 (1944), rehearing denied 321 U.S. 802, 64 S.Ct. 525, 88 L. Ed. 1089 (1944), noted 57 *Harv. L. Rev.* 574, 900 (1944); Morton Salt Co. v. Suppiger Co., 314 U.S. 488, 62 S.Ct. 402, 86 L. Ed. 363 (1942), noted 50 *Col. L. Rev.* 476 (1950).

43 See Moore, *Cyc. Law Dict.* (3d Ed.).

Definition and nature of franchise, license or permit, see more fully, McQuillin, *Municipal Corporations* (3d Ed.) Sec. 34.01 ff. Franchise and license distinguished, see State ex rel. Fairchild v. Wisconsin Automotive Trades Ass'n, 254 Wis. 398, 37 N.W.2d 98 (1949).

Common right to engage in particular business, see New State Ice Co. v. Liebmann, 285 U.S. 262, 52 S.Ct. 371, 76 L. Ed. 747 (1932).

property or as a substantial right having a pecuniary value which is in the nature of a property right. This is true even though the franchise or license is not an exclusive one.[44] One who interferes wrongfully with the exercise of the franchise or license or unlawfully competes with the franchise or license holder to his injury may be restrained in equity where there is no other adequate remedy. The injury is considered, as already indicated, one to a right of property or right of substance which is a proper subject of protection by equity.[45] It will be noticed that the wrong is either in the nature of unfair competition or is in the nature of a nuisance or trespass.

Where the franchise or license is an exclusive one, any competition is necessarily without authority of law and may be classified as wrongful. It is obvious that it must cause damage or injury to the franchise holder. Where the wrong is continuing it is undoubtedly one which will result in irreparable injury for which damages alone will not be adequate. Likewise, a resort to a criminal proceeding may not provide a sufficiently prompt and efficacious remedy which will prevent irreparable injury.[46] Even though the franchise or license is not exclusive, the franchise or license holder may enjoin one who competes against him without authority

---

[44] Frost v. Corporation Commission (Oklahoma), 278 U.S. 515, 49 S.Ct. 235, 73 L. Ed. 483 (1929); Phenix City v. Alabama Power Co. 239 Ala. 537, 195 So. 894 (1940); Puget Sound, etc., Co. v. Grassmeyer, 102 Wash. 482, 173 P. 504, L.R.A. 1918 F 469 (1918).

Liquor dealer's license not property so as to be within jurisdiction of equity. State ex rel. Zeller v. Montgomery Circuit Court, 223 Ind. 476, 62 N.E.2d 149 (1945), noted 46 Col. L. Rev. 301 (1946).

[45] Frost v. Corporation Commission (Oklahoma), 278 U.S. 515, 49 S.Ct. 235, 73 L. Ed. 483 (1929) (unauthorized competition); Boise Street Car Co. v. Van Avery, 61 Ida. 502, 103 P.2d 1107 (wrongful interference by others than competitors) (1940); Moundsville Water Co. v. Moundsville Sand Co., 124 W.Va. 118, 19 S.E.2d 217, 139 A.L.R. 1199 (1942) (unlawful obstructions and continuous trespasses).

Franchise or license to practice a profession is a property right protectible against infringement causing irreparable damage. Seifert v. Buhl Optical Co., 276 Mich. 692, 268 N.W. 784 (1936), noted 35 Mich. L. Rev. 497 (1937); Unger v. Landlords' Management Corp., 114 N.J. Eq. 68, 168 A. 229 (1933), noted 18 Minn. L. Rev. 227 (1933); Fitchette v. Taylor, 191 Minn. 582, 254 N.W. 910 (1934); Devorken v. Apartment House Owners Ass'n, 38 Ohio App. 265, 176 N.E. 577 (1931). But see Steinberg v. McKay, 295 Mass. 139, 3 N.E.2d 23 (1936).

See annotations, Right to enjoin practice of profession or conduct of business without a license or permit, 81 A.L.R. 292, 92 A.L.R. 173.

[46] Denver & R. G. W. Ry. Co. v. Linck, 56 F.2d 957 (1932); City Sanitary Service Co. v. Rausch, 10 Wash.2d 446, 117 P.2d 225 (1941).

or unlawfully, where he can show that he suffers irreparable damage or special injury therefrom for which there is no other adequate remedy.[47] For example, although those competing against him may be doing so unlawfully, they may be so numerous and the circumstances may be such that the prosecution of criminal actions against them may not be so speedy or so efficacious as the equitable remedy.[48] Although there is modern authority that one holding a non-exclusive franchise cannot enjoin unauthorized competition, this will usually be found to be based on the fact that no actual or irreparable injury was shown, or on the fact that the right is reserved by statute in the state, through a proper representative, to enjoin unauthorized operation by public service companies, ultra vires acts of corporations, or the like.[49]

Whether or not a franchise is exclusive, the franchise holder is entitled to injunctive relief against one unlawfully obstructing the franchise holder in the performance of its functions or continuously committing trespasses, to the irreparable injury of the franchise holder.[50]

Sec. 46.   Trade secrets.

A trade secret is some secret compound, process, formula, device, list, or data, or the like, used in a business and known only to the owner and to such employees to whom it must be made known in order to use it.[51] Whether trade secrets are, in themselves, prop-

---

[47] Frost v. Corporation Commission (Oklahoma), 278 U.S. 515, 49 S.Ct. 235, 73 L. Ed. 483 (1929); Farmers & Merchants Co-op. Tel. Co. v. Boswell Tel. Co., 187 Ind. 371, 119 N.E. 513 (1918), noted 32 Harv. L. Rev. 84 (1918); Puget Sound, etc., Co. v. Grassmeyer, 102 Wash. 482, 173 P. 504, L.R.A. 1918 F 469 (1918).

[48] See Puget Sound, etc., Co. v. Grassmeyer, 102 Wash. 482, 173 P. 504, L.R.A. 1918 F 469 (1918).

[49] Baxter Tel. Co. v. Cherokee County Mut. Tel. Ass'n, 94 Kan. 159, 146 P. 324, L.R.A. 1916 B 1083 (1915); Healey v. Sidone, — N.J. Eq. —, 127 A. 520 (1923), noted 25 Col. L. Rev. 1088 (1925).

That state statutes clearly did not reserve right in state but expressly gave right to sue for injunction to one injured, see Denver & R. G. W. Ry. Co. v. Linck, 56 F.2d 957 (1932), pointing out that in any event state statutes cannot restrict jurisdiction of federal court to grant injunction in proper case.

[50] Boise Street Car Co. v. Van Avery, 61 Ida. 502, 103 P.2d 1107 (1940); Moundsville Water Co. v. Moundsville Sand Co., 124 W.Va. 118, 19 S.E.2d 217, 139 A.L.R. 1199 (1942).

[51] Moore, Cyc. Law Dict., 3d Ed.; note 64 Harv. L. Rev. 976 (1951); 43 C.J.S., "Injunctions," Sec. 148; Walsh, Treatise on Equity (1930) Sec. 45. See also Rest. Torts, Sec. 757, comment b; Barton, "A Study in the Law of Trade Secrets," 64 Harv. L. Rev. 976 (1951).

erty has been the subject of dispute.[52]   However that may be, they do have a definite value as incidents of the business in which they exist and are used.   To the extent that they add to and increase the profits from the business, wrongful use of them or wrongful interference with them by another injures the owner of the business in his right to carry on a lawful business without wrongful or unreasonable interference.   Since a continued wrongful use or wrongful interference cannot be adequately compensated by money damages, equity will enjoin disclosure [53] or use [54] in such cases and, where necessary to give complete relief, order the restoration or return of the means of knowledge possessed by the wrongdoer [55] or require an accounting for profits,[56] or allow damages, according to the practice in the jurisdiction.[57]

Where disclosure or use by former employees is sought to be enjoined, varying grounds have been given to justify equity jurisdiction.[58]   In some cases the ground is said to be existence of a property right in the trade secret,[59] in others the ground is said to

---

[52] See McClintock, *Handbook of Equity* (2d Ed.) Sec. 152; Walsh, *Treatise on Equity* (1930) Sec. 45; note, 19 *Col. L. Rev.* 233 (1919).

[53] Riess v. Sanford, 47 Cal.App.2d 244, 117 P.2d 694 (1941) (species and source of supply of cactus spines used in manufacture of cactus phonograph needles).

"The word 'property' as applied to trade-marks and trade secrets is an unanalyzed expression of certain secondary consequences of the primary fact that the law makes some rudimentary requirements of good faith." E. I. Dupont De Nemours Powder Co. v. Masland, 244 U.S. 100, 37 S.Ct. 575, 61 L. Ed. 1016 (1917) per Holmes, J.

Temporary injunction to prevent geologist from revealing confidential information, see Superior Oil Co. v. Renfroe, 67 F. Supp. 277 (1946).

Protection and use of trade secrets, see also note, 64 *Harv. L. Rev.* 976 (1951).

[54] Riess v. Sanford, 47 Cal.App.2d 244, 117 P.2d 694 (1941); Simmons Hardware Co. v. Waibel, 1 S.D. 488, 47 N.W. 814, 11 L.R.A. 267, 36 Am.St.Rep. 755 (1891) (secret price code).

Secret or confidential list of customers wrongfully taken away by employee, see Sec. 44.

[55] Simmons Hardware Co. v. Waibel, 1 S.D. 488, 47 N.W. 814, 11 L.R.A. 267, 36 Am.St.Rep. 755 (1891) (copy of price code).

See annotation, Right of employer to have former employee deliver up information obtained during employment, 93 A.L.R. 1323.

[56] Irving Iron Works v. Kerlow Steel Flooring Co., 96 N.J. Eq. 702, 126 A. 291 (1924); *id.*, 103 N.J. Eq. 240, 143 A. 145 (1926).

[57] See Nims, "Damages and Accounting Procedure in Unfair Competition Cases," 31 *Cornell L.Q.* 431 (1946).

[58] See McClain, "Injunctive Relief against Employees Using Confidential Information," 23 *Ky. L.J.* 248 (1935); "Basis of Jurisdiction for Protection of Trade Secrets," 19 *Col. L. Rev.* 233 (1919).

[59] The trade secret as a property right itself, see Peabody v. Norfolk, 98 Mass. 452, 96 Am. Dec. 664 (1868); Simmons Hardware Co. v. Waibel, 1 S.D. 488, 47 N.W. 814, 11 L.R.A. 267, 36 Am.St.Rep. 755 (1891).

be the breach of contract by the employee, where he has agreed to secrecy,[60] and in others it is said to be the employee's breach of trust or confidence.[61] The last mentioned seems to be the preferred view today.[62] Frequently, of course, a combination of several of these grounds has been said to exist.[63] However, as already pointed out, it is the injury to the carrying on of a lawful business, resulting from the wrongful disclosure or use of the trade secret, that is the basis of equitable relief. The breach of contract, or of trust, or confidence is important in determining whether the disclosure or use is wrongful.

Just as an employee or former employee may be enjoined, a third person seeking to induce an employee to disclose a trade secret in violation of his contract with his employer or in breach of confidence, or using a trade secret so acquired, will be enjoined.[64] Likewise, one to whom the secret is revealed in confidence pending licensing negotiations with him will be enjoined from making an unauthorized use of the secret.[65] But one who purchases a trade secret in good faith without knowledge that it is imparted to him in violation of a contract or in breach of confidence will not be enjoined from making use of the secret.[66] It is also worth pointing out that the purchaser in good faith of a trade secret has exactly the same right to have it protected that the original owner of the secret had.[67]

---

[60] Enforcement of employee's promise of secrecy, see *infra*, Sec. 76.

[61] Horn Pond Ice Co. v. Pearson, 267 Mass. 256, 166 N.E. 640 (1929); Vulcan Detinning Co. v. American Can Co., 72 N.J. Eq. 287, 67 A. 339 (1907).
See annotation, Implied obligation of employee not to use trade secrets or confidential information for his own benefit or that of third persons after leaving the employment, 165 A.L.R. 1453.

[62] See Bispham, *Principles of Equity* (10th Ed.) Sec. 427; McClintock, *Handbook of Equity* (2d. Ed.), Sec. 152.

[63] See O. & W. Thum Co. v. Tloczynski, 114 Mich. 149, 72 N.W. 140 (1897), noted 11 *Harv. L. Rev.* 262 (1897).

[64] Taylor Iron & Steel Co. v. Nichols, 70 N.J. Eq. 541, 61 A. 946 (1905); Macbeth-Evans Glass Co. v. Schnelbach, 239 Pa. St. 76, 86 A. 688 (1913).

[65] Sandlin v. Johnson, 141 F.2d 660 (1944).

[66] Stewart v. Hook, 118 Ga. 445, 45 S.E. 369, 63 L.R.A. 265 (1903); Vulcan Detinning Co. v. American Can Co., 72 N.J. Eq. 387, 67 A. 339, 12 L.R.A.N.S. 102 (1906).

[67] Cincinnati Bell Foundry Co. v. Dodds, 19 *Ohio Wkly. Law Bul.* 84, 10 Ohio Dec. 154 (1887), per Taft, J.

Sec. 47. —Ordinary knowledge of business; names of customers.

It is necessary to distinguish a trade secret from knowledge gained by an employee which he is free to carry away and use for himself or in employment by another. Where the knowledge is such as he would have acquired in any other employment of the same nature, being common to all businesses of that type, or where the knowledge is such that anyone could discover it by mere process of observation, he is entitled to make use of it for his own benefit or for the benefit of a new employer, even though this use interferes to some extent with his former employer's business.[68] In this respect, the matter causing the greatest conflict among the courts relates to the acquisition of knowledge of or the names of customers. To what extent, if at all, can the employee make use of this knowledge or of these names to solicit their business for himself or for his new employer in the absence of any contract not to do so? [69]

Where the customers are known to all those engaged in the same type of business and are customarily solicited by all engaged in that business, the employee has obviously obtained no secret information or data by reason of his contact with these customers and carries into another employment no information not already generally known. This is particularly true in the case of a salesman employed by a wholesaler to call on retail dealers.[70] Similarly, where customers call at the premises of the employer and the employer has the opportunity to become personally acquainted with these customers himself or acquainted with them through his other employees and to hold their interest and their patronage through the exercise of his own personality and fair dealing or through the personality and fair dealing of his employees gen-

---

[68] Continental Car-Na-Var Corp. v. Moseley, 24 Cal.2d 104, 148 P.2d 9 (1944), noted 8 *Det. L.J.* 39 (1944); Victor Chemical Works v. Iliff, 299 Ill. 532, 132 N.E. 806 (1921); Southwest Specialties Co. v. Eastman, 130 Kan. 443, 286 P. 225 (1930).

[69] See annotations, Right in absence of express contract to enjoin former employee from soliciting complainant's customers, 23 A.L.R. 423, 126 A.L.R. 758. Enforcement of contract not to solicit customers, see *infra*, Sec. 78.

[70] Continental Car-Na-Var Corp. v. Moseley, 24 Cal.2d 104, 148 P.2d 9 (1944), noted 8 *Det. L.J.* 39 (1944); Boosing v. Dorman, 148 App. Div. 824, 133 N.Y.S. 910 (1912).

erally, he is at no disadvantage as compared with an employee who leaves and then seeks to obtain the patronage of the customers. The competition for their future patronage is on a reasonably equal basis.[71] However, the situation is entirely different where the employer has a secret list of customers which is an advantage to him in his business and the employee, having no or very little personal contact with these customers, takes away a copy of this list without permission and begins soliciting their business.[72]

Another variation, that causing the most difficulty, is where the employee has charge of a laundry or milk route, or the like, and is the only one who is in personal touch with the customers who do not know and are not known personally by the employer and are not known by competitors of the employer. The employer has to rely on the ability and personality of the employee to obtain and keep these customers. Having placed the employee in this favored position and having imposed trust and confidence in him, can the employee, upon leaving this employ, solicit these customers for himself or for a new employer? Some courts hold that the employee cannot solicit from a written list of customers which he has taken with him although he can solicit from memory,[73] others that he can do so either from memory or from a written list,[74] others that he cannot do so either from a written list or from memory.[75] The majority of the cases follow the holding first expressed. Whatever view is taken by a particular court depends

---

71 See Boone v. Krieg, 156 Minn. 83, 194 N.W. 92 (1923) (where employee took no copy of list of customers with him).

72 See United Bakeries v. Phillips, 5 Cal.2d 150, 53 P.2d 363 (1936); Boylston Coal Co. v. Rautenbush, 237 Ill. App. 550 (1925).

73 Progress Laundry Co. v. Hamilton, 208 Ky. 348, 270 S.W. 834 (1925); Garst v. Scott, 114 Kan. 676, 220 P. 277, 34 A.L.R. 395 (1923); Woolley's Laundry, Inc. v. Silva, 304 Mass. 383, 23 N.E.2d 899, 126 A.L.R. 752 (1939).

74 Di Angeles v. Scauzillo, 287 Mass. 291, 191 N.E. 426 (1934), noted 22 *Va. L. Rev.* 359 (1936).

75 People's Coat, etc., Supply Co. v. Light, 171 App. Div. 671, 157 N.Y.S. 15 (1916), aff'd 224 N.Y. 727, 121 N.E. 886 (1919); Colonial Laundries v. Henry, 48 R.I. 332, 138 A. 47, 54 A.L.R. 343 (1927). And see note, "Protection of Customer Lists in New York," 1 *Syracuse L. Rev.* 110 (1949).

Some courts make the distinction that the former employee, though taking no list, can be enjoined from soliciting but not from receiving patronage of the customers. New Method Laundry Co. v. McCann, 174 Cal. 26, 161 P. 990 (1916); Foster v. Peters, 47 Cal.App.2d 203, 117 P.2d 726 (1941); Brenner v. Stavinsky, 184 Okla. 509, 88 P.2d 613 (dictum) (1939). If he takes a list he can be enjoined, of course. Mackechnie Bread Co. v. Huber, 60 Cal. App. 539, 213 P. 285 (1923).

primarily upon whether it considers the information as to the customers to be of a confidential nature or whether it considers such information normally available to or ascertainable by anyone, and not of a confidential nature.[76]

Sec. 48. Interests in ideas.

In the case of an idea which may have value and utility if applied or used in a business, but which has not yet been so applied or used, we come to a matter of some difficulty. Is there a property right in the idea so as to make it the proper subject of negotiation and sale? Is there a property right in it so as to warrant resort to equity, to prevent its use by one to whom it has been revealed for the purpose of interesting him in its purchase and who thereupon appropriates and uses it without payment of compensation? [77] It is undoubted that uniformly in the past and widely at the present time it has been considered that there is no property right in a mere idea. Once uttered it has been said to be usable by anyone as part of the stock of common knowledge.[78] In itself it cannot be copyrighted or patented.[79] Its reduction to tangible form is said to be necessary in order to give rise to a property right, since it is the means of expressing the idea that is given protection, rather than the idea itself.[80]

But it has come to be considered in many jurisdictions that if it is revealed in confidence or pursuant to contract, its originator

---

[76] See annotation, Right in absence of express contract to enjoin former employee from soliciting complainant's customers, 126 A.L.R. 758.

[77] Property in ideas; ideas as subject matter of contrasts, see Comment, 31 *Cornell L.Q.* 382 (1946).

See also comment note, Common-Law Regulation of the Idea Market, 16 *U. Chi. L. Rev.* 323 (1949); Warner, "Legal Protection of Program Ideas," 36 *Va. L. Rev.* 289 (1950).

[78] In Bristol v. Equitable Life Assurance Co., 132 N.Y. 264, 30 N.E. 506 (1892), the court, without denying that there may be property in an idea, declared that upon disclosure it became the acquisition of whoever receives it, unless some contract should regulate or guard its disclosure.

[79] Affiliated Enterprises, Inc. v. Gantz, 86 F.2d 597 (1936).

Discussion of cases, see comment note, "Non-Patentable and Non-Copyrightable Business Ideas," 97 *U. Pa. L. Rev.* 94 (1948).

[80] O'Brien v. RKO Radio Pictures, Inc., 68 F. Supp. 13 (1946); Belt v. Hamilton Nat. Bank, 108 F. Supp. 689 (1954).

Effect of embodying ideas in a concrete plan, see Schonwald v. F. Burkart Mfg. Co., 356 Mo. 435, 202 S.W.2d 7 (1947).

may have ground for seeking to protect his interest in it. The breach of trust or the contract right, recognized as a form of property, provides the basis for equity jurisdiction,[81] even if it be considered that the idea itself is not property.[82]

In the former situation equity has intervened to prevent the breach of trust and confidence.[83] However, the breach of trust and confidence must be clearly alleged [84] and proven.[85] In the latter situation, that of contract, the requirement has been developed that the idea must be new, unusual, and valuable. If one of these elements is lacking, the contract will not be enforced or its violation prevented.[86] Moreover, there is frequently the difficulty of proving the contract.[87] Many of the cases, of course, are not suits for equitable relief but to recover compensation for the use of the idea revealed in confidence or pursuant to contract.[88] However, injunction may frequently be an appropriate remedy where it is sought to prevent the defendant from making an un-

---

[81] Rights and remedies independently of patent laws, of one conceiving idea or plan, against one using it industrially or commercially or who discloses it or threatens to do so, see annotation, 170 A.L.R. 449.

[82] Cf. Liggett & Myers Co. v. Myers, 101 Ind. App. 420, 194 N.E. 206 (1935), noted 44 *Yale L.J.* 1269 (1935), 15 *B. U. L. Rev.* 633 (1935), 21 *Cornell L.Q.* 486 (1936), taking a more advanced view as to an idea being property.

[83] See Booth v. Stutz Motor Car Co., 56 F.2d 962 (1932).

But even here, some courts have held that only if the idea is the subject of a contract can it be protected. Haskins v. Ryan, 75 N.J. Eq. 330, 78 A. 566 (1908); Stein v. Morris, 120 Va. 390, 91 S.E. 177 (1917).

And although an employer-employee relationship could certainly supply the necessary relationship of trust or confidence, it has been held that the employee has a prior duty to disclose his idea to his employer without charge. Keller v. American Chain Co., 255 N.Y. 94, 174 N.E. 74 (1930). Cf. National Development Co. v. Gray, 316 Mass. 240, 55 N.E.2d 783 (1944).

[84] Bristol v. Equitable Life Assurance Co., 132 N.Y. 264, 30 N.E. 506 (1892).

[85] See Moore v. Ford Motor Car Co., 43 F.2d 685 (1930), aff'g 28 F.2d 529 (1928).

[86] Masline v. New York, etc., R. R. Co., 95 Conn. 702, 112 A. 639 (1921); Thomas v. R. J. Reynolds Tobacco Co., 350 Pa. St. 262, 38 A.2d 61, 157 A.L.R. 1432 (1944).

Novelty of abstract idea not required where idea is reduced to a concrete plan, see Schonwald v. F. Burkart Mfg. Co., 356 Mo. 435, 202 S.W.2d 7 (1947).

Novelty of idea as affecting right to contract concerning it, see note, 36 *Geo. L.J.* 261 (1948).

[87] Grombach Productions v. Waring, 293 N.Y. 609, 59 N.E.2d 425 (1944), noted 31 *Cornell L.Q.* 382 (1945), 40 *Ill. L. Rev.* 130 (1945).

See comment, "Ideas as subject matter of contract," 31 *Cornell L.Q.* 382 (1946).

[88] See Havighurst, "Right to Compensation for an Idea," 49 *N. W. L. Rev.* 295 (1954).

authorized use of the idea.[89]   And where the idea has been made
the basis of a patent or copyright in the defendant's name (after
the idea has been obtained by him through breach of confidence
or contract) the originator may seek to have a constructive trust
impressed thereon in his favor and, as well, an accounting for
profits.[90]

In connection with interests in ideas, the following deserves
notice. As mentioned in a preceding section, courts do not consider a trade secret as in itself property. The right to its exclusive
use is a valuable incident or adjunct of the business. The unauthorized appropriation and use of the trade secret is not the
taking of property itself but is an injury to a property right, the
right to carry on a lawful business without being subjected to
unfair competition. In looking at a mere or abstract idea, the
courts have been influenced by the fact that it is not yet attached
to and used in a going business. But is this necessary? As pointed
out in the first section of this chapter, many of us do not own or
operate businesses. Many of us may work in the business of another. This ability to labor, to follow a trade, calling, or employment is as important to one individual for the purpose of earning
a living as the carrying on of a lawful business in order to earn
a living is to one owning a business. Anything which promotes
one's ability to earn a living or to increase his earning power is as
much an incident of a property right, his power to labor, as a trade
secret is an incident of the right to carry on a lawful business.
If one originates a new and original idea for use in commerce, he
has developed something which can increase his earnings or income
in the same way a trade secret, trademark, or the like may tend
to increase the earnings of a business. He is entitled to be fully
protected as to this idea as a valuable adjunct or incident of his
power to labor and to earn a living, just as is the owner of a business to be protected as to valuable adjuncts or incidents of his business.[91]

---

89 See cases cited in preceding notes.

90 See Becher v. Couture Laboratories, 279 U.S. 388, 49 S.Ct. 356, 73 L. Ed.
752 (breach of confidence by employee (1929); Bohlman v. American Paper
Goods Co., 66 F. Supp. 828 (alleged breach of contract and fraud) (1946).

91 Similar conclusion is reached in comment note, "Non-Patentable and Non-
Copyrightable Business Ideas," 97 *U. Pa. L. Rev.* 94 (1948).

Sec. 49. Trademarks and trade names—Use by competitors.

A trademark is some arbitrary name, symbol, or device affixed to goods for the purpose of identifying them as the goods of a particular manufacturer or producer [92] or of one whose established business is the selection and sale of an article of a certain standard and quality.[93] Or in the case of one engaged in the rendition of services of a particular kind or nature for compensation, the name, symbol, or device may be used to identify the one rendering such services.[94] A trade name, somewhat more broadly, is the name used to designate the particular business of an individual, corporation, partnership, or the like, but it may also designate specific goods or articles of merchandise or particular services.[95] The same fundamental principles of law and equity are applicable to both trademarks and trade names despite any technical distinctions between them.[96]

When a trademark or trade name has been used in business and the goods or services have become known to the public and sought for and obtained under that particular mark or name, the trademark

---

[92] Elgin National Watch Co. v. Illinois Watch Case Co., 179 U.S. 665, 21 S.Ct. 270, 45 L. Ed. 365 (1900); Italian Swiss Colony v. Italian Vineyard Co., 158 Cal. 252, 110 P. 913, 32 L.R.A.N.S. 439 (1910).

[93] Menendez v. Holt, 128 U.S. 514, 9 S.Ct. 143, 32 L. Ed. 526 (1888).

There has been criticism of such a definition on the ground that it overlooks the function of the trademark to create and retain customers without regard to ownership or origin of the goods. See note, 45 *Mich. L. Rev.* 239 (1946).

[94] As in the case of one engaged in the transportation of persons or goods, one engaged in repairing shoes or in repairing or "servicing" radios.

[95] Direct Service Oil Co. v. Honzay, 211 Minn. 361, 2 N.W.2d 434, 148 A.L.R. 1 (1941).

"It is sometimes confusing as to whether a name of a corporation is to be regarded as a trade-mark, a trade-name, or both. To some extent the two terms overlap, but there is a difference, more or less definitely recognized, which is that, generally speaking, the former is applicable to the vendible commodity, to which it is affixed, the latter to a business and its goodwill. A corporation name, therefore, seems to fall more appropriately into the latter class or that of a trade-name." Acme Chemical Co. v. Dobkin, 68 F. Supp. 601 (1946).

[96] Acme Chemical Co. v. Dobkin, 68 F. Supp. 601 (1946); Ball v. Broadway Bazaar, 194 N.Y. 429, 87 N.E. 674 (1909).

Firmly established trade name receives same protection as trademark. Stork Restaurant, Inc. v. Sahati, 166 F.2d 348 (1948); Eastern Columbia, Inc. v. Waldman, 30 Cal.2d 268, 181 P.2d 865 (1947).

No infringement of plaintiff's trademark shown but use of plaintiff's name on business enjoined. Thomas A. Edison, Inc. v. Shotkin, 69 F. Supp. 176 (1947).

or trade name becomes a valuable adjunct or incident of the business. Its value to the user in connection with an existing business is in the nature of a property right.[97] If a competitor uses the mark or name, he deceives the public into buying his goods or hiring his services in the belief that they are those of the original user of the trademark or trade name, to the competitor's own advantage and to the consequent loss of business by the original user.[98] This wrongful appropriation of a property right of an-

---

[97] Allen & Wheeler Co. v. Hanover Star Milling Co., 240 U.S. 403, 36 S.Ct. 357, 60 L. Ed. 713 (1916).

Trade name is a property right according to the general law. It is sometimes also made so by statute. Stork Restaurant, Inc. v. Sahati, 166 F.2d 348 (1948); Eastern Columbia, Inc. v. Waldman, 30 Cal.2d 268, 181 P.2d 865 (1947).

It is thus distinguishable from a patent which gives a monopolistic property right without user; there is no property right in a trademark or trade name not used in connection with an existing business. United Drug Co. v. Theodore Rectanus Co., 248 U.S. 90, 39 S.Ct. 48, 63 L. Ed. 141 (1918).

"It is well established that a trade-mark or tradename cannot be licensed or assigned except as an incident to the sale of the business and good will in connection with which it has been used." Purity Cheese Co. v. Frank Ryser Co., 57 F. Supp. 102 (1944). If it could be sold or transferred as a distinct property in itself it might be used to designate articles entirely different in origin or character from those to which it was originally given and thus the public would be deceived, according to the traditional view. However, there is some contention that a trademark is assignable of itself if the public is not deceived thereby. See note, 45 *Mich. L. Rev.* 239 (1946).

Abandonment of trademark or trade name, see annotation, 3 A.L.R.2d 1226.

[98] While, among the older cases, various equitable grounds were instanced as reasons for granting equitable relief, particularly the fraud practiced on the public (see Chadwick v. Covell, 151 Mass. 190, 23 N.E. 1068, 6 L.R.A. 839, 21 Am.St.Rep. 422 (1890)), at a later date it became common to deny that fraud on the public is the ground for equitable relief and, instead, that the real reason is the invasion of a property right, *i.e.*, the exclusive right to the use of the trademark or trade name, to the injury of the original user. See G. & C. Merriam & Co. v. Saalfield, 198 F. 369 (1912); Italian Swiss Colony v. Italian Vineyard Co. 158 Cal. 252, 110 P. 913, 32 L.R.A.N.S. 439 (1910). There has now been a return to recognition of the fraud on or deceit of the public as an important factor in warranting equitable relief, but on the basis that this fraud or deceit or creation of confusion in the public mind is causing or will bring about loss to the business of the original user. This may be so even without actual intent on the defendant's part to cause loss to the plaintiff. See Academy of Motion Picture Arts and Sciences v. Benson, 15 Cal.2d 685, 104 P.2d 650 (1940); Hartman v. Cohen, 350 Pa. 41, 38 A.2d 22 (1944), noted 30 *Iowa L. Rev.* 120 (1944); 43 *Mich. L. Rev.* 409 (1944). The federal courts now frequently stress the likelihood of confusion as the test; actual deceit of anyone or actual intent to defraud need not appear. Majestic Mfg. Co. v. Kokenes, 67 F. Supp. 282 (1946); LaTouraine Coffee Co. v. Lorraine Coffee Co., 157 F.2d 115 (1946), noted 60 *Harv. L. Rev.* 308 (1946), 35 *Geo. L.J.* 580 (1947).

No loss suffered, see Caron Corp. v. Ollendorff, 160 F.2d 444 (1947).

other to his injury is an act of unfair competition.[99]   Although an action, of a legal nature, for damages can be brought, it is obvious that this remedy at law is inadequate.   The injury flows from the continued invasion of the property right and only equitable relief can restrain this continued invasion.[100]   Equity can also, of course, to the extent that it is feasible in the particular case, award damages for the injury so far incurred or require an accounting of profits made by the competitor through his wrongful use of the trademark or trade name, according to the practice in the particular jurisdiction.[101]

Except as may be provided by statutes authorizing or permitting registration of trademarks and trade names,[102] according to the

---

[99] Allen & Wheeler Co. v. Hanover Star Milling Co., 240 U.S. 403, 36 S.Ct. 357, 60 L. Ed. 713 (1916) ("the common law of trademarks is but a part of the broader law of unfair competition").

"On one thing there seems to be complete agreement; that is, that the common law of trademarks is but a part of the broader law of unfair competition." Griesdieck Western Brewery Co. v. Peoples Brewery Co., 56 F. Supp. 600 (1944).

See Glenn, "Pre-emption in Connection with Unfair Trade," 19 *Col. L. Rev.* 29 (1919); "The Relation of the Technical Trademark to the Law of Unfair Competition," 29 *Harv. L. Rev.* 763 (1916).

The actual spelling or number of letters or syllables is not determinative. If there is similarity in ordinary speech, that may be sufficient. LaTouraine Coffee Co. v. Lorraine Coffee Co., 157 F.2d 115 (1946), noted 60 *Harv. L. Rev.* 308 (1946).

If less than the whole of plaintiff's mark is used it must appear that the part taken is sufficient to identify the owner's product. Caron Corp. v. Ollendorff, 160 F.2d 444 (1947).

[100] "To establish infringement, plaintiff need show only that the name adopted by defendants is so similar to its trade-mark as to be likely to cause confusion among reasonably careful purchasers. Defendants urge that there has been no showing of actual instances of confusion; but no such evidence is required." La-Touraine Coffee Co. v. Lorraine Coffee Co., 157 F.2d 115 (1946), noted 60 *Harv. L. Rev.* 308 (1946), 35 *Geo. L.J.* 580 (1947).

[101] Liberty Oil Corp. v. Crowley, Milner & Co., 270 Mich. 187, 258 N.W. 241, 96 A.L.R. 645 (1935); L. Martin Co. v. L. Martin & Wilckes Co., 75 N.J. Eq. 257, 72 A. 294, 20 Ann. Cas. 57, 21 L.R.A.N.S. 526 (1908).

See Nims, "Damages and Accounting Procedure in Unfair Competition Cases," 31 *Cornell L.Q.* 431, 32 *Cornell L.Q.* 24 (1946).

[102] The statutes of one's own state should be examined. Frequently, they do not change the common law rule that use as well as selection must be present.

Nor do they commonly confer any right to use a name already appropriated and used by another, although not registered under the statute. See Acme Chemical Co. v. Dobkin, 68 F. Supp. 601 (1946).

Registration under Federal Trade-Mark Act does not enlarge plaintiff's substantive rights but merely confers jurisdiction on federal court on basis of federal question being involved. See Best & Co. v. Miller, 67 F. Supp. 809 (1946). See also Callman, "The New Trade-Mark Act of July 5, 1946," 46 *Col. L. Rev.* 929 (1946).

developed rule an exclusive right in a trademark or trade name is not acquired instantly, by mere selection. It must be used long enough to become identified in the public mind with the article, services, or business to which it is affixed.[103] But what is the territorial extent of this public knowledge as related to sales of goods, articles, or services to which the mark or name is affixed? The rule has been laid down that the use of the mark or name in one area or territory confers no right to prevent its subsequent use by one in the same business in an area or territory where the prior user has not been selling the goods, articles, or services to which his mark or name is affixed. As the United States Supreme Court put it, the trademark, "of itself, cannot travel to markets where there is no article to wear the badge and no trader to offer the article." [104] Such a rule is based, obviously, on the fact that in the latter territory the public is unaware of the goods, articles, or services of the prior user doing business elsewhere and, thus, does not identify or associate the mark or name with his goods, articles, or services.[105] However, it is now well recognized that one who first appropriates a trademark or trade name may enjoin its use by a subsequent user even in an area or territory where the senior appropriator is not selling his goods, articles, or service, if the

---

Lanham Act creates a national substantive law of unfair competition which confers federal jurisdiction, notwithstanding lack of diversity of citizenship; it creates federal cause of action for unfair competition even though unrelated to registered trademark if defendant's activities affect interstate commerce. Stauffer v. Exley, 184 F.2d 962 (1950), noted 64 *Harv. L. Rev.* 1209 (1951); 51 *Col. L. Rev.* 1053 (1950).

[103] Kellogg Co. v. National Biscuit Co., 305 U.S. 111, 59 S.Ct. 109, 83 L. Ed. 73 (1938), rehearing denied, 305 U.S. 674, 59 S.Ct. 246, 83 L. Ed. 437 (1938), noted 24 *Cornell L.Q.* 255 (1939).

To what extent a preliminary advertising campaign will or will not supply this identification, see *infra*, Sec. 52.

[104] Allen & Wheeler Co. v. Hanover Star Milling Co., 240 U.S. 403, 36 S.Ct. 357, 60 L. Ed. 713 (1916); Griesdieck Brewery Co. v. Peoples Brewery Co., 56 F. Supp. 600 (1944); Yellow Cab Co. v. Sachs, 191 Cal. 238, 216 P. 33, 28 A.L.R. 105 (1923); Direct Service Oil Co. v. Honzay, 211 Minn. 361, 2 N.W.2d 434, 148 A.L.R. 1 (1941); *Rest. Torts*, Sec. 732, comment a.

It is not within the scope of this section to discuss what constitutes an area or territory. See cases, annotation, 148 A.L.R. 12, at p. 104 ff.

[105] United Drug Co. v. Theodore Rectanus Co., 248 U.S. 90, 39 S.Ct. 48, 63 L. Ed. 141 (1918). See also cases cited in preceding note.

Registration of a trademark under the Federal Trademark Act does not alter the rule or extend the rights delimited by equitable principles. Griesdieck Brewery Co. v. Peoples Brewery Co., 56 F. Supp. 283 (1944).

public there, or even any appreciable portion of the public, identifies or associates the mark or name with the business of the senior appropriator. This has variously or cumulatively been put upon such grounds as that the senior appropriator's good reputation is known in the area or territory where he does not operate and the subsequent appropriator is seeking to take advantage of that reputation for his own profit, that the subsequent appropriator is acting in bad faith to deceive the public, that the senior appropriator's reputation may suffer injury, and that there is some inimical design, as to forestall expansion of the senior appropriator's business to the area or territory.[106] Indeed, it is argued that the Lanham Trade-Mark Act of 1946, in providing for constructive notice and incontestability, has the effect of overruling previous case law as represented by the Supreme Court's opinion in the *United Drug Co. v. Theodore Rectanus Co.*[107] and that the purpose of the Act is to give nationwide protection.[108]

A trademark or trade name must be a proper one. It is therefore necessary, in adopting one, to select one which no one else will thereafter have an equal right to use.[109] An entirely original or invented name, word, device, or symbol, known as a pure or technical trademark, may answer this requirement.[110] Ordinarily, no name which is merely descriptive of the qualities of an article can be appropriated as a trademark or trade name.[111] Likewise,

---

[106] Stork Restaurant v. Sahati, 166 F.2d 348 (1948); Stork Restaurant v. Marcus, 36 F. Supp. 90 (1941); Good Housekeeping Shop v. Smitter, 254 Mich. 592, 236 N.W. 872 (1931); *Rest. Torts*, Sec. 732. And see, Brooks Bros. v. Brooks Clothing of California, 60 F. Supp. 442 (1945), aff'd 158 F.2d 798.

See comment, "Protection accorded to prior user," 19 *So. Calif. L. Rev.* 272 (1946); annotation, "Actual competition as necessary element of trademark infringement or unfair competition," 148 A.L.R. 12.

Application of same principle in use by noncompetitor, see section following.

[107] See note 105, *supra*.

[108] See comment, 35 *Cornell L.Q.* 618 (1950), to S. C. Johnson & Son, Inc. v. Johnson, 175 F.2d 176 (1949), which as a matter of fact takes the view that the Act does not extend the right of a trademark user to pre-empt new markets.

[109] See Franklin Knitting Mills v. Fashionit Sweater Mills, 297 F. 217 (1923). Abandonment of trademark, see note 22 *Va. L. Rev.* 102 (1935).

[110] Vide the word "Kodak." But compare invention of a word, such as "aspirin" or "cellophane," used in connection with a patented article and becoming word of common usage so as to be available to anyone when the patent expires. Bayer Co. v. United Drug Co., 272 F. 505 (1921); Dupont Cellophane Co. v. Waxed Products Co., 85 F.2d 75 (1936).

[111] Whole Grain Wheat Distributing Co. v. Bon Marche, 154 Wash. 455, 282 P. 914 (1929); *Rest. Torts*, Sec. 721.

ordinarily, words and phrases in common use cannot be appropriated.[112] Nevertheless, words of description or ordinary use may, from long and exclusive use, come to be so associated or identified in the public mind with the source or origin of the goods to which they are affixed that they have what is termed a "secondary meaning," so that their subsequent use by another on a similar product will be enjoined.[113]

While a mere color or shape of a container cannot be appropriated as a trademark,[114] an original combination of several things or words may constitute a protectible trademark.[115]

Although it has formerly been stated that no one can acquire an exclusive right to a merely geographic name, certain exceptions have been developed. When one has truly applied the name of his town or district to his goods and they have become known by that name, he will be protected as against one whose goods are produced elsewhere and which have fraudulently and falsely affixed to them the same name in order that they may pass as the goods made by the original user of the name.[116] Even where the subsequent use is by a competitor who has established himself in

Applied even where the name as used by defendant was falsely descriptive of his product. American Washboard Co. v. Saginaw Mfg. Co., 103 F. 281 (1900). It is hard to see what equities exist in the defendant's favor in such a situation.

Foreign word, see Italian Swiss Colony v. Italian Vineyard Co., 158 Cal. 252, 110 P. 913, 32 L.R.A.N.S. 439 (1910).

Phonetic spelling of descriptive word does not change the principle applied. Lusta-Foame Co. v. Wm. Filene's Sons Co., 66 F. Supp. 517 (1946).

[112] Purity Spring Water Co. v. Redwood Ice Co., 203 Cal. 286, 263 P. 810 (1928); *Rest. Torts*, Sec. 721.

[113] Wisconsin Electric Co. v. Dumore, 35 F.2d 555 (1929), certiorari dismissed, 282 U.S. 813, 51 S.Ct. 214, 75 L. Ed. 728 (1931).

"To entitle a private party to equitable relief, there must be wrong added to incidental confusion in the use of similar names, such as fraud, deception, or palming off, or the name which it has sought to protect must have acquired a secondary meaning." General Industries Co. v. 20 Wacker Drive Bldg. Corp., 156 F.2d 474 (1946).

See comment note, Doctrine of secondary meaning in law of trademarks and unfair competition, 150 A.L.R. 1067.

[114] Sun-Maid Raisin Growers v. Mosesian, 84 Cal. App. 485, 258 P. 630 (1927). But compare functional design, *infra*, Sec. 51.

[115] Lusta-Foame Co. v. Wm. Filene's Sons Co., 66 F. Supp. 517 (1946); *Rest. Torts*, Sec. 724.

[116] La République Française v. Saratoga Vichy Springs Co., 107 F. 459, 65 L.R.A. 830 (1901), aff'd 191 U.S. 427, 24 S.Ct. 145, 48 L. Ed. 247 (1903). But compare California Apparel Creators v. Wieder of California, 163 F.2d 893 (1947), noted 48 *Col. L. Rev.* 158 (1948), relating to impossibility of proof of injury.

the same town or district, the subsequent user may be enjoined from using the same geographic name because it has acquired a "secondary meaning" or, at least, required to distinguish his goods from those of the prior appropriator so that the public may not be deceived and the prior appropriator injured.[117]

A kindred question arises as to how far one may use his own name as a trademark or trade name so as to be protected against the use of the same or a similar name by another.[118] It is conceded that a person cannot acquire an exclusive right to the use of his mere name as against another of the same name. A second comer in the field has the right to use his name to identify his business or goods so long as he does not thereby deceive the public or others to the detriment of the first user.[119] However, if the name of the prior user has become so well associated in the public mind with his goods that confusion is unavoidable, the court may require the second comer to distinguish or identify his goods in such way that the confusion or mistake will be prevented.[120] If the second comer resorts to any further imitation or to any artifice whatever, calculated to represent his goods as being those of the first user, he will in all probability be enjoined absolutely from the use of the name.[121] One will, of course, be protected against the use of his name by persons not bearing that name. In such a case,

---

[117] American Waltham Watch Co. v. United States Watch Co., 173 Mass. 85, 53 N.E. 141, 43 L.R.A. 826, 73 Am.St.Rep. 263 (1899).

[118] See Annotations, Right, in absence of self-imposed restraint, to use one's own name for business purposes to detriment of another using the same or a similar name, 47 A.L.R. 1189, 107 A.L.R. 1279.

In respect of corporations, see annotations, Protection of business or trading corporation against use of same or similar name by another corporation, 115 A.L.R. 1241, 66 A.L.R. 948.

[119] Ida May Co. v. Ida May Ensign, 20 Cal.App.2d 339, 66 P.2d 727 (1937).

[120] Waterman Pen Co. v. Modern Pen Co., 235 U.S. 88, 35 S.Ct. 91, 59 L. Ed. 142 (1914); Brown Sheet Iron & Steel Co. v. Brown Steel Tank Co., 198 Minn. 276, 269 N.W. 633, 107 A.L.R. 1276 (1936).

[121] Jackman v. Mau, 78 Cal.App.2d 234, 177 P.2d 599 (1947); Sellers v. McCormick, 19 Del. Ch. 238, 165 A. 569 (1933); Healer v. Bloomberg Bros., Inc., 321 Mass. 476, 73 N.E.2d 895 (1947); L. Martin Co. v. L. Martin & Wilckes Co., 75 N.J. Eq. 257, 72 A. 294, 20 Ann. Cas. 57, 21 L.R.A.N.S. 526 (1908); Flora v. Flora Shirt Co., 141 Okla. 58, 283 P. 1013 (1930).

Where defendant's use of his own name was motivated by desire to divert business from plaintiff and he could not use his name without inevitably confusing public, his use of his name was absolutely enjoined. Hoyt Heater Co. v. Hoyt, 68 Cal.App.2d 523, 157 P.2d 657 (1945), noted 59 Harv. L. Rev. 140 (1946).

assumption of his name is without any pretence of right.[122] Protection will also be accorded against one not of the same name who makes a point of employing or associating with him someone of the same name as the prior user, in order to take advantage of the good will and reputation of the prior user.[123]

A trademark may be infringed without imitating it, as where a dealer in response to requests for a particular trademarked article of plaintiff hands over another's product,[124] or where a dealer removes identifying labels, marks, or the like from the plaintiff's goods and sells them as the product of another or as his own product.[125] In this respect, litigation frequently results from the sale of repaired or reconditioned goods. The dealer may be removing the trademark and selling the reconditioned or repaired goods as his own or another's product,[126] or he may be leaving the trademark on the goods but selling them as, or in a manner to lead to the belief that they are, new goods.[127]

It is an essential of a valid trademark that it contain no false statement as to the character of the article itself, or as to the person by whom or the place where it is made. No property right can be asserted in such a false statement and it would be contrary to public policy for equity to lend its aid to one who is deceiving

---

122 See Brooks Bros. v. Brooks Clothing of California, 60 F. Supp. 442 (1945), aff'd 158 F.2d 798.

123 De Nobili Cigar Co. v. Nobile Cigar Co., 56 F.2d 324 (1932), noted 31 *Mich. L. Rev.* 292 (1932).

Use of a stockholder's name, see Ford Motor Co. v. Ford Insecticide Corp., 69 F. Supp. 935 (1947).

124 Barnes v. Pierce, 164 F. 214 (1908).

In Enoch Morgan's Sons' Co. v. Wendover, 43 F. 420, 10 L.R.A. 283 (1890), the plaintiff, who made a soap known as "Sapolio," proved that on several occasions customers who asked for "Sapolio" were handed the soap of a different maker which was marked "Pride of the Kitchen" and was in a package not resembling that of plaintiff's soap.

Similarly, where products of another are placed in a container bearing the plaintiff's mark or name, see annotation, 60 A.L.R. 285.

125 Jantzen Knitting Mills v. A. Balmuth, Inc., 257 N.Y.S. 611 (1932).

126 Injunction granted to prevent infringement of trademark by one dealing in repaired goods, but dealer permitted to identify origin of goods. Champion Spark Plug Co. v. Sanders, 56 F. Supp. 782, 787 (1944), noted 34 *Geo. L.J.* 118 (1944).

127 Champion Spark Plug Co. v. Sanders, 156 F.2d 488 (1946), affirmed 331 U.S. 125, 67 S.Ct. 1136, 91 L. Ed. 1386 (1947), pointing out that reconditioned goods may be sold with the original trademark thereon if plainly stamped as repaired or used goods.

the public.[128]   It is not necessary that the deception should inhere
in the trademark itself.   If misleading words or symbols are used
in connection with it, the trademark will not be protected.[129]
Similarly, the use of a trademark or trade name in connection with
a business which is in its nature illegal or contrary to public policy
will not be protected in equity.[130]

Sec. 50.   —Use by noncompetitors.

Formerly, since the term "unfair competition" was considered
to presuppose actual competition of some kind,[131] equitable relief
was not available against one who used another's trademark or
trade name on distinctly different articles, goods, or services.[132]
There being no actual competition it was evidently believed that
there could be no loss of business to the prior user of the mark
or name which would supply the property injury which in some
form is so frequently said to be a necessary element of equitable
jurisdiction.

Probably one of the earliest, if not the earliest, American departure from this view is to be found in a case involving the famous
inventor, Thomas A. Edison.   Edison sought to enjoin the unauthorized use of his name and picture on a drug manufactured
and sold by the defendant.   Obviously hard pressed to find precedent to justify the giving of equitable relief, the court touched upon
such matters as whether there was a property interest in a name
or a picture or reputation, as well as upon the right of privacy,
without obtaining any fully satisfactory justification therefrom for

---

[128] Clinton E. Worden & Co. v. California Fig Syrup Co., 187 U.S. 516, 23 S.Ct.
161, 47 L. Ed. 282 (1903).

[129] Applied in case of a "fruit" pudding under the name of "Puddine" which,
as chemical analysis disclosed, contained no fruit.   Clotworthy v. Schepp, 42 F. 62
(1890).

[130] Affiliated Enterprises, Inc. v. Gantz, 86 F.2d 595 (1936); Affiliated Enterprises,
Inc. v. Gruber, 86 F.2d 958 (1936).   In these cases plaintiff sought to establish
a protectible property right in the use of the term "Bank Night" in connection
with a scheme which the court considered in the nature of a lottery.   Incidentally,
in 1938, plaintiff discontinued operations when a "fraud order" was issued against
it by the Post Office Department.

[131] See *supra*, Sec. 46.

[132] See Plumb, "Unfair Competition from Non-Competing Goods," 2 *Wyo.
L.J.* 66 (1948).

This seems to be stated as the rule in Nims, *Unfair Competition* (2d Ed.) Sec.
221; Walsh, *Treatise on Equity* (1930) Sec. 46.

equitable relief.   Analysis of the court's opinion shows its decision to give equitable relief to be based on the view that one's name and reputation come to have a pecuniary value in connection with one's business, in the nature of a property right, and that reasonable probability of future injury results from the unauthorized use of the name, even by a noncompetitor.[133]

When it is considered that the prior user of a mark or name has no control over the subsequent user's methods of doing business or the quality of the articles, goods, or services that he dispenses, it is plain that the prior user is at the mercy of one who may discredit the mark or name in the mind of the public, whose dissatisfaction or ill will may thereupon attach to every article with that mark or name.   Moreover, it is necessary to consider that the subsequent user, though a noncompetitor, is usually intentionally and deliberately attempting to profit himself, in deceit of the public, by appropriating to his own benefit the good will and business value of an established mark or name.   So far as the equities are concerned, they are all on the side of the prior user. It is now well settled that, even though there is no actual market competition, where one passes off his goods, services, or his business as the goods, services, or business of another, equity will intervene to protect the good will and business reputation of the latter from any injury liable to be caused thereby.[134]   Prior to the Lanham

[133] Edison v. Edison Polyform Mfg. Co., 73 N.J. Eq. 136, 67 A. 392 (1907), wherein the injunction extended to the use of Edison's name in the name of the defendant company. Compare Edison v. Thomas A. Edison, Jr., Chemical Co., 128 F. 957 (1904), where an injunction was denied against use of name "Edison," though defendants were injuring Edison's business reputation. The court did not recognize the right to enjoin "defamation" injurious to business.

[134] Standard Oil Co. of New Mexico v. Standard Oil Co. of California, 56 F.2d 973 (1932); California Fruit Growers Exchange v. Sunkist Baking Co., 68 F. Supp. 946 (1946); Great Atlantic & Pacific Tea Co. v. A. & P. Radio Stores, 20 F. Supp. 703 (1937), noted 86 U. Pa. L. Rev. 444 (1938); Academy of Motion Picture Arts and Sciences v. Benson, 15 Cal.2d 685, 104 P.2d 650 (1940); Colorado Nat. Co. v. Colorado Nat. Bank of Denver, 95 Colo. 386, 36 P.2d 454 (1934); Lady Esther, Ltd. v. Lady Esther Corset Shoppe, 317 Ill. App. 451, 46 N.E.2d 165, 148 A.L.R. 6 (1943); Churchill Downs Distilling Co. v. Churchill Downs, Inc., 262 Ky. 567, 90 S.W.2d 1041 (1936), noted 25 Ky. L. J. 280 (1937); H. Milgrim & Bros. v. Schlesinger, 168 Or. 476, 123 P.2d 196 (1942). Compare Schwartz v. Slenderella Systems of California, 43 Cal.2d 107, 271 P.2d 857 (1954), criticized 6 Hastings L.J. 115 (1954).

See Callman, "Unfair Competition without Competition?" 95 U. Pa. L. Rev. 443 (1947); comment, "Extension of Trademark Protection to Non-Competitive Rela-

Act of 1946,[135] the qualification was sometimes added, particularly in the federal courts, that the relation between the owner's use and the borrower's use of the mark or name must not be so remote or foreign as concerns the nature of the goods or services as to insure against any identification in the mind of the public. Or, to put it another way, the goods of both should have the same or common descriptive properties.[136] However, very liberal construction was given in the owner's favor, as witness the equitable relief given where the plaintiff's mark or name on fountain pens was used on razor blades,[137] where the plaintiff's mark or name on watches was used on shoes,[138] where the plaintiff's mark or name on automobiles was used on an insecticide,[139] where the plaintiff's mark or name on locks was used on flashlights,[140] and other such situations.[141] The effect of the Lanham Act would seem to change the test of trademark infringement from use on goods of the same descriptive property to use likely to cause con-

---

tionships," 44 *Ill. L. Rev.* 182 (1949); annotation, Actual competition as necessary element of trademark infringement or unfair competition, 148 A.L.R. 12; note, 38 *Harv. L. Rev.* 370 (1925): note, 24 *Notre Dame Law.* 110 (1948).

Although Acme Chemical Co. v. Dobkin, 68 F. Supp. 601 (1946), involved the sale of essentially similar products, the court sets out a long list of cases in which defendants not engaged in competition with plaintiffs were nevertheless enjoined from using the same or similar trademarks or trade names.

"It is true that under the early English and American cases absence of direct competition in the same identical field of business was a good defense to a charge of unfair competition. But in this country that rule has been progressively relaxed in many jurisdictions in suits to enjoin unfair competition." General Finance Loan Co. v. General Loan Co., 163 F.2d 709 (1947).

[135] U. S. C., Title 15, Sec. 1051.

[136] See discussion and illustrations in Bulova Watch Co. v. Stolzberg, 69 F. Supp. 543 (1947). See also note, "Goods of the Same Descriptive Properties," 35 *Ky. L.J.* 330 (1947).

In Philco Corp. v. F. & B. Mfg. Co., 170 F.2d 958 (1948), injunction was denied to the plaintiff against the defendant's use of his name "Filko" used on goods of different descriptive properties, not sold in competition and sold to a different class of purchasers.

[137] L. E. Waterman Co. v. Gordon, 72 F.2d 272 (1934).

[138] Bulova Watch Co. v. Stolzberg, 69 F. Supp. 543 (1947).

[139] Ford Motor Co. v. Ford Insecticide Corp., 69 F. Supp. 935 (1947).

[140] Yale Electric Corp. v. Robertson, 26 F.2d 972 (1928).

[141] Hanson v. Triangle Publications, Inc., 163 F.2d 74 (1947) (name of plaintiff's magazine that had acquired secondary meaning used by defendant on dresses); Triangle Publications, Inc. v. Rohrlich, 167 F.2d 969 (1948), noted 24 *Notre Dame Law.* 110 (1948), 35 *Va. L. Rev.* 120 (1949), 34 *Cornell L.Q.* 447 (1949) (same magazine's name used by manufacturer of girdles).

fusion or mistake or to deceive purchasers as to the source or origin of such goods.[142]

So far as concerns the territorial extent of protection in the case of subsequent use by a noncompetitor, it will be found that the same rules govern as in the case of subsequent use by an actual competitor.[143]

It will have been noticed that even where subsequent use of a mark or name is by a noncompetitor, nevertheless both parties are engaged in business or commerce of some kind. It is the probability of pecuniary damage, however slight, to the business of the prior user of the mark or name which justifies equity in giving relief. Can there be any pecuniary damage resulting from the use of the mark or name of one not engaged in business for profit? According to what may be described as a leading case of some years ago, the answer is in the negative. Vassar College sought to enjoin the Loose-Wiles Biscuit Company from using its name and a crude imitation of its college seal on boxes of chocolate which the defendant sold under the name of "Vassar Chocolates." The court declared that there was no such property right in its name and insignia, in the nature of a business right, to which any injury was done so as to entitle it to injunctive relief. The injury, if any, was described as being psychological rather than real and the plaintiff was said to be oversensitive.[144]

Nevertheless, the same factors and the same probabilities are present in such a case as in the case where both parties are engaged in business for profit. The reputation of the plaintiff may suffer, the public may conceivably be deceived, the defendant may be deliberately attempting to profit himself from the established reputation and good will of the plaintiff. The plaintiff, though en-

---

[142] See note, 34 *Minn. L. Rev.* 77 (1949), to S. C. Johnson & Son v. Johnson, 175 F.2d 176 (1949). The Johnson case is criticized in a note, 35 *Cornell L.Q.* 618 (1950), as unduly limiting the effect and application of the Lanham Act.

Use of similar trademark not enjoined where goods not possessing same descriptive properties and there was little chance of confusion. Consolidated Cosmetics v. Neilson Chemical Co., 109 F. Supp. 132 (1952), noted 29 *Notre Dame Law.* 132 (1952).

[143] See, *e.g.*, Tillman & Bendel v. California Packing Corp., 63 F.2d 498 (1933), certiorari denied 290 U.S. 638, 54 S.Ct. 55, 78 L. Ed. 554 (1933). And see preceding section.

[144] Vassar College v. Loose-Wiles Biscuit Co., 197 F. 982 (1912).

gaged in nonprofit activities, is usually dependent on continued public support and patronage, in other words, on continued public good will.   Injury to the plaintiff's reputation or otherwise can decrease public support and patronage to actual pecuniary loss on the part of the plaintiff.   And since the plaintiff's activities will usually be educational, religious, or otherwise in the public benefit, the public may suffer an incalculable loss through diminution of the nonprofit activities.   This is by far the better view and is the modern view.[145]

Sec. 51. —Design or appearance of goods; business system.

Closely akin to the matter of trademarks and trade names is that of design or appearance of goods.   It is necessary to distinguish, however, between "functional" and "non-functional" design. The former may be described as an essential feature which serves a substantial and desirable use which prevents it from being a mere matter of dress or appearance.   If purely functional elements or designs are copied, without more, no charge of unfair competition because of resemblance can be supported.[146]

The non-functional design or aspect, on the other hand, is not essential to the use of the product but is adopted for the purpose of identifying the product in the mind of the public.   Where goods of a certain design or appearance, although not protected by patent, in course of time become identified in the public mind with their manufacturer or source, the one responsible therefor is entitled to equitable relief against another who subsequently simulates the design or appearance for the purpose of deceiving the public to his own profit.[147]   Where the deception is flagrant or

---

[145] *E.g.*, Academy of Motion Picture Arts and Sciences v. Benson, 15 Cal.2d 685, 104 P.2d 650 (1940).

That a voluntary association for religious, fraternal, benevolent, or social purposes may enjoin another person, association, or corporation from using its name or emblem or any name or emblem so similar as to cause confusion, see Most Worshipful Hiram of Tyre, etc. v. Most Worshipful Sons of Light, etc., 94 Cal.App.2d 25, 210 P.2d 34 (1949).

[146] Warner & Co. v. Eli Lilly & Co., 265 U.S. 526, 44 S.Ct. 615, 68 L. Ed. 1161 (1924).

[147] Singer Mfg. Co. v. June Mfg. Co., 163 U.S. 169, 16 S.Ct. 1002, 41 L. Ed. 118 (1895); Netterville, "Unprivileged Imitation," 28 *So. Calif. L. Rev.* 240 (1955).

where it is accompanied by other deceptions, such as use of the same mark or name or similar mark or name, the defendant may be enjoined from further simulation.[148] Frequently, however, it is considered sufficient relief to require the defendant to mark or identify his goods with sufficient clarity to show that they are not those of the plaintiff.[149] Indeed, one may usually avoid charges of unfair competition made by a first comer by adequately marking or distinguishing his goods.[150] While some cases hold to the contrary in respect to such voluntary marking, it will usually be found that in such cases the marking was not actually sufficient or in good faith.[151]

It is immaterial that the simulation on the part of the manufacturer or wholesaler of the goods will not deceive retail dealers and that as to them no deception is attempted or practiced. If the former designedly enables the retail dealer to palm off the simulated goods or articles as those of the plaintiff, it is an act of unfair

---

Copyright structural design, form, shape, and color of plaintiff's taxicabs. Yellow Cab Co. v. Creasman, 185 N.C. 551, 177 S.E. 787, 28 A.L.R. 109 (1923).

As in the case of the use of a trademark, the first user of a particular design must have had it on the market for a sufficient length of time for the public to become familiar with it as his product. Rathbone, Sard & Co. v. Champion Steel Range Co., 189 F. 26, 37 L.R.A.N.S. 258 (1911). Ephemeral dress design, see Cheney Bros. v. Doris Silk Corp., 35 F.2d 279 (1929), cert. den. 281 U.S. 728, 50 S.Ct. 245, 74 L. Ed. 1145 (1930), noted 30 Col. L. Rev. 135 (1930), 43 Harv. L. Rev. 330 (1930), 16 Va. L. Rev. 617 (1930).

Only if the style of a bottle has acquired a secondary meaning through use can the first user enjoin competitor from using that style of bottle upon expiration of design patent of bottle. Lucien Lelong, Inc. v. Lander & Co., 164 F.2d 395 (1947).

148 Kyle v. Perfection Mattress Co., 127 Ala. 39, 28 So. 545, 50 L.R.A. 628, 85 Am.St.Rep. 78 (1900).

149 Flagg Mfg. Co. v. Holway, 178 Mass. 83, 59 N.E. 667 (1901). See Crescent Tool Co. v. Kilborn & Bishop Co., 247 F. 299 (1917).

150 Crescent Tool Co. v. Kilborn & Bishop Co., 247 F. 299 (1917).

In Kellogg Co. v. National Biscuit Co., 305 U.S. 111, 59 S.Ct. 109, 83 L. Ed. 73 (1938), noted 6 U. Chi. L. Rev. 310, 52 Harv. L. Rev. 536, it was held that reasonable means were taken to distinguish the defendant's goods, where it sold shredded wheat biscuits of the same shape as those of the plaintiff but they were of a different size, there were a different number of biscuits in the carton, and the carton was dissimilar and carried a slightly different name.

151 In Yale & Towne Mfg. Co. v. Alder, 154 F. 57 (1907), the defendant copied all the external details of the plaintiff's Yale Lock but put the word "Yap" on it in place of the word "Yale" and placed its name and address on the shackle in the same size letters used by plaintiff. It will be noticed that the simulation of appearance was accompanied by a name that might be easily misread as "Yale."

competition on the part of the manufacturer or wholesaler. He who induces another to commit fraud and furnishes the means is equally guilty.[152]

With reference to a business system, the design or shape of an article usually continues to be important. The point is that the first comer in the field has built up the probability of future demand for a given article and subsequently a competitor produces, usually at a cheaper price and perhaps of inferior quality, parts which will fit into the article or system devised and established by the first comer. Examples are the manufacture and sale of a system of sectional bookcases over a period of time whereupon, after the establishing of a demand therefor, a second comer in the field produced and sold sectional bookcases of the same styles and sizes which could be used to extend those already bought from the originator of the system;[153] and the manufacture of a toy construction set, named "Meccano," sold in various units, any one of which would fit into and expand any of the others, whereupon, after a demand was established therefor, a second comer manufactured and sold at a cheaper price a similar toy under a different name but of the same dimensions which could be fitted into units of the first comer.[154] The decisions were not entirely harmonious. In the first example given, although there was found to be an intent on the defendant's part to deceive the public into thinking they were buying the plaintiff's goods, equitable relief was denied. The right of anyone to produce goods or articles of a similar nature, not the subject of patent, was asserted, despite the deception. In the second example, the deliberate attempt to palm off the defendant's goods as those of the plaintiff warranted injunctive relief. The better view is undoubtedly that a second comer is entitled to get the benefit of the demand created by the first comer, so long as he does not intend to deceive the public by passing off

---

[152] Yale & Towne Mfg. Co. v. Alder, 154 F. 57 (1907); American Philatelic Soc. v. Claibourne, 3 Cal.2d 689, 46 P.2d 135 (1935), noted 25 *Cal. L. Rev.* 340 (1936), 34 *Mich. L. Rev.* 296 (1935), 9 *So. Calif. L. Rev.* 407 (1936), 84 *U. Pa. L. Rev.* 428 (1936).

See annotation, Right to enjoin competitor from selling his produce to dealers with whom plaintiff has exclusive contract or in such form as to enable dealers to palm off competitor's produce on customers as that of plaintiff, 84 A.L.R. 472.

[153] Globe-Wernicke Co. v. Macey, 119 F. 696 (1902).

[154] Meccano, Ltd. v. Wagner, 234 F. 912 (1916).

his goods as those of the first comer. If he is proceeding in good faith and clearly marks his goods to show unmistakably that they are his and not the goods of the first comer he may compete without equity's intervention.[155]

Sec. 52. —Advertising.

Although advertising may create popular demand for articles of a particular nature, shape, size, or form, or bearing a particular trademark, it appears that advertising alone has not been considered to entitle the advertiser to prevent a competitor from reaching the market first and capitalizing on this demand.[156] This can hardly be justified as an equitable view where the advertiser has first originated the idea, has expended money on preparations for production and has expended money on his advertising campaign and another unfairly attempts to capitalize on the advertising to pass his goods off as those advertised. Where both come into the field, in good faith, approximately at the same time, it is another matter. It was long before the development of the scope and extent of advertising on its present-day scale that the rule became established that mere selection of a mark or name does not give an exclusive right of use and that it must be used long enough to become identified in the public mind with the article, goods, or services to which it is affixed. Modern advertising campaigns can identify a mark or name with the articles, goods, or services in the mind of the public, and create a demand. It would then seem to become a fraud on the public to the injury of the advertiser to permit another to capitalize on the advertising.[157] Of course, if advertising has been confined to the retail trade only, it could hardly be argued that identification has been built up in the public mind.[158]

---

155 See, *e.g.*, Flagg Mfg. Co. v. Holway, 178 Mass. 83, 59 N.E. 667 (1901).

156 See Upjohn Co. v. Wm. S. Merrell Chemical Co., 269 F. 209 (1920); Gotham Music Service, Inc. v. Denton & Haskins Music Pub. Co., 259 N.Y. 56, 181 N.E. 57 (1932).

157 See Stork Restaurant, Inc. v. Sahati, 166 F.2d 348 (1948). See also Derenburg, *Trade-Mark Protection and Unfair Trading* (1936) 108, 109; Brown, "Advertising and the Public Interest: Legal Protection of Trade Symbols," 57 *Yale L.J.* 1165 (1948); Callman, "He Who Reaps Where He Has Not Sown: Unjust Enrichment in the Law of Unfair Competition," 55 *Harv. L. Rev.* 595 (1942).

158 See Upjohn Co. v. Wm. S. Merrell Chemical Co., 269 F. 209 (1920).

In another sense advertising may enter the unfair competition picture, as where a competitor advertises falsely. Aside from remedies available before the Federal Trade Commission or in the field of operation of Better Business Bureaus, the fact is, as pointed out by a distinguished authority, that "false advertising injures every competitor" and tends to increase the business of the one falsely advertising at the expense of honest businessmen.[159] While it has not been so recognized in the past,[160] or even currently,[161] the importance of advertising in the business field today warrants recognition of the fact that false advertising is a form of unfair competition, against which equity should interpose.[162]

Sec. 53.   Interference with contractual relations.

Where the plaintiff, in the course of carrying on a lawful business, enters into a contract with another, and a stranger to the contract deliberately seeks to induce the other contracting party to breach the contract or otherwise seeks to interfere with the contract to the irreparable injury of the plaintiff, the stranger may be enjoined from interfering with the plaintiff's business or his rights under the contract, if the remedy by way of damages is not adequate and complete. Not only is the right to carry on a lawful business free from wrongful interference a right of property or a substantial right in the nature of a property right, but the contract, with the rights thereunder, is a property right. Accordingly, the property element is more than adequately present to justify equitable consideration.[163]   The contracts may be those entered

---

[159] See Callman, "False Advertising as a Competitive Tort," 48 *Col. L. Rev.* 876 (1948).

[160] See, *e.g.*, American Washboard Co. v. Saginaw Mfg. Co., 103 F. 281 (1900).

[161] Mr. Callman remarks that the decision in the American Washboard Co. case still represents the law today, in the absence of disparagement or intent to drive a competitor out of business or in the absence of special legislation. See Callman, *op. cit., supra*, footnote 159.

[162] See, *e.g.*, Cal. Civ. Code, Sec. 3369, authorizing preventive relief in a case of unfair competition and providing that "unfair competition shall mean and include . . . unfair, untrue or misleading advertising. . . ."

[163] See annotation, Liability for procuring breach of contract, 84 A.L.R. 43; Carpenter, "Interference with Contract Relations," 41 *Harv. L. Rev.* 728 (1928); Sayre, "Inducing Breach of Contract," 36 *Harv. L. Rev.* 663 (1923).

The fact that in some jurisdictions there is said to be no right of action for damages against one maliciously inducing breach of a contract other than for

into with employees, or with customers or with manufacturers or wholesalers, in short, contracts lawfully and properly entered into for the purpose of furthering the business. It is immaterial that the contract is terminable at will, even though terminable at the will of the one induced to breach it.[164]

Where a competitor of the plaintiff seeks to induce the breach of or interfere with the plaintiff's contracts with others, it becomes an act of unfair competition, as where the competitor seeks to induce customers of the plaintiff to breach their contracts with the plaintiff and deal with the competitor,[165] or where the competitor seeks to induce one to breach a contract he has made with the plaintiff which gives the latter an exclusive right or agency.[166] Where the act or acts complained of will result in irreparable injury to the plaintiff, as will assuredly be the case where they represent a continued course of conduct, equity will enjoin the act or acts.[167] The plaintiff, of course, must not himself come into court with unclean hands, as where he himself has been inducing customers

---

employment, and that action for damages resorted to must be against the party to the contract who breaches it, provides ground for equitable relief, since there is no remedy at law, at all, against one pursuing a deliberate or malicious course of conduct to the irreparable injury of the plaintiff. Origin and growth of action at law for damages, see Sayre, "Inducing Breach of Contract," 36 *Harv. L. Rev.* 663 (1923).

164 E. L. Hustings Co. v. Cocoa Cola Co., 205 Wis. 356, 237 N.W. 85, 238 N.W. 626, 84 A.L.R. 22 (1931), certiorari denied 285 U.S. 538, 52 S.Ct. 311, 76 L. Ed. 931 (1932).

165 California Grape Control Board v. California Produce Corp., 4 Cal.App.2d 242, 40 P.2d 846 (1935); American Law Book Co. v. Edward Thompson Co., 41 Misc. 396, 84 N.Y.S. 225 (1903).

166 Westinghouse Electric & Mfg. Co. v. Diamond State Fibre Co., 268 F. 121 (1920); Beekman v. Marsters, 195 Mass. 205, 80 N.E. 817, 11 L.R.A.N.S. 201, 122 Am.St.Rep. 232, 11 Ann. Cas. 332 (exclusive agency) (1907); E. L. Hustings Co. v. Coca Cola Co., 205 Wis. 356, 237 N.W. 85, 238 N.W. 626, 84 A.L.R. 22 (1931), certiorari denied 285 U.S. 538, 52 S.Ct. 311, 76 L. Ed. 931 (exclusive bottling and sales right) (1932). Compare Philadelphia Dairy Products v. Quaker City Ice Cream Co., 306 Pa. 164, 159 A. 3, 84 A.L.R. 466 (1932).

In Montgomery Enterprises v. Empire Theater Co., 204 Ala. 566, 86 So. 880, 19 A.L.R. 987 (1920), it does not appear specifically that defendant induced the breach of an exclusive contract that plaintiff had for "first run" motion pictures, but defendant was enjoined from knowingly profiting from such breach by showing such pictures.

Fact that the contract is unenforceable does not justify malicious interference by a third person who induces breach of the contract. Schecter v. Friedman, 141 N.J. Eq. 318, 57 A.2d 251 (1948), noted 34 *Va. L. Rev.* 605 (1948).

167 See cases cited in two preceding notes.

to breach their contracts with the defendant,[168] or where he is carrying on a business which is a fraud on the public,[169] or where the contract is entered into for the purpose of restraining competition or creating a monopoly, against the public interest.[170]

So far as interference with contracts enters the field of labor law or disputes, the matter is not within the scope of this work. However, it is proper to notice that a competitor may be enjoined from a continued course of conduct of inducing employees of the plaintiff to breach their contracts of employment, to the irreparable injury of the plaintiff.[171] Or in the case of an employee whom the defendant has already induced to breach his contract, the defendant may be enjoined from employing him.[172] The employee himself may be enjoined from working for another in violation of his contract with the plaintiff where the employee's services are of an unusual or unique nature and he has negatively covenanted not to work for another during the period of his contract with the plaintiff. This is dealt with subsequently.[173]

---

[168] American Law Book Co. v. Edward Thompson Co., 41 Misc. 396, 84 N.Y.S. 225 (1903).

[169] Relief denied to plaintiff against defendant charged with diverting students from the plaintiff where plaintiff's school was simply a correspondence school carried on in fraud of the public. American University v. Wood, 294 Ill. 186, 128 N.E. 330 (1920).

[170] Dr. Miles Medical Co. v. John D. Park & Sons Co., 220 U.S. 373, 31 S.Ct. 376, 55 L. Ed. 502 (1911); Fairbanks, Morse & Co. v. Texas Electric Service Co., 63 F.2d 702 (1933).

Compare Kinner v. Lake Shore & M. S. R. Co., 69 Ohio St. 339, 69 N.E. 614 (1903), where defendant was interfering in contractual arrangement between plaintiff and purchasers of round trip railway tickets and defendant charged plaintiff with being involved in monopoly to give freight rebates, etc. The wrong, if any, of the plaintiff, had no connection with the subject matter of the present action, according to the court.

[171] An interesting example of this was the attempt to enjoin the Pasquel brothers, operators of a Mexican baseball league, and their alleged agent, from inducing baseball players under contract with the plaintiff to breach their contracts and go to Mexico to play baseball. See Brooklyn Nat. League Baseball Club v. Pasquel, 66 F. Supp. 117 (1946), wherein the action was dismissed on the ground that the alleged agent was the only party served with process in the district and that he was not in fact a party to the tortious acts. On the other hand, in American League Baseball Club of New York v. Pasquel, 63 N.Y.S.2d 537 (1946), an injunction was granted against inducing or attempting to induce the breach of their contracts by baseball players.

[172] Lumley v. Wagner, (1852) 1 De G. & Sm. 485, 64 Eng. Rep. 1209, aff'd (1852) 1 De G., M. & G. 604, 42 Eng. Rep. 687, followed as the leading case on the subject.

[173] See *infra*, Sec. 73.

Since the employee's power to earn a living is as important to him as the carrying on of a lawful business is to the owner of the business, the employee has a right recognized as a property right [174] which is entitled to protection by injunction against one seeking to interfere with the employee's contract of employment to the irreparable injury of the employee.[175] The employee's own conduct, of course, may be such as to render him guilty of coming into court with unclean hands and so not entitled to equitable relief.[176]

Sec. 54. Defamation.

As in the past, equity does not at the present time—except as modified by the doctrine of the right of privacy—enjoin the publication of defamatory matter which affects merely the personal reputation and personal character of the plaintiff. This matter, however, is discussed at another place.[177] What we are concerned with here is whether equity will enjoin publication of defamatory matter relative to the business, goods, or services of the plaintiff or to his financial standing and so be directly injurious to him in his property.

In England when the matter became one of first impression, it was pointed out that the business of a merchant is the most valuable kind of property that he can have. A libel which would injure his business reputation was declared to be an injury to his property and equity had jurisdiction to protect him in his property by enjoining the threatened publication.[178] Subsequently, the correctness of this decision was denied,[179] and still later the decision was expressly overruled in *Prudential Assurance Co. v. Knott*,[180] frequently cited and relied on in the American decisions. Nevertheless, under authority of the English Judicature Act of 1873, there has been a return to the view first expressed, and courts of equity

---

174 See *supra*, Sec. 41.
175 Truax v. Raich, 239 U.S. 33, 36 S.Ct. 7, 60 L. Ed. 131, L.R.A. 1916 D 545, Ann. Cas. 1917 B 283 (1915).
176 See Carmen v. Fox Film Corp., 269 F. 928, 15 A.L.R. 1209 (1920), certiorari denied 255 U.S. 569, 41 S.Ct. 423, 65 L. Ed. 790 (1921).
177 See *infra*, Sec. 58.
178 Dixon v. Holden, (1869) L. R. 7 Eq. 488.
179 Mulkern v. Ward, (1872) L. R. 13 Eq. 619.
180 (1875) 10 Ch. App. 142.

in England enjoin not only libelous publications but also oral slanders which injuriously affect one's business.[181] Indeed, courts of law in England have been authorized to grant an injunction pendente lite in an action of libel and a permanent injunction after verdict by the jury in the plaintiff's favor.[182]

In this country the courts for very long and with unanimity refused to enjoin the publication of defamatory matter even where it was clearly injurious to the plaintiff's business or business reputation. The chief ground for refusal was that the constitutional guaranties of freedom of speech and freedom of the press would be infringed or interfered with.[183] Another ground, however, was the very force and weight of precedent which had so long declared that equity did not enjoin defamatory matter injurious to one's reputation that the courts were inclined to feel that this principle was settled even where injury to business or business reputation appeared.[184]

This American view which was once so firmly established has been whittled away in some jurisdictions and attacked outright in other jurisdictions.[185] Some courts have declared that where libelous matter is an incident or part of an attack on the plaintiff's

181 Loog v. Bean, (1884) L. R. 26 Ch. D. 306, 316; Thorley's Cattle Food Co. v. Massam, (1877) L. R. 6 Ch. D. 763.

182 See Bonnard v. Perryman, [1891] 2 Ch. 269; Pound, "Equitable Relief Against Defamation," 29 *Harv. L. Rev.* 665 (1916); annotation, 148 A.L.R. 853, at p. 866.

183 Willis v. O'Connell, 231 F. 1004 (1916); Dailey v. Superior Court, 112 Cal. 94, 44 P. 458, 32 L.R.A.N.S. 273, 53 Am.St.Rep. 160 (1896); Life Association v. Boogher, 3 Mo. App. 173 (1876) (where insolvency of defendant did not sway the court); Marlin Fire Arms Co. v. Shields, 171 N.Y. 384, 64 N.E. 163, 59 L.R.A. 310 (1902).

That this view is still followed in some jurisdictions, see Montgomery Ward & Co. v. United Retail, etc., Employees, CIO, 330 Ill. App. 49, 70 N.E.2d 75 (1946).

But once a plaintiff had established in an action at law that the publication was libelous, he could then obtain injunction against further publication of it or similar matter which was shown to be injurious to him in his business. Flint v. Hutchinson Smoke Burner Co., 110 Mo. 492, 19 S.W. 804, 16 L.R.A. 243, 33 Am.St.Rep. 476 (1892).

In Brandreth v. Lance, 8 Paige (N.Y.) 24, 34 Am. Dec. 368 (1839), the court is careful to point out that the bill did not allege any injury to business, although counsel insisted at the trial that the publication was injurious to business.

See annotation, Injunction as remedy in case of trade libel, 148 A.L.R. 853.

184 See, *e.g.*, Boston Diatite Co. v. Florence Mfg. Co., 114 Mass. 69, 19 Am. Rep. 310 (1873), considered a leading case. Notice, however, that it is no longer followed in Massachusetts.

185 For excellent collection of cases, see annotation, Injunction as remedy in case of trade libel, 148 A.L.R. 853.

business or is part of a plan to injure the plaintiff's business, the publication can be enjoined along with the other incidents or parts.[186] This has been especially true in labor disputes where the false statements enjoined were said by the court to be part of a plan to injure the employer's business.[187] The further view has been arrived at that, whatever the view as to non-enjoinability of the publication of defamatory matter injurious to personal reputation that may also be injurious to property or business, where the defamatory matter is deliberately directed at the business itself or the articles, goods, or services dealt in and is thus classifiable as unfair competition by a competitor or as an unjustifiable and wilful attempt at injury by a noncompetitor, injunction will issue

---

[186] Beck v. Railway Teamsters Protective Union, 118 Mich. 497, 77 N.W. 17, 42 L.R.A. 407, 74 Am.St.Rep. 421 (1898) (At this time, the Michigan Constitution of 1850, art. IV, sec. 42, expressly provided that no one could be enjoined from publishing a libel. However, the court took the view that if the libelous printed statements were part of a plan of coercion and intimidation, the circulation of the statements could be enjoined); J. C. Pitman & Sons v. Pitman, (1946; Del. Ch.) 47 A.2d 721 (libelous or defamatory matter treated as an incident of unfair competition); Gibraltar Sav. & Bldg. Ass'n v. Isbell, (1937; Tex. Civ. App.) 101 S.W.2d 1029.

Defamation of lawyer's professional reputation not enjoined where not connected with factors of conspiracy, coercion, or intimidation. Kwass v. Kersey, — W.Va. —, 81 S.E.2d 237 (1954), noted 39 *Minn. L. Rev.* 580 (1955), and criticized by Professor Redden, *1954 Annual Survey of American Law*, "Equity," 30 N.Y.U.L. Rev. 888.

"Equity does not intervene to restrain the publication of words on a mere showing of their falsity. It intervenes in those cases where restraint becomes essential to the preservation of a business or of other property interests threatened with impairment by illegal combinations or other tortious acts, the publication of the words being merely an instrument or incident." Nann v. Raimist, 255 N.Y. 357, 174 N.E. 690, 73 A.L.R. 669 (1931), per Cardozo, J.

This method of approach is not always consistent with the expressed view of some of these very same courts that libelous publications, even if injurious to business, are not enjoinable because to do so would infringe on the constitutional guaranties of freedom of speech and press. It is not clearly explained why it infringes these guaranties to enjoin a libelous publication which is the sole cause of injury, but not so where the publication is one of several causes of injury.

[187] See Beck v. Railway Teamsters Protective Union, in preceding note; Sachs Quality Furn. Co. v. Hensley, 269 App. Div. 264, 55 N.Y.S.2d 450 (1945).

In Magill Bros., Inc. v. Building Service Employees International Union, 20 Cal.2d 506, 127 P.2d 542 (1942), noted 31 *Cal. L. Rev.* 220 (1943), the false and misleading statements were on signs carried by pickets. The view of the court seems to be that if the union members had sat at home and issued the false statements there would have been nothing to enjoin; but combining the publication of the false statements with picketing warranted injunctive relief. Cf. Cafeteria Employees Union v. Angelos, 320 U.S. 293, 64 S.Ct. 126, 88 L. Ed. 58 (1943).

against the publication.[188] Thus it has become well established that defamatory or false statements directed at the business or business rights of the plaintiff will be enjoined where such statements are issued for the purpose of persuading or inducing customers or the public generally not to do business with the plaintiff,[189] or for the purpose of intimidating them from doing business with the plaintiff.[190] Some courts, in enjoining, as injurious, false statements which are directed against a business or its product, have termed the wrong a "disparagement of property" or "disparagement of a business" and thus, by avoiding the terms "libel," "slander" or "defamation," have neatly evaded many of difficulties presented by precedent as represented in the older cases.[191] Others

---

[188] Carter v. Knapp Motor Co., 243 Ala. 600, 11 So.2d 383, 144 A.L.R. 1177 (1943); Menard v. Houle, 298 Mass. 536, 11 N.E.2d 436 (1937), noted 24 *Va. L. Rev.* 452 (1938), 17 *Tex. L. Rev.* 97 (1938); Yood v. Daly, 37 Ohio App. 574, 174 N.E. 779 (1930) (rule stated but petition not sufficient to set out cause of action).

Consider distinctions made in American Malting Co. v. Keitel, 217 F. 672 (1914); Saxon Motor Sales Co. v. Torino, 166 Misc. 863, 2 N.Y.S.2d 885 (1938).

[189] Carter v. Knapp Motor Co., 243 Ala. 600, 11 So.2d 383, 144 A.L.R. 1177 (1943); Menard v. Houle, 298 Mass. 536, 11 N.E.2d 436 (1937), noted 24 *Va. L. Rev.* 452 (1938), 17 *Tex. L. Rev.* 97 (1940); Lawrence Trust Co. v. Sun-American Pub. Co., 245 Mass. 262, 139 N.E. 655 (1923), noted 9 *Cornell L.Q.* 66 (1923).

Untrue, as well as unfair or misleading, advertising is defined as unfair competition by Cal. Civ. Code, Sec. 3369(2).

An interesting example of disparagement or defamation accomplished in a negative manner appears in Davis v. New England Ry. Pub. Co., 203 Mass. 470, 89 N.E. 565, 25 L.R.A.N.S. 1024, 133 Am.St.Rep. 318 (1909). Defendant published a list which purported to contain the names of all reputable express companies in and around Boston, but deliberately and purposely omitted plaintiff's name from the list. One might compare with that case the Southwestern Bell Tel. Co. v. Texas State Optical, (1954; Tex. Civ. App.) 253 S.W.2d 877, where listing in classified section of telephone directory was compelled. However, defamation does not seem to have been involved.

[190] Emack v. Kane, 34 F. 46 (1888); Shoemaker v. South Bend Spark Arrester Co., 135 Ind. 471, 35 N.E. 280, 22 L.R.A. 332 (1893); J. C. Pitman & Sons v. Pitman (1946; Del. Ch.) 47 A.2d 721 (on the ground that the defamatory threats were an incident of unfair competition). See also American Mercury v. Chase, 13 F.2d 224 (1926), noted 25 *Mich. L. Rev.* 74 (1926); 75 *U. Pa. L. Rev.* 258 (1926), where statements were made in good faith by one not a competitor. Similarly, see New American Library of World Literature, Inc. v. Allen, 114 F. Supp. 823 (1953).

[191] See, *e.g.*, Paramount Pictures, Inc. v. Leaker Press, Inc., 106 F.2d 229 (1939), noted 40 *Col. L. Rev.* 341 (1940), 18 *N.C.L. Rev.* 153 (1940), 25 *Iowa L. Rev.* 668 (1940), 14 *St. Johns L. Rev.* 410 (1940); Lawrence Trust Co. v. Sun-American Pub. Co., 245 Mass. 262, 139 N.E. 655 (1923). See also Smith, "Disparagement of Property," 13 *Col. L. Rev.* 13, 121 (1913); Wham, "Disparagement of Property," 21 *Ill. L. Rev.* 26 (1926); annotation, Injunction against acts or conduct, in street

designate the wrong a "trade libel" to differentiate it and to justify giving equitable relief.[192]

There is no sound reason why the publication or making of defamatory statements, whether written or oral, should not be enjoined where injurious to property rights, including the right to carry on a lawful business and as well the right to earn a living.[193] The gradual arrival at this point of view by the American courts brings about uniformity in equity's protection of property rights, particularly of the right to carry on a lawful business.[194] And the ability to earn a living, as by carrying on a trade or occupation or practicing a profession, is as equally important to the one concerned as is the right of another to carry on a lawful business. Defamatory matter charging professional misconduct is in no wise different from that which defames a business or its goods or services.[195] Constitutional guaranties of freedom of speech and press do not confer unlimited rights. On the contrary, the law

or vicinity, tending to disparage plaintiff's business or his merchandise, 144 A.L.R. 1181; notes, 38 *Col. L. Rev.* 1291 (1939), 24 *Cornell L.Q.* 252 (1939).

[192] See, *e.g.*, Black & Yates, Inc. v. Mahogany Ass'n, Inc., 129 F.2d 227, 148 A.L.R. 841 (1941). See annotation, Injunction as remedy in case of trade libel, 148 A.L.R. 853.

[193] See Walsh, *Treatise on Equity* (1930) Sec. 51.

[194] "We are quite willing to repudiate the 'waning doctrine that equity will not restrain the trade libel.' We are further willing to do so directly and without hiding behind the other equitable principles put forward in some of the cases." Black & Yates, Inc. v. Mahogany Ass'n, Inc., 129 F.2d 227, 148 A.L.R. 841 (1941).

"The defendant relies upon Boston Diatite Co. v. Florence Mfg. Co., 114 Mass. 69, 19 Am. Rep. 310, wherein it was held that equity jurisdiction does not extend to cases of libel or slander or of false representations as to the character or quality of the plaintiff's property or as to his title thereto which involve no breach of trust or of contract. . . . But later cases have held that equity will take jurisdiction where there is a continuing course of unjustified and wrongful attack upon the plaintiff motivated by actual malice, and causing damage to property rights as distinguished from 'injury to the personality affecting feelings, sensibility and honor,' Choate v. Logan, 240 Mass. 131, 133 N.E. 582, 583, even though false statements and false announcements are the means or among the means employed, and that in such cases there is no adequate remedy at law." Menard v. Houle, 298 Mass. 536, 11 N.E.2d 436 (1937), noted 24 *Va. L. Rev.* 452 (1938), 17 *Tex. L. Rev.* 97 (1938), where defendant both by oral statements and signs upon a car purchased from plaintiff attacked the business reputation and goods of plaintiff. To same effect, see Carter v. Knapp Motor Co., 243 Ala. 600, 11 So.2d 383, 144 A.L.R. 1177 (1943).

[195] Defamatory matter charging professional misconduct damages a property right or a substantial right in the nature of a property right with a pecuniary value, and certainly may be distinguished from defamation of personal reputation alone. It is difficult to understand such cases as Gariepy v. Springer, 318 Ill. App. 523, 48 N.E.2d 572 (1942); Wolf v. Harris, 267 Mo. 405, 184 S.W. 1139 (1916).

sets limits beyond which one may not go without violating the law
and becoming subject to penalty. As Dean Pound has pointed
out, if the law is free to penalize as it pleases any publication after
the act, it can prevent publications violating the standards or limits
the law has set.[196]   And if a court, after an act, is considered capable of determining whether the act violates the standard set by law,
it is certainly equally capable of determining beforehand that the
contemplated act will violate the standard and is enjoinable because
of the irreparable injury it will do. To any argument that the
latter situation is one in which the defendant will not have the
benefit of a jury trial, one may well ask whether a person has some
legal or constitutional right to commit some injurious or offensive
act in order that he may then claim the enjoyment of a constitutional right of trial by jury.[197]   Certainly, equity has not proceeded on any such basis in regard to other contemplated or
threatened methods of inflicting irreparable injury to property
or property rights.[198]

Sec. 55.   Miscellaneous business rights; modern developments.

As we have already seen, there are many well-recognized incidents or assets of business, such as trademarks, trade secrets, and the
like, which have value in connection with the business and the misappropriation or unauthorized use of which will irreparably injure
the business of which they are rightful incidents.   Some others not
previously dealt with are mentioned here, including some of recent
origin.   The growth and the complexity of our economic life have
introduced many new assets or incidents of value into various businesses.   Indeed, a business today may be altogether based on new
facilities or processes not formerly existent.   These are as much
entitled to equitable protection as the better-known incidents or
assets.[199]

---

[196] Pound, "Equitable Relief against Defamation," 29 *Harv. L. Rev.* 640 (1916).

[197] Consider concurring opinion of Valliant, J., in Crow v. Canty, 207 Mo. 439,
105 S.W. 1078 (1907).

[198] It will be recalled that one of the reasons for enjoining unauthorized use of
a trade name or trademark by a noncompetitor has been the probable injury to
the reputation of the prior user. See *supra*, Sec. 53.

[199] Listing plaintiff's professional and trade name under classified heading in

The growth of radio is an outstanding illustration of the foregoing. Thus, those engaged in the business of presenting athletic contests or operating athletic teams of various sorts have found that the public interest coupled with the existence of radio offers a new source of income. The exclusive radio broadcasting rights of athletic contests can be sold to operators of radio broadcasting stations and to businesses wishing to advertise their products to radio listeners. The right to restrict the broadcasting privilege to those with whom it contracts for a consideration and the right obtained under the contract by those obtaining the exclusive broadcasting privilege are property rights which equity will protect from interference from others who seek to broadcast the same information.[200] The same situation exists as to exclusive or restricted rights to make motion pictures of athletic contests.[201] Nevertheless, some courts, frequently influenced by an English decision,[202] hold that anyone may broadcast or take pictures inside the enclosure where the contest or event takes place unless all admission tickets expressly prohibit the right or privilege and may, in any event, do so from outside the enclosure from some convenient vantage point.[203] However, the first view, recognizing the property rights of the plaintiff and characterizing the defendant's acts as unfair competition, is undoubtedly more equitable. Consistent with the first view is the decision of the United States Supreme Court that an association engaged in main-

---

telephone directory compelled on part of telephone company. Southwestern Bell Tel. Co. v. Texas State Optical, (1952; Tex. Civ. App.) 253 S.W.2d 877.

An odd case is that in which a newspaper conducting a puzzle contest enjoined professional puzzle solvers from soliciting participants to buy purported solutions, on ground of wrongful interference with right to conduct lawful business. Philadelphia Record Co. v. Leopold, 40 F. Supp. 346 (1941).

[200] Pittsburgh Athletic Co. v. KQV Broadcasting Co., 24 F. Supp. 490 (1938), noted 24 *Cornell L.Q.* 288 (1939), 27 *Geo. L.J.* 381 (1939), 33 *Ill. L. Rev.* 475 (1938), 24 *Iowa L. Rev.* 388 (1939), 23 *Minn. L. Rev.* 395 (1939), 37 *Mich. L. Rev.* 988 (1939), 17 *Tex. L. Rev.* 370 (1939), 25 *Va. L. Rev.* 243 (1938); Twentieth Century Sporting Club v. Transradio Press Service, 165 Misc. 71, 300 N.Y.S. 159 (1937), noted 38 *Col. L. Rev.* 530 (1938); Southwestern Broadcasting Co. v. Oil Center Broadcasting Co., (1948; Tex. Civ. App.) 210 S.W.2d 230.

[201] Madison Square Garden Corp. v. Universal Pictures Co., 255 App. Div. 459, 7 N.Y.S.2d 845 (1938), noted 16 *N.Y.U.L.Q.* 503 (1939).

[202] Sports & General Press Agency v. "Our Dogs" Pub. Co., L. R. 2 K. B. 880 [1916]. See also Victoria Park Racing, etc., Co. v. Taylor (1936; New South Wales) 37 S. R. 322, noted 51 *Harv. L. Rev.* 755 (1938).

[203] National Exhibition Co. v. Teleflash, Inc., 24 F. Supp. 488 (1936).

taining an organization to gather news all over the world and distribute it to members of the association has something in the nature of a property in such news as against a competitor who was obtaining such news from early bulletins of the plaintiff or from employees and using it as its own.   The peculiar value of the news, the court pointed out, was in spreading it while it was fresh.[204]

Just as radio has produced new problems in the field of equity, the development of television is producing problems for the consideration of equity.   The existence of protectible property rights has already come into question and will continue to do so.[205]   So far as televising news events is concerned, it has been suggested that the principle laid down in the *International News Service v. Associated Press* may have application.[206]

In the field generally of art, literature, and music, equity recognizes and protects from unfair competition such matters as the use of a name, distinctive style or manner of rendition and interpretation, creation of characterization, and similar matters.[207]

---

[204] International News Service v. Associated Press, 248 U.S. 215, 39 S.Ct. 68, 63 L. Ed. 211, 2 A.L.R. 293 (1918), noted 18 *Col. L. Rev.* 257 (1918), 4 *Cornell L.Q.* 223 (1919), 32 *Harv. L. Rev.* 566 (1919), 13 *Ill. L. Rev.* 708 (1919), 17 *Mich. L. Rev.* 490 (1919), 67 *U. Pa. L. Rev.* 191 (1919), 28 *Yale L.J.* 387 (1919).

Similarly as to rights in quotations collected by trading exchange, see Moore v. New York Cotton Exchange, 270 U.S. 593, 46 S.Ct. 367, 70 L. Ed. 750, 45 A.L.R. 1370 (1926).

[205] See discussions by Warner, "Legal Protection of Content of Radio and Television Programs," 36 *Iowa L. Rev.* 14 (1950), and "Protection of Radio and Television Programs by Common Law Copyright," 3 *Vand. L. Rev.* 209 (1950); note, "Unauthorized rediffusion of live and film telecasts to home viewers," 68 *Harv. L. Rev.* 712 (1955); note, "Property rights in a sports telecast," 35 *Va. L. Rev.* 246 (1949).

Video tape recording, so-called, see Meagher, "Copyright Problems Presented by a New Art," 30 *N.Y.U. L. Rev.* 1081 (1955).

[206] See interesting discussion by Solinger, "Unauthorized Uses of Television Broadcasts," 48 *Col. L. Rev.* 848 (1948).

[207] See innumerable examples, annotation, Application of principles of unfair competition to artistic or literary property, 19 A.L.R. 949.

As to cartoons or comic strips, see Fisher v. Star Co., 231 N.Y. 414, 132 N.E. 133, 19 A.L.R. 937 (1921), certiorari denied 257 U.S. 654, 42 S.Ct. 94, 66 L. Ed. 419.

Distinctive style of nationally known orchestra conductor as subject of exclusive radio contract, see Waring v. Dunlea, 26 F. Supp. 338 (1939); Waring v. WDAS, 327 Pa. 433, 194 A. 631 (1937).

Compare an interesting situation presented in Shostakovitch v. Twentieth Century-Fox Film Corp., 80 N.Y.S.2d 575 (1948), concerning the motion picture, "The Iron Curtain," based on the exposure of the Soviet Russian spy ring in Canada which sought to obtain atomic bomb secrets. Shostakovitch and other

Membership in a trade or labor union, aside from any benefits in the way of insurance or the like to which it may entitle the member, in itself is a valuable right. Wrongful expulsion may prevent the member from following his trade or occupation to his incalculable damage. Since the power to earn a living, free from unwarranted interference or injury, is recognized nowadays as a right or property,[208] a wrongful expulsion from a trade or labor union which would affect the member's ability to earn a living is an injury to a property right as to which equity will provide relief.[209] Exactly the same point may be made as to membership in a business exchange or trade association, as concerns either the power to earn a living or the right to carry on a lawful business.[210]

In respect to the power to earn a living, seniority rights are said to be a property right since they tend to promote the opportunity to earn a living and to increase one's earning power. Consequently, seniority rights are entitled to the protection of equity when invaded, since such invasion threatens to diminish one's earning power and is thus an attack on one's means or ability to earn a livelihood.[211]

---

famous Soviet Russian music composers sought unsuccessfully to enjoin the use of their compositions as background music and their names on credit lines in the picture, on the ground it implied their approval of the picture and their disloyalty to Soviet Russia.

208 See *supra*, Sec. 41.

209 Recovery of damages for expulsion from labor union where membership was essential in order to gain employment, see Sweetman v. Barrows, 263 Mass. 349, 161 N.E. 272, 62 A.L.R. 311 (1928).

210 Professional association, see Blenko v. Schmeltz, 362 Pa. 365, 67 A.2d 99, 20 A.L.R.2d 523 (1949), and annotation at p. 531.

Motion picture association expelling a member for use of unapproved advertising revealing too much of the female anatomy, see Hughes Tool Co. v. Motion Picture Ass'n, 66 F. Supp. 1006 (1946).

211 Grand International Brotherhood, etc. v. Mills, 43 Ariz. 379, 21 P.2d 971 (1934). See also Piercy v. L. & N. R. R. Co., 198 Ky. 477, 248 S.W. 1042 (1923); Gleason v. Thomas, 117 W.Va. 550, 186 S.E. 304 (1936), noted 23 *Va. L. Rev.* 1935. Compare Donovan v. Travers, 285 Mass. 167, 188 N.E. 705 (1934); Mosshamer v Wabash Ry. Co., 221 Mich. 407, 191 N.W. 210 (1922).

Chapter 8.

PROTECTION OF PERSONAL OR INDIVIDUAL RIGHTS

Sec. 56. In general.

Equity, as has already been remarked, developed as a system of jurisprudence to supply the deficiencies in the remedial relief available at common law and in the common law courts. The common law might give a right but with the powers of the common law courts not sufficient to give a complete remedy or the common law gave no right but upon principles of universal justice the interference of some judicial power was necessary to prevent a wrong. Thus, one prerequisite of equitable relief came to be that there was no remedy at law or else only an incomplete or inadequate remedy.

Unfortunately, when equity was developing and emerging as a full-fledged system of jurisprudence, rights of property rather than human rights were paramount. The personal, the individual, the civil, the social, the political rights of the common man were in that day vague and more or less formless. Consequently, equity, while supplying the deficiencies or lack of remedies in the common law courts, found itself engaged solely with matters of property and rights incidental thereto. From this arose the second prerequisite of the exercise of equity jurisdiction, that property or property rights must be in question.[1] While the concept of what are property and property rights has necessarily been broadened by the great economic, industrial and mercantile growth of Anglo-American life—and duly recognized by courts in the exercise of equity jurisdiction—courts of equity continue to be burdened, like Coleridge's ancient mariner, with a dead albatross hung around their necks. That is, to repeat the rule, courts of equity intervene only to protect property and property rights and not to prevent injuries of a purely personal or individual nature which have no connection or association with property interests. The rule continues to be reiterated by numerous writers and courts at the present day.[2] Although frequently asserted by courts at the very moment they are seeking to evade its stultifying effect, its constant assertion apparently demands that the law student and the lawyer accept it as having been established. Then it is necessary to begin the study of the ways and situations in which it is frequently evaded or abandoned outright in some jurisdictions.[3]

That this restriction on the exercise of equity jurisdiction should be removed would seem to be obvious. Equity developed to

---

[1] See *supra*, Chapter 3.

[2] See High, *Injunctions* (4th Ed.) Sec. 20b, who appears to approve of the rule. Other writers seem to accept it without comment or criticism. See Bispham, *Principles of Equity* (10th Ed.) Secs. 37, 465; Merwin, *Principles of Equity* (1895). However, most present-day writers are critical of the rule. See authorities cited *infra*, Footnote 4.

A number of courts still seem to cling resolutely to this rule. See, *e.g.*, Bank v. Bank, 180 Md. 254, 23 A.2d 700 (1942); Snedaker v. King, 111 Ohio 225, 145 N.E. 15 (1924), noted 19 *Ill. L. Rev.* 587 (1925), 34 *Yale L.J.* 327 (1925).

[3] Lawrence, in his *Equity Jurisprudence* (1929) Sec. 53, asserts that equity is not confined to the protection merely of property rights, but his illustrations to demonstrate this are mainly instances wherein equity accomplished its purpose by expanding or stretching the concept of what is property.

"The rule that equity will not afford relief by injunction except where property rights are involved is known chiefly by its breach rather than by its observance; in fact, it may be regarded as a fiction, because courts with greatest uniformity have based their jurisdiction to protect purely personal rights nominally on an alleged property right, when, in fact, no property rights were invaded." Hawks v. Yancey (1924; Tex. Civ. App.) 265 S.W. 233, noted 19 *Ill. L. Rev.* 679 (1924).

relieve the inadequacies of remedies available at common law. That this was in instances of property rights or property interests was due to the fact that society of that day gave weight principally only to such rights. But the very development of our way of life which has brought about recognition of new property rights or rights of substance in the nature of property rights has also brought a recognition of human rights, of personal and individual rights. Since these rights may be subjected to interference, to injury, to infringement, justice demands that the judicial power protect these rights. If the power or limits of the common law, or statutory provisions, do not provide the adequate remedies, equity is the proper source of remedy, just as it was once before in comparable situations.[4] This has, indeed, been very widely recognized by the courts and frequently by the legislatures. The result has been the establishment of some situations, although not in all jurisdictions, in which the power of equity has been made available to relieve against violation or threatened violation of rights not connected with property interests. It has also led many courts to read into a situation some alleged property right which will justify it in giving relief. There is thus a definite modern trend to extend equitable relief to protect personal rights, although most courts are not as yet at the point where they unanimously renounce the surface rule that property is prerequisite to equity jurisdiction.[5] Some few courts, however, have been outspoken in declaring that personal rights recognized by law will be protected by equity upon the same conditions upon which property rights will be protected.[6] These conditions, of course, are that unless relief is

---

[4] See Brandeis & Warren, "The Right to Privacy," 4 *Harv. L. Rev.* 193 (1890); Pound, "Equitable Relief against Defamation and Injuries to Personality," 29 *Harv. L. Rev.* 668 (1916); Long, "Equitable Jurisdiction to Protect Personal Rights," 33 *Yale L.J.* 115 (1923); Chafee, "Does Equity Follow the Law of Torts," 75 *U. Pa. L. Rev.* 1 (1926); Moscovitz, "Civil Liberty and Injunctive Protection," 39 *Ill. L. Rev.* 144 (1944); Oberfell, "Jurisdiction of Equity to Protect Personal Rights," 20 *Notre Dame Law.* 56 (1944); note, 20 *Rocky Mt. Law Rev.* 304 (1948); annotations, 37 L.R.A. 783 (1897), 14 A.L.R. 295 (1921); 175 A.L.R. 438 (1948).

[5] See illustrative cases throughout succeeding sections. And see annotation, Jurisdiction of equity to protect personal rights; modern view, 175 A.L.R. 438 (1948); Eames, "The Protection of Personal Rights in Equity Since 1949," 32 *B.U. L. Rev.* 419 (1952).

[6] In Alabama, see Henley v. Rockett, 243 Ala. 172, 8 So.2d 852 (1942).
In California, see Orloff v. Los Angeles Turf Club, 30 Cal.2d 110, 180 P.2d 321,

granted, a substantial right of the plaintiff will be impaired to a material degree; that the remedy at law is inadequate; and that injunctive relief can be applied with practical success and without imposing an impossible burden on the court or bringing its processes into disrepute.[7]

The distinction has been made, no doubt properly, that where there is no personal right present there is no ground upon which to base equitable relief. It is, indeed, apparent that even if equity will protect personal rights, there must be a personal right existent and judicially cognizable to warrant the interposition of equity.[8]

---

171 A.L.R. 913 (1947), noted 15 *U. Chi. L. Rev.* 227 (1947), in which statutes providing for equitable relief are cited as authorizing protection of personal as well as property rights. Further, see Orloff v. Los Angeles Turf Club, 36 Cal.2d 734, 227 P.2d 449 (1951), in favor of injunction to restrain defendant from refusing plaintiff admission to race track in violation of his statutory rights.

In the District of Columbia, the decision of the trial court that it had no jurisdiction to grant an injunction because it could interfere only to protect property rights was reversed as error in Berrien v. Pollitzer, — U.S. App. D.C. —, 165 F.2d 21 (1947), noted 34 *Va. L. Rev.* 352 (1948), wherein the appellate court makes clear its view that equity must and shall protect personal rights where there is no adequate remedy by way of damages.

In Massachusetts, it has been definitely announced that "we cannot believe that personal rights recognized by law are in general less important to the individual or less vital to society or less worthy of protection by the peculiar remedies equity can afford than are property rights. We are impressed by the plaintiffs' suggestion that if equity would safeguard their right to sell bananas it ought to be at least equally solicitous of their personal liberties guaranteed by the Constitution. We believe the true rule to be that equity will protect personal rights by injunction upon the same conditions upon which it will protect property rights by injunction." Kenyon v. City of Chicopee, 320 Mass. 528, 70 N.E.2d 241, 175 A.L.R. 430 (1946), noted 27 *B.U. L. Rev.* 241 (1947), 20 *Rocky Mt. Law Rev.* 304 (1948).

In Louisiana, where the civil law, as distinguished from the Anglo-American common law, prevails, the courts have not been hampered by the restrictions existing in the Anglo-American law. Injunction may be granted to protect personal rights. See, *e.g.*, Itzkovitch v. Whitaker, 117 La. 708, 42 So. 228, 116 Am.St.Rep. 215 (1906).

In England, the Judicature Act of 1873, Sec. 25, subsec. 8, confers power on the courts to grant injunction in all cases "in which it shall appear to the court to be just or convenient that such order should be made." It has been said in Texas that the Texas statutes confer equivalent power. Ex parte Warfield, 40 Tex. Cr. 413, 50 S.W. 933, 76 Am.St.Rep. 724 (1899); Hawks v. Yancey (1924; Tex. Civ. App.) 265 S.W. 233. And in Oklahoma, the power to protect against injury to personal rights is said to result from statute. See Nation v. Chism, 154 Okla. 50, 6 P.2d 766 (1931).

[7] Kenyon v. City of Chicopee, preceding note.

[8] See annotations, Jurisdiction of equity to protect personal rights, 14 A.L.R. 295; 175 A.L.R. 438. For an interesting analysis of situation, see Moscovitz, "Civil Liberties and Injunctive Protection," 39 *Ill. L. Rev.* 144 (1944).

And, certainly, equity will not concern itself with trivial matters.[9] However, an examination of many of the cases holding that there is no personal right present or no legal injury to be redressed reveals situations as to which a more enlightened view would consider a personal right was present.[10] Much the same may be said of the often-repeated statements of the courts that equity does not grant protection of purely moral or ethical rights.[11] Changes of viewpoint might bring about a consideration that what was once dismissed as a purely moral or ethical right is instead a personal right of substance worthy of equity's protection. Moreover, differences frequently exist between courts of law and courts of equity in the interpretation of the existence of a personal right which is judicially cognizable. The former may deny the existence of a right for the injury of which an action for damages will lie, whereas on similar facts the latter may find a right deserving of equitable protection in the absence of any remedy at law. This dissimilarity of view tends to disappear in a court in which powers of law and equity have been merged.[12]

The existence of an adequate legal remedy may naturally result in the refusal to give equitable aid.[13] Here again, changes in viewpoint, as well as the effect of the merger of legal and equitable powers in the same court, may lead to belief that although a legal remedy may be available it is nevertheless not so adequate, effective, and complete as that which equity can afford.[14]

---

[9] Use of insulting language, as to which in any event there was other adequate relief available, see Smith v. Hamm, 207 Ark. 507, 181 S.W.2d 475 (1944); Randall v. Freed, 154 Cal. 299, 97 P. 669 (1908).

[10] For example, the unauthorized use of one's picture or the publication of matter injurious to one's reputation. Whereas, formerly, it was usually held that there was no right present or existent, many jurisdictions now consider that the one complaining has a personal right of privacy which should be protected. See *infra*, Sec. 59.

[11] Statement of rule, see Benj. T. Crump Co. v. Lindsay, 130 Va. 144, 107 S.E. 679, 17 A.L.R. 747 (1921). Interesting note, see "Moral Right of Artists," 49 *Col. L. Rev.* 132 (1949).

[12] Chafee, "Does Equity Follow the Law of Torts," 75 *U. Pa. L. Rev.* 1 (1926).

[13] See Snedaker v. King, 111 Ohio 225, 145 N.E. 15 (1924), noted 19 *Ill. L. Rev.* 587 (1925), 34 *Yale L.J.* 327 (1925). See also Smith v. Hamm and Randall v. Freed, *supra*, footnote 9.

[14] Compare with view of court in Snedaker v. King, *supra*, that of Texas courts, *supra* and *infra*, Sec. 60.

Sec. 57.   Injuries to the physical person.

Where physical injury has been inflicted by a completed act, there is no ground for equitable relief, for in any event equity does not concern itself with an injury which is over and done, with no reasonable probability of repetition.   There is an adequate remedy at law by way of damages for the physical injury inflicted by the completed act.   If the act constitutes a crime, as is usually the case, criminal proceedings may be instituted to punish the act.   Is the situation different where physical injury has been inflicted and will, with reasonable probability, again be inflicted or, although none has yet been inflicted, there is reasonable probability that it will be?

If property is in question, whether or not a threatened act is a crime or will give rise to an action for damages, equity will enjoin its commission if the commission of the act will cause irreparable injury to the property.   The remedy at law or the resort to criminal proceedings comes too late and is thus inadequate as a remedy.[15]   Human life or safety is not less important than property, at least by present-day standards in this country.   Hence, if the only remedy available is an action for damages or a criminal proceeding after the threatened physical injury actually occurs, the remedy is totally inadequate and equity should intercede.   But if there are other methods available for preventing the threatened physical injury, there is no need to resort to equity.   For instance, if there is time to apply to equity before the threatened injury will occur, there is certainly also time in which to call a policeman or to file a criminal complaint.   This may provide adequate protection and adequate remedy, since the threat of the physical injury may come within the definition of disorderly conduct or assault or may be made in connection with a criminal trespass.[16]   Adequate relief may also exist under statutory provisions for placing the threatener under bond or security to keep the peace.

There may, of course, be situations in which calling a policeman, filing a criminal complaint, or placing one under a bond to keep

---

[15] See *supra*, Sec. 19.
[16] Randall v. Freed, 154 Cal. 299, 97 P. 669 (1908).

the peace will not be appropriate methods of relief. If this is true and no other adequate means of protection are afforded except by equitable remedies, then assuredly equitable relief should be granted.[17] Illustrations of such situations may be found in the granting of an injunction against the use of a rifle range until it was made safe to use without endangering the lives of those occupying adjoining property,[18] granting injunction against a course of conduct which not only involved threatened physical injury but which included defamation designed to accomplish the arrest of the complainant and the loss of her job and other matters of persecution,[19] and the granting of an injunction against removing an elderly woman to a pesthouse which was dangerously unsuitable for habitation by her.[20]

Sec. 58. Injuries to personal reputation.

The principle has, with much seeming firmness, been announced from the earliest cases [21] to the present day [22] that equity will not enjoin the threatened publication of matter defamatory of the personal reputation. An exception has sometimes been stated, to the effect that equity will enjoin publication of the defamatory matter

---

[17] It is interesting to note that in Harris Stanley Coal & Land Co. v. Chesapeake & O. R. Co., 154 F.2d 450 (1946), the granting of injunctive relief to the plaintiff was largely influenced by the protection of human life which would result.

[18] McKillop v. Taylor, 25 N.J. Eq. 139 (1874).

Although it appears that the personal danger to such occupants was the reason for granting the injunction, it will be observed that this type of case would permit an approach based on the element of a property right if that is considered necessary. That is, it might be alleged that the use of the rifle range was a nuisance, in that it prevented the plaintiff's reasonable use and enjoyment of his property. This view of the maintenance of a rifle range as a nuisance was taken, in allowing damages for injury, in Gaines v. Village of Wyoming, 147 Ohio St. 491, 72 N.E.2d 369 (1947).

[19] Hawks v. Yancey (1924; Tex. Civ. App.) 265 S.W. 233, noted 19 *Ill. L. Rev.* 679 (1924).

The greater liberality of the Texas courts in granting injunctive relief in other than property matters is instanced also in other sections of this chapter.

[20] Kirk v. Wyman, 83 S.C. 372, 65 S.E. 387, 23 L.R.A.N.S. 1188 (1909).

Compare Stuart v. Board of Supervisors, 83 Ill. 341 (1876), denying injunction against confinement in unhealthful jail, on ground there was an adequate remedy at law.

[21] Brandreth v. Lance, 8 Paige (N.Y.) 24, 34 Am. Dec. 368 (1839).

[22] Howell v. Bee Pub. Co., 100 Neb. 39, 158 N.W. 358, L.R.A. 1917 A 160 (1916), Ann. Cas. 1917 D 655; League for Peace with Justice in Palestine v. Newspaper PM, 65 N.Y.S.2d 480 (1946).

as an incident to the specific enforcement of a trust or contract.[23]

This refusal has been based on the ground that equity protects property rights only (a contention having less validity today than when originally announced), and on such grounds as that the constitutional rights of freedom of the press and right of trial by jury would be interfered with.[24] The validity of such grounds or reasons has been seriously questioned.[25] It is undoubtedly true that there have been many departures from the rule. The recognition in many jurisdictions of the doctrine of the right of privacy has brought about the equitable restraint of many acts as invasions of the right of privacy, where actual consequence of the acts would be to injure personal reputation.[26] Protecting one from charges of paternity of an illegitimate child is in fact equitable prevention of defamation of personal reputation.[27] Restraining the wrongful expulsion of one from a club or social organization is frequently the restraint of an act which would be injurious to the personal reputation of the expelled member.[28] Likewise, restraining the unauthorized publication of private letters, on the ground that the writer's right of property in the letter is being protected, may actually be the prevention of an injury to the personal reputation of the writer.[29]

Sec. 59. Right of privacy.

The right of privacy or the right to privacy may be defined as the right of the individual to be let alone, or the right to live one's life in seclusion free from unwarranted and undesired publicity,[30]

---

23 See Choate v. Logan, 240 Mass. 131, 133 N.E. 582 (1921), where it was said that the facts disclosed no contract or trust which was violated by the defamatory matter.

24 See cases in preceding notes.

25 Pound, "Equitable Relief Against Defamation," 28 *Harv. L. Rev.* 665 (1916). Discussion of obligatory correction of errors in books, magazines, and newspapers, on the radio, and in governmental "press releases," in the form of a right of reply or of compulsory retraction, see Professor Chafee's article, 60 *Harv. L. Rev.* 1 (1947).

26 See Sec. 59.

27 See *infra*, Sec. 60.

28 See *infra*, Sec. 61.

29 See *supra*, Sec. 17; *infra*, Sec. 59.

30 See Melvin v. Reid, 112 Cal. App. 285, 297 P. 91 (1931); Brandeis and Warren, "The Right to Privacy," 4 *Harv. L. Rev.* 193 (1890).

or the right of a person to be secure from invasion by the public into matters of a private nature.[31]   The consequence of such invasion or publicity may be to hold the individual up to public ridicule or even scorn or contempt, in short in some way to attack or damage his personal reputation.   To a lesser extent it may make him an object of public curiosity, or otherwise interfere with his peace of mind and his right to the pursuit of happiness.[32]

In the past there was no recognition of the existence of such a right so as to afford a basis of judicial jurisdiction, whether legal or equitable.   Courts of equity refused to enjoin invasions of privacy on the ground that no property or property right was involved to which irreparable injury was threatened.[33]   Courts of law, short of a clear case of libel, refused to recognize any right which could be the subject of injury.

The change in viewpoint which has now come about is generally attributed to an article written in 1890 by the late Justice Brandeis and Professor Warren.   They pointed out that it is a principle as old as the common law that the individual shall have full protection in person and in property.   And that it is necessary from time to time to define anew this protection where political, social, and economic changes entail the recognition of new rights.   The time had now come, they argued, to consider anew the need for increased protection of the person, rendered necessary by such modern developments as the growth of photography and the press —to which we may now add radio, television and even newsreels.[34]   The weight and validity of their arguments were very

---

[31] Pavesich v. New England Life Ins. Co., 122 Ga. 190, 50 S.E. 68, 106 Am.St.Rep. 104, 2 Ann. Cas. 561, 69 L.R.A. 101 (1905).

[32] Invading right of privacy by publishing another's literary efforts or letters or by using his name, see annotation, 138 A.L.R. 96.

[33] See, *e.g.*, Chappell v. Stewart, 82 Md. 323, 33 A. 542, 51 Am.St.Rep. 476, 37 L.R.A. 783 (1896) (The principle there stated that equity will not grant relief for wrongs affecting the person was reaffirmed in Bank v. Bank, 180 Md. 254, 23 A.2d 700 (1942)); Roberson v. Rochester Folding-Box Co., 171 N.Y. 538, 64 N.E. 442, 89 Am.St.Rep. 828, 59 L.R.A. 478 (1902) (which led to enactment of New York statute establishing limited right of privacy).

[34] See Brandeis and Warren, "The Right to Privacy," 4 *Harv. L. Rev.* 193 (1890). Innumerable articles of much excellence have appeared in the years since. It may suffice to cite Nizer in 39 *Mich. L. Rev.* 526 (1941), and Feinberg in 48 *Col. L. Rev.* 713 (1948), which review the developments since the article by Brandeis and Warren. A very comprehensive collection of cases on the subject will be found in the annotations in 138 A.L.R. 22, 168 A.L.R. 446. See also comment, "Right of Privacy," [1952] *Wis. L. Rev.* 507.

shortly thereafter judicially recognized and given concrete effect,[35] and this has continued to be the case. In the majority of courts in which the question has arisen, the courts have recognized that a justiciable right exists and have afforded protection against invasions or violations of the right. While many of these courts, plagued by doubt that equity should protect purely personal rights, have founded their decision on the existence of some real or technical property right,[36] others have made the personal right itself the basis of their decision.[37]

Of course, where the right of privacy is recognized as judicially cognizable, the relief sought may be by way of damages for the invasion,[38] or by way of injunctive relief in equity where the remedy by way of damages affords inadequate relief. If the invasion of one's privacy is as yet only threatened, but threatened with reasonable probability, equitable relief is the proper remedy to prevent the violation of one's rights from taking place. Or if the invasion has already taken place but is of a continuing nature, again equitable relief provides the proper remedy.

The recognition and protection of the right has been primarily by

---

[35] Pavesich v. New England Life Ins. Co., 122 Ga. 190, 50 S.E. 68, 106 Am.St.Rep. 104, 2 Ann. Cas. 561, 69 L.R.A. 101 (1905).

[36] Munden v. Harris, 153 Mo. App. 652, 134 S.W. 1076 (1911).

Breach of contract rights, see McCreery v. Miller's Groceteria Co., 99 Colo. 499, 64 P.2d 803 (1936), noted 16 *Tex. L. Rev.* 263 (1938), where it is clear that one of the defendants who was nevertheless enjoined had no contractual relations with the plaintiff.

It is interesting to notice the well-known case of Gee v. Pritchard, (1818) 2 Swanst. 402, 36 Eng. Rep. 670, wherein the plaintiff sought to enjoin the unauthorized publication of private letters of the plaintiff. This, as is well recognized today, was in reality an effort to prevent an invasion of the plaintiff's privacy, which would have been violated by such publication. Lord Eldon, although declaring that equity protects only rights of property, then found that the writer of a letter has a property right therein and that such right, however nominal, is a proper subject of equitable protection. This view as to a property right in letters has been uniformly followed by the American courts. The most cited American illustration is undoubtedly Baker v. Libbie, 210 Mass. 599, 97 N.E. 109, Ann. Cas. 1912 D 551, 37 L.R.A.N.S. 944 (1912), noted 12 *Va. L. Rev.* 656 (1926).

[37] Reed v. Real Detective Publishing Co., 63 Ariz. 294, 162 P.2d 133 (1946), noted in 46 *Col. L. Rev.* 315 (1946), 41 *Ill. L. Rev.* 144 (1946).

The California court has based its decision on the state constitutional provision guaranteeing the fundamental right to pursue and obtain happiness, which it declares includes the right to live one's life free from unwarranted attacks on one's liberty, property and reputation. Melvin v. Reid, 112 Cal. App. 285, 297 P. 91 (1931).

[38] As in O'Brien v. Pabst Sales Co., 124 F.2d 167 (1942). See also cases collected in annotations in 138 A.L.R. 22; 168 A.L.R. 446.

judicial action,[39] but in several states this recognition and protection has been afforded by statute.[40]   However, this statutory recognition and protection is usually much narrower in scope than that provided by judicial action.[41]   This is not to say, however, that the right as developed by many courts is by any means broad.   The doctrine of the right of privacy, as so developed by judicial action, has been summarized by one court, as follows: [42] An incident of the person and not of property; a purely personal action which does not survive the person injured; [43] the right does not exist where the person has himself published or consented to publication of the matter objected to; [44] the right does not exist where the person has become so prominent that by his very prominence he has dedicated his life to the public; [45] the right can only be violated by printings, writings, pictures, or other permanent publications or reproductions and not by word of mouth;[46] and—in some jurisdictions only

---

[39] See preceding notes.

[40] See N. Y. Civil Rights Law, Secs. 50, 51; Utah Code Ann. 1943, Tit. 103, c. 4, Secs. 7–9; Va. Code Ann. 1942, Sec. 5782.

[41] The New York statute, for example, goes no further than to protect against the unauthorized use of one's name or picture for advertising or commercial uses. The prohibition of the statute has been held not to apply to a newspaper or to a news film. Jeffries v. New York Evening Journal Pub. Co., 67 Misc. 540, 124 N.Y.S. 780 (1910); Humiston v. Universal Film Mfg. Co., 189 App. Div. 467, 178 N.Y.S. 752 (1919). And see note, "Use of Name in Newspaper Advertisement without Consent," 49 Col. L. Rev. 282 (1949).

[42] Melvin v. Reid, 112 Cal. App. 285, 297 P. 91 (1931).

[43] Metter v. Los Angeles Examiner, 35 Cal.App.2d 304, 95 P.2d 491 (1939).

But the right of action has been held to survive the death of the wrongdoer and may be revived against his administrator. Reed v. Real Detective Pub. Co., (Ariz.) supra, Footnote 37.

[44] O'Brien v. Pabst Sales Co., 124 F.2d 167 (1942) (tort action for damages).

[45] This is applied to all those who become what has been described as objects of legitimate public interest, either by voluntarily following a course of conduct or an occupation of public interest, as in O'Brien v. Pabst Sales Co., in preceding note, or by involuntarily attracting public interest, as by some anti-social act, as in Elmhurst v. Pearson, 153 F.2d 467 (1946), noted 46 Col. L. Rev. 1040 (1946) (where person seeking relief was defendant in sedition trial of national interest). In this latter regard, reference may also be made to Melvin v. Reid, supra, note 42, as to incidents of a woman's life which appeared in the records of her criminal trial and were thus open to the public as part of the public records.

See also note, 32 Va. L. Rev. 1045 (1946), as to right of privacy not being enforceable where public interest involved.

[46] See criticism of this in paragraph following.

Taking and retention of fingerprints and photographs by police as invasion of right of privacy, see State ex rel. Mavity v. Tyndall, 224 Ind. 364, 66 N.E.2d 755 (1946), noted 21 Tulane L. Rev. 289 (1946), 26 B.U. L. Rev. 526 (1946); McGovern v. Van Riper, 140 N.J. Eq. 341, 54 A.2d 469 (1947), noted 23 Notre Dame Law. 380 (1948).

—that the right of action accrues only when publication or repro-duction is made for gain or profit.[47]

Objection may certainly be made to any such requirement as that the publication must be one made for gain or profit. It should be entirely immaterial what purpose or motive brings about the invasion of privacy. Certainly, so long as it is knowingly done or continued, it is as much a wrong in one instance as in the other. The point is not whether the defendant is making a profit from his invasion of the right of another, but whether the right of another is violated. In protecting property rights, equity does not make its relief dependent on whether or not the defendant profits from his wrongful act.

Similarly, it should be entirely immaterial whether the wrong is accomplished by writings, pictures, or printings on the one hand or by word of mouth on the other. The point is not the method by which one violates the rights of an innocent person but the fact that he violates the rights to the latter's injury. It is interesting to notice in this regard that the right of privacy has been held to have been violated by a radio broadcast.[48]

Another legitimate object of criticism is the view of many courts that only one's name and picture are comprised within one's right of privacy. One's privacy must assuredly comprise more than the mere right to object to the unauthorized use of one's name or picture, since it is the right to be let alone and to maintain one's seclusion. On a radio program recently, the master of ceremonies announced that one of the contestants would toss away 200 dollars in dimes—supplied by the sponsor, of course—in front of the contestant's home on a certain day and hour. As reported on the program the following week, a large crowd had gathered for hours at the place named, overflowing into the yards of the neigh-bors to their obvious disturbance, inconvenience, and discomfiture. Aside from any injury to the property of these neighbors and the blocking of their ingress and egress, it would clearly appear that the radio program and the broadcasting company were respon-sible for the invasion of the neighbors' rights of privacy, and that

---

[47] As under the New York statutory provision, *supra*, footnote 40.
[48] Mau v. Rio Grande Oil, Inc., 28 F. Supp. 845 (1939).
"Defamation by Radio," see comment, 33 *Va. L. Rev.* 612.

without any use of their names or pictures.[49]   Indeed, in these days of commercial advertising, with the policy of using individuals' indorsements of a product, one's name and picture must be considered to have a definite value and to constitute a property right. The value of this property right naturally varies and as to most individuals will have only a nominal value.   Nevertheless, as a property right which each of us has, it may be clearly distinguished from that right of privacy which each of us has.   The right of privacy must, logically, go beyond the mere use of names and pictures and must relate to all disturbance to or interference with one's right to be let alone.[50]

Sec. 60.   Domestic or family rights and relationships.

In the matter of domestic or family rights and relationships, courts of equity usually have no trouble in finding present a property right or interest of some sort.   The right to or duty of support, rights of inheritance, rights to services, are common examples. Nevertheless, it is not infrequent to find courts announcing that the personal rights involved are alone sufficient to warrant equitable protection, although the weight of this is usually weakened by the court hurrying on to point out the property rights that are involved.   An example of this practice is the well-known case of *Vanderbilt v. Mitchell*,[51] in which the plaintiff sought the cancellation of a birth certificate placed on the public records which charged him with the paternity of the child.   He also sought a permanent injunction against the mother and child claiming under this certificate the status, name, property, or privilege of a lawfully begotten child of his, as well as an injunction against the appropriate official from issuing copies of the certificate from the public record.   This case is much cited as an outright example of equity's departure from the rule that equity protects only prop-

---

[49] That causing the collection of a crowd of people to the annoyance of one's neighbors may be a nuisance, see Lyons Sons & Co. v. Gulliver, [1914] 1 Ch. 631, noted in 48 L. J. 666; Shamhart v. Morrison Cafeteria Co., 159 Fla. 629, 32 So.2d 727 (1948); Tushbant v. Greenfield's, Inc., 308 Mich. 626, 14 N.W.2d 520 (1944).

[50] See dissenting opinion in O'Brien v. Pabst Sales Co., *supra*, footnote 38; note, 35 *Ore. L. Rev.* 42 (1955), when right of privacy invaded by publication of news items and photographs.

[51] 72 N.J. Eq. 910, 67 A. 97, 14 L.R.A.N.S. 304 (1907), noted 7 *Col. L. Rev.* 533 (1907), 21 *Harv. L. Rev.* 54 (1907).

erty rights.[52]   The court does say that if the plaintiff's status and
personal rights were alone threatened or invaded by the filing of
the false certificate, nevertheless a court of equity would protect
those rights.   However, it continues, "But it is not necessary to
place the decision upon this ground, because there are sufficient
facts presented to enable us to put this case upon the technical
basis that the jurisdiction we are exercising is the protection of
property rights."   These property interests were considered to
be the burden of support that might be imposed upon the plaintiff
and the rights of inheritance that might subsequently be claimed.[53]

Another example wherein the property element was supplied
by a contract arose in Kentucky.   The defendant lived with her
mother in a house jointly owned by them.   The plaintiff, another
daughter, obtained an injunction against the defendant molesting
and annoying her when she visited their mother.   The court said,
"As a general rule, equitable remedies deal with property rights
rather than with personal rights and obligations, and at one time
the rule was broadly stated that equity will not interfere to enforce
a strictly personal right where no property right is involved, but
that rule has been greatly relaxed and many cases can be found
where a court of equity has assumed jurisdiction to protect purely
personal rights from invasion. . . . But, even if some property
right is requisite to equity jurisdiction, this element is not wholly
lacking in the present case.   Appellant and appellee entered into
a written contract in which the former agreed that appellee should

---

[52] See Walsh, *Treatise on Equity* (1930) Sec. 52; annotation, 14 A.L.R. 295
(1921).

[53] Similarly, to annul and cancel an instrument purporting to be a contract of
marriage, on the ground that it was a forgery, see Sharon v. Hill, 20 F. 1 (1884).
In overruling a demurrer to the bill, the court stated that a proper case for
equitable relief was stated, since there was no adequate remedy at law and the
contract, after the death of the complainant, who was far older, might be made
the basis of a claim to the large property interests of complainant. See also Ran-
dazzo v. Rappolo, 105 N.Y.S. 481 (1906), where defendant had gone through a
marriage ceremony with a man impersonating the plaintiff; Burns v. Stevens, 236
Mich. 443, 210 N.W. 482 (1926).
    The converse of Vanderbilt v. Mitchell, *supra*, is presented by Morecroft v.
Taylor, 225 App. Div. 562, 234 N.Y.S. 2 (1929), where plaintiff sought a declaratory judgment that she was the daughter, albeit illegitimate, of defendant and that
defendant be compelled to execute and deliver to plaintiff a certificate of plaintiff's birth. Motion to dismiss complaint as not stating a cause of action was
denied.

have the right to visit her mother . . . without molestation by appellant, in consideration of the settlement of certain litigation which was then pending. The natural right of appellee to visit her mother was fortified by a written contract executed for a valuable consideration." [54]

In neither of the situations presented by the two foregoing cases should the existence of an actual or pretended property interest be necessary to warrant equitable protection. In the first situation, the injury to the personal reputation and, in all reasonable probability, the inestimable injury to one in his business life should provide sufficient reason for equitable relief. In the second situation, even in the absence of any contract to provide a property element, the right to visit one's mother in her own home, free from interference, is in itself sufficient basis for aid from the courts. So-called debunkers frequently ridicule the alleged fetish that Americans make of "Mother." Nevertheless, the affection of the child for the mother is a genuine affection which equity, certainly, should protect from wrongful interference. The "natural right," as the court terms it, to visit one's mother is worthy of recognition in any civilized country.

Where personal rights of infants are involved, courts of equity have never hesitated to give relief. Undoubtedly, rights of property might be adduced to support the equity jurisdiction and sometimes the courts do adduce such matters. However, it has been for centuries considered that the welfare of infants is peculiarly within the purview of the equity court's jurisdiction and within the protection of its equity powers. It is immaterial whether this is put on the ground that infants are the wards of the courts or on the ground of public policy. A court of equity will exercise its power to determine and protect the personal rights of infants.[55]

---

[54] Reed v. Carter, 268 Ky. 1, 103 S.W.2d 663 (1937), noted 51 *Harv. L. Rev.* 166 (1937), 32 *Ill. L. Rev.* 496 (1937), 22 *Minn. L. Rev.* 566 (1938).

[55] Ex parte Badger, 286 Mo. 139, 226 S.W. 936, 14 A.L.R. 286 (1920); Dovi v. Dovi, 245 Wis. 50, 13 N.W.2d 585, 151 A.L.R. 1368 (1944).

See Moreland, "Injunctive Control of Family Relations," 18 *Ky. L.J.* 207 (1930); annotation, Jurisdiction of equity to protect personal rights, 14 A.L.R. 295, at p. 308.

Injunction to prevent further debauching of plaintiff's minor daughter, see Stark v. Hamilton, 149 Ga. 227, 99 S.E. 861, 5 A.L.R. 1041 (1919).

Much the same is true, incidentally, in regard to the mentally incompetent.[56]

In regard to the marital relation, it has not been infrequent for courts to enjoin interference with the relationship by a third person, especially where the third person is alienating the affections of one spouse. This has been especially true of lower courts, as shown by Dean Pound's collection of newspaper accounts of such occurrences.[57] The basis or reason of the court's action in such cases does not appear. In the appellate courts where such injunctive relief has been granted it has been based either on the public policy of protecting and furthering the marriage relation or on the ground of the husband's right in the services and society of his wife or the wife's right to society of and support from the husband.[58] In some jurisdictions which adhere strictly to the requirement that protection of a property right is essential to equity jurisdiction, relief in such cases has been denied as involving purely personal rights and on the grounds that remedies are available at law and the difficulty of enforcing the injunctive decree.[59]

Insofar as concerns suits between spouses for equitable relief, the grant or denial of such relief usually has been dependent upon the existence of property interests or pecuniary loss. Whether the

---

[56] See Watson v. Watson, 183 Ky. 516, 209 S.W. 524, 3 A.L.R. 1575 (1919).

[57] Pound, *Cases on Equitable Relief against Defamation and Injuries to Personality* (2d Ed., Chafee, 1930) 127–137.

[58] Henley v. Rockett, 243 Ala. 472, 8 So.2d 852 (1942); Ex parte Warfield, 40 Tex. Cr. 413, 50 S.W. 933, 76 Am.St.Rep. 724 (1899) (injunction obtained by husband); Smith v. Womack (1925; Tex. Civ. App.) 271 S.W. 209, writ of error denied by Texas Supreme Court (injunction obtained by wife), noted 74 *U. Pa. L. Rev.* 97 (1925), 10 *Minn. L. Rev.* 163 (1925); Witte v. Bauderer (1923; Tex. Civ. App.) 255 S.W. 1016 (injunction obtained by husband), noted 24 *Col. L. Rev.* 431 (1924), 37 *Harv. L. Rev.* 770 (1924), 72 *U. Pa. L. Rev.* 451 (1924).

The Texas courts also interpret the statutory authorization to grant injunction where it shall appear that the party "is entitled to the relief demanded," or in all cases where he shows himself enitled thereto under principles of equity, as giving them a wide power, equivalent to that of the English courts under the Judicature Act of 1873. See Ex parte Warfield, *supra*. Actually, this seems to grant no different powers from that possessed by courts of other jurisdictions to grant relief "under principles of equity." The difference merely lies in the willingness of the Texas courts to extend equitable principles to the protection of rights not formerly recognized by equity.

[59] Bank v. Bank, 180 Md. 244, 23 A.2d 700 (1942); Snedaker v. King, 111 Ohio 225, 145 N.E. 15 (1924), noted 19 *Ill. L. Rev.* 587 (1925), 34 *Yale L.J.* 327 (1925).

property interest or probability of pecuniary loss is real or is more or less invented to justify equitable relief is another matter. A close approach to ignoring of the property element appears in a New Jersey case wherein the wife obtained an injunction against her husband continuing the prosecution of a suit for divorce in another state allegedly having no jurisdiction. It was remarked that the wife would either have to go to the "trouble and expense" of appearing in the other state to fight the suit or to allow it to go by default which would leave her in a position described as a "hardship" to which the "husband has no right in equity to subject her." It may also be noticed that the court was concerned about the rights and interests of the children of the marriage.[60]

However, on a similar state of facts the New York court denied the wife an injunction on the ground that no injury was shown except it be to her feelings.[61] Even where a husband had already obtained a divorce in another state and returned and married a second time, the New York court contented itself with rendering a declaratory judgment at the suit of the wife that she was still the lawful wife of the defendant husband and denied her an injunction against the husband and the other woman holding themselves out as husband and wife. Injunction is warranted, the court held, only where some substantial legal right is to be protected. It does not intervene to restrain conduct merely injurious to one's feelings and causing mental anguish.[62]

[60] Kempson v. Kempson, 58 N.J. Eq. 94, 43 A. 97, *id.* (1899), 63 N.J. Eq. 783, 52 A. 625 (1902).

In Dandini v. Dandini, 86 Cal.App.2d 478, 195 P.2d 871 (1948), where wife had obtained a decree of separate maintenance with an award for support and husband was in arrears, wife was granted injunction against husband re-marrying after obtaining invalid foreign divorce decree. Although a property right may be seen to be present and was referred to by the court, the court also points out that it would protect the personal right of the wife which was said to be involved.

[61] Goldstein v. Goldstein, 283 N.Y. 146, 27 N.E.2d 969 (1940) (with strong dissent by Conway, J.). It does not appear, incidentally, that the right of any children were present.

A different trend or change in the point of view may be indicated by the decision of an intermediate appellate court, in Pereira v. Pereira, 70 N.Y.S.2d 763 (1947), noted 47 *Col. L. Rev.* 1236 (1947), wherein the view seems to have been taken that the husband's divorce action did sufficiently threaten injury to warrant enjoining him.

[62] Baumann v. Baumann, 250 N.Y. 382, 165 N.E. 819 (1929) (with strong dissent by O'Brien, J.), noted 14 *Cornell L.Q.* 503 (1929), 29 *Col. L. Rev.* 214 (1929). And see Somberg v. Somberg, 263 N.Y. 1, 188 N.E. 137 (1933) noted 47 *Harv. L.*

The situation presented by the foregoing cases would seem to boil down to the question whether the marital status itself is a substantial legal right which equity should protect. Since marital property rights, the right of support, and rights and interests of children of the marriage may also be involved, it would appear that there is ample justification for the intervention of equity.

Sec. 61. —Interment, disinterment, etc.

Whether this is the appropriate place to make reference to the subject of dead bodies is open to considerable doubt. However, it is dealt with here, briefly, because of the fact that equity's quickness and ever-present willingness to lend its aid in regard to bodies of the dead really rests on a recognition of personal feelings of affection and respect toward the dead on the part of the surviving spouse and members of the family, feelings which may necessitate the aid of the courts in respect to matters of interment and disinterment and the like.[63] It has frequently been stated that there is no property right in a dead body but to justify their interference in behalf of surviving members of the family it has been common for courts to recognize a so-called quasi-property interest or that the charge of a dead body is a trust.[64] This is really no more than the injection of a sufficient property interest to justify the court in giving its aid and protection in the matter of personal feelings

Rev 1059 (1934), 34 Mich. L. Rev. 85 (1935), 82 U. Pa. L. Rev. 542 (1934), where there was no divorce, husband was living with another woman, and he and woman were representing themselves to be husband and wife. The court refused even a declaratory judgment to the lawful wife as to her marital status.

Compare a variant situation in Bartholomew v. Workman, 197 Okla. 267, 169 P.2d 1012 (1946), wherein a minor, suing by his mother as next friend, sought to enjoin the defendant, who falsely claimed to be married to plaintiff's father, from using the name "Mrs. George A. Workman." This seems to have been based on the contention that the minor's privacy was invaded, which the court denied. It may be noticed that the plaintiff's mother was divorced from his father and had remarried. It is also to be noticed that the court admitted that equity may protect personal rights even though no property rights are invaded.

[63] Disputes among relatives, etc., as to disinterment and re-interment of body, see, e.g., Bradley v. Burgis, (1946; La. App.) 25 So.2d 753; Koon v. Doan, 300 Mich. 662, 2 N.W.2d 878 (1942); Yome v. Gorman, 242 N.Y. 395, 152 N.E. 126, 47 A.L.R. 1165 (1926) (with reference to previous annotations), noted 11 Minn. L. Rev. 171 (1927).

Disinterment of dead body buried on another's land, see note, 47 Mich. L. Rev. 418 (1949), to Glatzer v. Dinerman, 142 N.J. 88, 59 A.2d 242 (1948).

[64] For full discussion of the matter, see the topic "Dead Bodies" in American Jurisprudence and Corpus Juris Secundum.

and emotions. It is, in short, protecting personal rights in the nature of family rights. That this is the real interest which is being given protection is more frankly recognized today by courts of equity.[65]

Sec. 62. Civil rights.

Civil rights are those rights one enjoys as regards other individuals rather than those in relation to the establishment and administration of the government, the latter being political rights. Civil rights are the rights accorded to every member or citizen of a community or nation with reference to such matters as property, marriage, family, education, religion, and designed to assure happiness, equality, freedom from discrimination, and so on.[66] The term is sometimes used to designate those rights of the individual guaranteed by the federal constitution and, as well, by the various state constitutions. The term "civil liberties" is also used in this latter connection.[67]

When the law gives a civil right, it is recognized that a violation of the right gives rise to a cause of action for damages, even if not expressly so stated by the law itself. Since the amount of damage may be only nominal, rendering such remedy somewhat ineffectual to afford protection and discourage violations, it is common to provide by statute that penal or punitive damages in some flat sum shall also be recoverable as well as actual damages. As an alternative means of protecting civil rights and discouraging their violation, or sometimes in addition to the right of action for penal or

---

[65] See Bradley v. Burgis (1946; La. App.) 25 So.2d 753; Brownlee v. Pratt (1946; Ohio App.) 68 N.E.2d 798.

[66] Moore, *Cyc. Law Dict.* (3d Ed.); "Civil Rights," 10 Am. Jur. 894.

[67] See Moore, *Cyc. Law Dict.* (3d Ed.); Moscovitz, "Civil Liberties and Injunctive Protection," 39 *Ill. L. Rev.* 144 (1944).

Judge Yankwich, in Hardyman v. Collins, 80 F. Supp. 501 (1948), distinguishes between purely personal rights which are within the domain of the state power to protect, and the civil rights or liberties which come under the protection of the federal constitution and legislation.

The scope of this work does not permit consideration of the sociological and political aspects of civil rights or liberties. Reference is recommended to such works as those by Konvitz, *The Constitution and Civil Rights* (1947), and *The Alien and the Asiatic in American Law* (1946).

punitive damages, it is frequently provided that the violation shall constitute a crime.[68]

In ordinary circumstances, the violation of the right having already occurred, such remedies may be entirely adequate. Even if the wrongdoer is determined to continue his course of conduct, the loss to him in damages from successive actions against him may well cause him to stop and consider. Nevertheless, occasions have arisen in which the foregoing remedies have not been adequate to prevent violations. Repeated violations may require successive actions at law for damages; violations by a great number which are repeated or continued may require a multiplicity of actions at law for damages. Or an initial violation may be threatened with reasonable probability. Must the individual resign himself to an initial violation or to repeated violations of his civil rights and content himself thereafter with attempts to obtain compensation which may be difficult of ascertainment? Certainly, constitutional or legal guaranties of civil rights mean little if violation must be submitted to and cannot be prevented.[69] In many of the cases asserting that equity does not protect purely personal or individual rights, it has been stated that equity protects "only civil rights and property rights" or words to that effect.[70] Since civil rights were not involved in those cases, the statements amount only to dicta, but they raise the question whether these courts of equity recognized a field of operation in between property rights and political rights.[71] But despite these dicta, when the question of enjoining violation of a civil right has squarely arisen we find the property question frequently influencing the court. In a jurisdiction where the rule is strictly followed that property rights but not personal

[68] See "Civil Rights," 10 Am. Jur. 917; annotation, Constitutionality of "civil rights" legislation by State, 49 A.L.R. 505; annotation, Private right of action for violation of civil rights statute, 53 A.L.R. 188.

[69] See Orloff v. Los Angeles Turf Club, 30 Cal.2d 110, 180 P.2d 321, 171 A.L.R. 913 (1947), noted 15 U. Chi. L. Rev. 227 (1947), 21 So. Calif. L. Rev. 409 (1948), placing stress on difficulty of ascertaining compensation, even where statute provides for a flat sum as punitive damages since additional punitive damages may be recoverable in excess of those provided by statute upon a proper showing.

[70] Chappell v. Stewart, 82 Md. 323, 33 A. 542, 37 L.R.A. 783, 51 Am.St.Rep. 476 (1896); Moscovitz, "Civil Liberties and Injunctive Protection," 39 Ill. L. Rev. 144, at p. 149 (1944).

[71] See Moscovitz, supra, footnote 70.

rights are protected by equity, injunctive relief to prevent violation of a civil right has been denied.[72]

In other jurisdictions, however, civil rights have been considered rights of substance, to be distinguished from personal rights involving trivial issues or for which adequate remedies at law do actually exist, and preventive equitable relief determined to be the only adequate and suitable relief, as where a continued policy of violating the civil rights of a complainant is shown.[73]   Certainly, if the remedy at law is patently inadequate or may not be resorted to successfully, as where the violation is under color of law, equity is the proper source of relief and has provided relief.[74]   Judicial

[72] Tate v. Eidelman, 32 Ohio N. P., N. S. 478 (1934), noted 1 *Ohio S.U.L.J.* 59 (1935), wherein the court seemed favorably inclined to giving equitable relief but declared it could not do so until the state Supreme Court overruled its view that equity protects only property rights.

In White v. Pasfield, 212 Ill. App. 73 (1918), wherein negroes were excluded from a public swimming pool in violation of a civil rights statute, injunctive relief was denied on the ground that equity does not protect personal rights. It was indicated, however, that an adequate remedy by way of mandamus against the public officials was available.

[73] Orloff v. Los Angeles Turf Club, 30 Cal.2d 110, 180 P.2d 321, 171 A.L.R. 913 (1947), noted 15 *U. Chi. L. Rev.* 227 (1947), 21 *So. Calif. L. Rev.* 409 (1948), replacing prior opinion by District Court of Appeal, 172 P.2d 355 (1946), in which it had been held that it had not been shown that resort to the legal remedy would be inadequate. Plaintiff had twice been ejected allegedly without cause from a race course, after buying a ticket, in violation of his statutory rights.

In Farrall v. District of Columbia Amateur Athletic Union (1946; U.S. App. D.C.) 153 F.2d 647, the complaint was held to state a cause of action where Negro members of the defendant association sought equitable and declaratory relief in the case of a rule of the association that allegedly barred plaintiffs from engaging in amateur athletic competition in the District.

[74] Kenyon v. City of Chicopee, 320 Mass. 528, 70 N.E.2d 241, 175 A.L.R. 430 (1946) (enjoining interference with distribution of handbills by religious sect), noted 27 *B.U. L. Rev.* 241 (1947); Harjst v. Hoeger, 349 Mo. 808, 163 S.W.2d 609 (1942) (enjoining use of school funds for sectarian religious purposes); Garrett v. Rose (1942; Tex. Civ. App.) 161 S.W.2d 893 (enjoining interference with religious practices).

Interference, under color of law, with civil rights guaranteed by the federal constitution is ground for suit in equity in the federal courts, according to the federal statutes. U. S. Code, Title 28, Sec. 1343. See also Cyc. Fed. Proc., 2d Ed., Sec. 252; Moscovitz, "Civil Rights and Injunctive Protection," 39 *Ill. L. Rev.* 144 (1944). Federal court enjoining city officials from denying use and enjoyment of municipal playground and swimming pool to citizens of Mexican and Latin descent, see Lopez v. Seccombe, 71 F. Supp. 769 (1947).

Mandamus has also been resorted to in order to compel public officials to discontinue racial discrimination or the like. Stone v. Board of Directors, 47 Cal.App.2d 749, 118 P.2d 866 (1941) (where mandamus issued to compel city officials to admit Negroes to public swimming pool); Pearson v. Murray, 169 Md. 478, 182 A. 590, 103 A.L.R. 706 (1936) (proper remedy where state refused to admit Negro law students to state-maintained law school).

language on the point has tended to become more and more emphatic in favor of equitable relief.[75] It is submitted that in a case where it can be shown with reasonable probability that an initial violation will occur, equity should interpose to protect the civil right, rather than letting the violation occur and directing the injured person to seek relief by way of damages.

Sec. 63. Social rights.

Social rights, for our purposes, may be defined briefly as those rights arising from companionship or relationship with others, in clubs, social or fraternal organizations, and the like.

Where the right asserted is merely the right to be allowed to continue this association or companionship, as where expulsion is threatened or has taken place, no property right really exists to warrant equitable protection in a jurisdiction wherein property is an essential prerequisite to equity jurisdiction.[76] Even in a more liberal jurisdiction, equitable relief might well be denied on the basis that there is no injury which warrants judicial remedy of any kind and that, in any event, it would not lie within the power of a court of equity to compel men to associate with each other when they are disinclined or unwilling to do so.[77] Moreover, as is well known, courts are uniformly unwilling to interfere in the internal affairs of clubs and associations.[78]

---

[75] See particularly, Orloff v. Los Angeles Turf Club and Kenyon v. City of Chicopee, preceding notes.

Equitable aid in the enforcement of fair employment practice legislation, designed to prevent discrimination in employment on racial or religious grounds, may well become of frequent occurrence. As to this type of legislation, see note, "The Trend in State Fair Employment Practice Legislation," 23 *Notre Dame Law.* 107 (1947).

[76] See Baird v. Wells (1890) L. R. 44 Ch. Div. 661.

[77] See Chafee, "Internal Affairs of Associations not for Profit," 43 *Harv. L. Rev.* 993 (1930); note 1 *Minn. L. Rev.* 513 (1917); note 37 *Yale L.J.* 368 (1927).

The late Professor Walsh, in his *Treatise on Equity* (1930) 275, note 37, asks if equity would intervene in the case of wrongful expulsion from a petty card club having only a handful of members who have contributed a small sum for prizes and argues that a remedy by way of damages should be adequate and that any injury to the personality would be too petty to warrant injunctive relief. Certainly one may agree with this, for it is but a reminder of the principle that equity does not concern itself with trivial matters. Some of the English decisions denying relief may well be put upon this ground.

Admission to membership cannot be compelled. See Chapman v. American Legion, 244 Ala. 553, 14 So.2d 225, 147 A.L.R. 585 (1943).

[78] See note, 7 *Cornell L.Q.* 261 (1922).

Nevertheless, there is one aspect of this situation which has a strong appeal for a court of equity. The expulsion of one from a club, social organization, or the like, implies that he cannot get along with his fellows, or even worse, that he is unfit to be associated with. Once the news of his expulsion is bruited about, the consequences in his personal and in his business life can be very harmful. If the expulsion is wrongful, the situation is highly inequitable as to him. Thus, when an expulsion is wrongfully threatened or attempted, an expulsion which may blacken the victim's character, destroy his peace of mind, injure him in his private and his business life, an injury or wrong is threatened to him for which all fair-minded men will agree there should be a judicial remedy somewhere. Equity is the logical place to obtain this remedy or relief and equity has risen to the challenge.[79]

Many courts interpose in the situation of an expulsion without a hearing or without a fair hearing, on the ground that such conduct is contrary to "natural justice" or "fair play." [80] The difficulty concerning the existence of a property right has frequently been surmounted by determining that the constitution or by-laws of the club or organization providing for membership or the agreement by which one becomes a member constitutes a contract between the member and the club or organization. An attempt wrongfully to expel the member is said to be a breach of his contract and thus an injury to a property right, since the contract or the right under it constitute a property right. Upon this basis, many courts of equity have been willing to examine the rightfulness or wrongfulness of a threatened expulsion or of an accomplished

---

[79] See Chafee, *op. cit.*, footnote 77, *supra*, p. 993; comment note, 58 *Yale L.J.* 999 (1949); Blenko v. Schmeltz, 362 Pa. 365, 67 A.2d 99, 20 A.L.R.2d 523 (1949), with annotation at p. 531.

Whether wrongfully expelled or merely wrongfully excluded from essential privileges, and irrespective of the presence or absence of so-called property interests or rights, the aid of equity is available in the absence of adequate legal remedy. Berrien v. Pollitzer, — U.S. App. D.C. —, 165 F.2d 20 (1947).

In Alabama, see Mitchell v. Jewish Progressive Club, 253 Ala. 195, 43 So.2d 529, 20 A.L.R.2d 339 (1949).

[80] See note, 30 *Yale L.J.* 202 (1920); Pound, "Equitable Relief Against Defamation and Injuries to Personality," 29 *Harv. L. Rev.* 640 (1916).

Expulsion because of exercise of constitutional rights as citizens, see Spayd v. Ringing Rock Lodge, etc., 270 Pa. St. 67, 113 A. 70, 14 A.L.R. 1443 (1921), noted 35 *Harv. L. Rev.* 332 (1922), 6 *Minn. L. Rev.* 241 (1921).

expulsion and to enjoin threatened or pending expulsion proceedings if found to be wrongful or to enforce performance of the contract by compelling reinstatement of the member if the wrongful expulsion has been accomplished. Any remedy at law by way of damages is a totally inadequate remedy in the circumstances.[81] In some cases, some other technical property interest has been found, such as some interest in assets or property of the organization.[82]

Where, as is frequently the case these days, membership in an organization or society carries with it concrete benefits, such as health, accident, hospital, medical or life insurance or the like, the loss of such benefits from a wrongful expulsion definitely deprives the member of property rights. This is a deprivation or loss against which equity will give relief, since the remedy at law is inadequate.[83] As to membership in labor unions, trade associations and the like, the matter goes beyond mere social relationships and enters the realm of the power to earn a living or the right to carry on a lawful business and so is dealt with elsewhere.[84]

When any remedy exists within the club, association or organization, the member must first exhaust it before applying to the courts, unless the procedure whereby this remedy is obtained is too burdensome or is unfairly conducted.[85]

---

[81] Lawson v. Hewell, 118 Cal. 613, 50 P. 763, 49 L.R.A. 400 (1897); Blenko v. Schmeltz, 362 Pa. 365, 67 A.2d 99, 20 A.L.R.2d 523 (1949). See also Pound, op. cit., footnote 80, supra, pp. 640, 680; Walsh, Treatise on Equity (1930), 275–277 and notes thereto.

[82] Weiss v. Musical Mutual Protective Union, 189 Pa. St. 446, 42 A. 118 (1899). See Pound, op. cit., footnote 80, supra, pp. 640, 677; Chafee, Internal Affairs of Associations not for Profit, 43 Harv. L. Rev. 993 (1930).

That a substantial property right must be involved, see Howard v. Betts, 190 Ga. 530, 9 S.E.2d 742 (1940).

The dispute within a society or association may, of course, concern other matters than expulsion of a member. If the dispute between the society or association and the member involves property rights, a court of equity will take cognizance of it. See Ryan v. Cudahy, 157 Ill. 108, 41 N.E. 760, 49 L.R.A. 353, 48 Am.St.Rep. 305 (1895).

[83] Ayres v. Order of United Workmen, 188 N.Y. 280, 80 N.E. 1020 (1907).

[84] See supra, Sec. 55.

[85] Fales v. Musicians Protective Union, etc., 40 R.I. 34, 99 A. 823 (1917).

Where a fair hearing would be prevented by animosity, prejudice, and prejudgment of his case, the plaintiff is not required to exhaust his remedies within an association before seeking equitable relief. Blenko v. Schmeltz, 362 Pa. 365, 67 A.2d 99, 20 A.L.R. 523 (1949).

See annotation, Exhaustion of remedies within labor union as condition of resort to civil courts by expelled or suspended member, 168 A.L.R. 1462.

Sec. 64.   Political rights.

Political rights are the rights of participation in the establishment and administration of the government and include such rights as the right to vote, the right to be a candidate for public office, the right to hold public office, the right to see to the proper disposition of public funds, and similar matters.   They are to be distinguished from civil rights.[86]

In the past, courts in the exercise of equity jurisdiction have refused to grant injunctive relief against the violation or denial of political rights.[87]   This has variously been put upon the ground that no property rights or interests in property are involved,[88] that there are other adequate remedies available,[89] or that the matter is properly within the jurisdiction of other branches of the government and that equity cannot interfere or should not interfere as a matter of public policy.[90]

So far as the so-called extraordinary remedies, particularly mandamus, prohibition and quo warranto, are available, as to enforce one's right to register or to vote or to try title to public office, it may be conceded that there are adequate remedies which

---

[86] Winnett v. Adams, 71 Neb. 817, 99 N.W. 681 (1904); Moore, *Cyc. Law Dict.* (3d Ed.); Moscovitz, "Civil Liberty and Injunctive Protection," 39 *Ill. L. Rev.* 144 (1944).

[87] "Notwithstanding the array of authorities which support it, we should not care to commit ourselves unqualifiedly to the doctrine that a court of equity will not under any circumstances interfere for the protection of political rights. But, we think it is perfectly safe to adopt the doctrine to the extent of holding that a court of equity will not undertake to supervise the acts and management of a political party, for the protection of a purely political right." Winnett v. Adams, 71 Neb. 817, 99 N.W. 681 (1904). What if the right denied or threatened by the political party is actually a substantial civil right?

[88] Fletcher v. Tuttle, 151 Ill. 41, 37 N.E. 683, 42 Am.St.Rep. 220, 25 L.R.A. 143 (1894); Dunn v. Bd. of County Commissioners, 162 Kan. 254, 177 P.2d 207 (1947).

[89] Fletcher v. Tuttle, 151 Ill. 41, 37 N.E. 683, 42 Am.St.Rep. 220, 25 L.R.A. 143 (1894); Ryan v. Hennepin County, 224 Minn. 444, 29 N.W.2d 385 (1947).

[90] Walls v. Brundidge, 109 Ark. 250, 160 S.W. 230 (1913); Duggan v. Emporia, 84 Kan. 429, 114 P. 235, Ann. Cas. 1912 A 719 (1911).

Reapportionment of congressional districts as a political question not justiciable in the courts, see Colegrove v. Green, 328 U.S. 549, 66 S.Ct. 1198, 90 L. Ed. 1432 (1946), noted 41 *Ill. L. Rev.* 578 (1946), 45 *Mich. L. Rev.* 368 (1947), 56 *Yale L.J.* 127 (1946).

Scope of judicial power in matters of a political nature, see comment, 33 *Va. L. Rev.* 625 (1947); political questions as distinguished from judicial questions, see comment, 24 *Notre Dame Law.* 231 (1949).

render unnecessary a resort to equity.[91]   It may also be conceded that matters sometimes arise which are properly within the jurisdiction or cognizance of some other branch of the government, such as the legislative branch, and are not within the jurisdiction or cognizance of equity or for that matter of the judicial branch at all.[92]   It may well be doubted, however, in view of modern developments, that the property element is any longer a requisite for the protection of personal or individual rights, certainly where such rights are recognized as legal rights, as political rights are. If there is no other adequate remedy, as by way of mandamus or quo warranto, for example, to prevent the loss of or injury to a political right and there is no question of invading the province of another branch of the government, equitable relief should be awarded.[93]

It will be found that equitable relief is being increasingly given, at least as part of the relief, where political rights are in dispute.[94] This is particularly true in code states where law and equity powers are merged in one court.   Thus, despite some authority to the contrary, where title to a public office is in dispute, an injunction will usually issue to protect the possession of the incumbent while the title is determined in a court of law or on the law side of the court.[95]   Sometimes the political question may give rise to tax liability and on the ground that a property question is involved as the main issue of the case, the equity court has passed on the

---

[91] As these remedies, see specific treatises thereon or on the subject of Elections.
[92] See Spies v. Byers, 267 Ill. 627, 122 N.E. 841 (1919).
[93] See Thompson v. Talmadge, 201 Ga. 867, 41 S.E.2d 883 (1947), noted 33 *Va. L. Rev.* 625 (1947); Gilmore v. Waples, 108 Tex. 167, 188 S.W. 1037 (1916).
[94] Illustrations of equitable protection of political rights, and some of the judicial reasoning to justify it, are given by Moscovitz, *op. cit.*, footnote 86, *supra*, pp. 154, **155.**
Determination, in injunction proceeding, of length of term of public official, see Bailey v. Knight, 118 Mont. 594, 168 P.2d 843 (1946).
Enjoining use of name and emblem of political party, see Chambers v. I. Ben Greenman Ass'n, 58 N.Y.S.2d 637 (1945), aff'd 269 App. Div. 938, 58 N.Y.S.2d 3 (1945); Rich v. Storer, 186 Misc. 87, 58 N.Y.S.2d 643 (1945).
[95] Heyward v. Long, 178 S.Ct. 351, 183 S.E. 145, 114 A.L.R. 1130 (1935), and annotation thereto at p. 1147.   And see annotation, Injunction as remedy against removal of public officer, 34 A.L.R.2d 554.
Equity may protect the occupant of a public office from dispossession pending determination at law of a dispute as to his right to the office.   Scott v. Sheehan, 145 Cal. 691, 79 P. 353 (1905).

political question as being merely incidental to the main issue of the property right involved.[96] The property interest of the taxpayer has also frequently provided the basis for enjoining the holding of an invalid election relating to the expenditure of public funds,[97] or for enjoining the unconstitutional or invalid use or expenditure of public funds.[98] Whether placed on the ground of protection of a legal right or on the ground of protecting a property right, the increasing tendency, as already remarked, is to extend equitable relief to political rights as in the case of other personal rights.[99]

---

[96] Coleman v. Board of Education, 131 Ga. 643, 63 S.E. 41 (1908).

[97] It is frequently asserted that the rule is that injunction will not issue to enjoin the holding of an election but such rule is open to serious question in view of the many decisions allowing injunction. The matter seems to boil down to the question of whether or not there is any other adequate remedy except in equity to protect the political right of the plaintiff or to the question whether the matter is one placed by governing law beyond the jurisdiction of the judiciary generally. See annotation, Power to enjoin holding of election, 33 A.L.R. 1376; note, 32 *Col. L. Rev.* 138 (1932); note, 18 *Cornell L.Q.* 278 (1933); note, [1921] 1 *Wis. L. Rev.* 309; McClintock, *Handbook of Equity* (1936) Sec. 161.

[98] See comment, "Taxpayer's Action Against State Officials to Prevent Alleged Unconstitutional Use of State Funds," 17 *Fordh. L. Rev.* 107 (1948); Clapp v. Town of Jeffrey, 97 N.H. 456, 91 A.2d 464 (1952).

[99] Power of equity court to enjoin unlawful expenditure of public funds in holding invalid election, see note, 18 *Fordh. L. Rev.* 298 (1949), justifiably criticizing the holding in City of Austin v. Thompson, 147 Tex. 639, 219 S.W.2d 57 (1949). And see note, 62 *Harv. L. Rev.* 133 (1948), criticizing Caven v. Clark, 78 F. Supp. 295 (1948).

CHAPTER 9.

POSSESSORY RELIEF

Sec. 65. Realty.
Sec. 66. Personalty.

Sec. 65. Realty.

Where one is entitled to possession of realty of which he has been wrongfully dispossessed, adequate relief usually may be obtainable through the legal action of ejectment or its statutory counterpart. But if the dispossession has been accomplished by an encroachment of such a substantial nature that restoration by enforcement of the judgment in ejectment is not feasible or the encroachment is above the surface, in jurisdictions which do not recognize ejectment as lying in such a case, it is clear that successful and adequate possessory relief is obtainable only in equity. However, these matters have been discussed previously.[1]

There may also be situations in which the plaintiff has not been wrongfully dispossessed of property of which he was previously in lawful possession so as to bring him within the realm of ejectment and consideration of its adequacy or inadequacy, but is nevertheless entitled to obtain possession of realty. This, however, involves us in such fields as resulting and constructive trusts which are not within the scope of this work.[2]

---

[1] See *supra*, Chapters 3, 4.

[2] In the early days in Pennsylvania, when there was no chancery court, the common law courts of necessity assumed chancery powers and developed the practice of allowing the legal action of ejectment to be used in a situation in which a court of chancery would execute a trust or compel a conveyance. The court determined whether the plaintiff was entitled to relief and only the ascer-

Sec. 66. Personalty.

There is little, if any, distinction in the principles governing actions to recover possession of personalty wrongfully withheld from the plaintiff and actions to compel the performance of contracts to sell or deliver personalty.[3] But since the former may be considered to involve a tort or, at least, an act in the nature of a tort, it is pertinent to consider the extent to which equitable relief is available.[4]

In a possessory action for personalty, it seems to be incumbent on the plaintiff to show that there is no adequate remedy at law. This results from the fact that ordinarily in the case of personalty, personalty of like kind or quality is easily obtainable on the open market at a more or less uniform price. Accordingly, adequate relief exists in that the plaintiff may purchase such personalty on the open market and obtain adequate compensation in an action for damages incurred from having to pursue that method or in that the plaintiff may sue for the value of the personalty and with the damages obtained thereby purchase similar personalty on the open market.[5] But if it can be shown that the personalty wrongfully withheld from the plaintiff is of some unique or unusual nature so that personalty of like kind or quality is not obtainable elsewhere, or where damages must necessarily be conjectural or speculative, the remedy at law is obviously inadequate and the aid of equity is necessary and appropriate as a means of relief.[6]

---

tainment of the facts was left to the jury. See Peebles v. Reading, 8 S. & R. (Pa.) 484 (1822).

[3] Accordingly, some writers treat cases of possessory actions to recover personalty, without distinction, along with discussion of specific performance of contracts for the sale of personalty. See Walsh, *Treatise on Equity* (1930) Sec. 60. On the other hand, see Glenn and Redden, *Cases and Materials on Equity* (2d Ed.) 96; Cook, *Cases and Materials on Equity* (4th Ed., 1948) 19.

[4] For thorough discussion, see Van Hecke, *Equitable Replevin*, 33 *N.C. L. Rev.* 57 (1954).

Professors Chafee and Simpson, in their *Cases on Equity* (2d Ed., 1946) 151, point out that upon title passing to a buyer upon conclusion of the contract, failure of the seller to deliver the personalty constitutes a tort as well as breach of contract and that frequently the buyer proceeds in equity for reparation rather than for specific performance of a contract.

[5] See Rawll v. Baker-Vawter, 187 App. Div. 330, 176 N.Y.S. 189 (1919).

[6] See Van Hecke, *Equitable Replevin*, 33 *N.C. L. Rev.* 57 (1954).

In Denver Milk Bottle, Case & Can Exchange, Inc. v. McKinzie, 87 Colo. 379,

Illustrations commonly considered to present situations where no adequate remedy at law exists are those wherein the personalty has sentimental value or association, such as an heirloom or article of antiquity,[7] papers or documents necessary to establish title,[8] evidences of debt,[9] or personalty of like nature.[10]

The various common law or statutory remedies available at law, such as detinue, replevin and the like, are not considered adequate if they do not assure recovery of possession of the personalty itself but may result only in the recovery of its value.[11] The equitable decree ordering the surrender of the personalty provides the only adequate relief in such cases.[12]

But even where the personal property has no special value beyond what might be compensated for in damages, where it is wrongfully withheld from the owner by one standing in a fiduciary relation toward him, as an agent or trustee, an equitable suit will lie for its delivery. It does not lie in the mouth of one breaching his fiduciary obligations virtually to force the sale to himself of such property, by requiring the injured party to accept its value.[13]

It is also pertinent here to recall that possessory relief may be

---

287 P. 888 (1930), the plaintiff successfully recovered from the defendant milk bottles stamped with the plaintiff's name that the defendant was using without permission and intended to continue to do so.

[7] Berman v. Leckner, 188 Md. 321, 52 A.2d 464 (1947); Burr v. Bloomsburg, 101 N.J. Eq. 615, 138 A. 876 (1927).

[8] Pattison v. Skillman, 34 N.J. Eq. 344 (1881); Coven v. First Sav. & Loan Ass'n, 141 N.J. Eq. 1, 55 A.2d 244 (1947). See also Pierce v. Lamson, 5 Allen (Mass.) 60, 81 Am. Dec. 732 (1862).

[9] Farnsworth v. Whiting, 104 Me. 488, 72 A. 314 (1908).

[10] Business records and correspondence, see Industrial Electronics Co. v. Harper, 137 N.J. Eq. 171, 43 A.2d 883 (1945), aff'd 137 N.J. Eq. 530, 45 A.2d 671 (1946).

Key of safe deposit box, see Farnsworth v. Whiting, 104 Me. 488, 72 A. 314 (1908).

Maps and plans, see McGowin v. Remington, 12 Pa. 56, 51 Am. Dec. 584 (1849).

[11] Denver Milk Bottle, Case & Can Exchange, Inc. v. McKinzie, 87 Colo. 379, 287 P. 888 (1930); McGowin v. Remington, 12 Pa. 56, 51 Am. Dec. 584 (1849).

Application and interpretation of statute granting equitable jurisdiction to compel redelivery of goods or chattels where they cannot be replevined, see Broomfield v. Checkoway, 310 Mass. 68, 38 N.E.2d 563 (1941).

[12] Denver Milk Bottle, Case & Can Exchange, Inc. v. McKinzie, *supra*.

"The foundation of this (equitable) doctrine is that the article in question, from its character or associations, has some peculiar interest or value to the owner, and therefore mere damages at law for its intrinsic value furnish no adequate compensation." Merwin, *Principles of Equity* (1895) 422.

[13] This enters into the specific field of Trusts, as to which reference may be made in the standard works on that subject.

given in connection with or as incidental to preventive relief against acts threatening irreparable or permanent injury to property rights or substantial rights in the nature of property rights. For example, we have seen that where equitable relief is granted to prevent the unauthorized use of trade secrets, the defendant may be compelled to deliver into the plaintiff's possession any material relative to the trade secret.[14] Likewise, in enjoining infringement, misappropriation, unauthorized use, or the like, of a common law copyright, surrender to the plaintiff of material in the defendant's possession may be ordered.[15] In fact, where infringement of a statutory copyright is involved, the statute authorizes an order to deliver copies, plates, etc. in the defendant's hands to possession of the plaintiff.[16] Other illustrations might be given, but the foregoing should suffice.

---

[14] See Sec. 46.
[15] See Sec. 43.
[16] U. S. Code, Title 17.

Chapter 10.

SPECIFIC PERFORMANCE–CONTRACTS ENFORCEABLE

Sec. 67. Specific performance generally.

The only remedy which the common law can give where a party refuses to perform his contract is to award to the injured party damages for the breach. On the other hand it is one of the great distinctions of equity that it can compel a refractory party to do what he has agreed to, that is, specifically to perform his contract, or it can place the parties in the same position as if the contract had actually been performed.

However, the foregoing statement must not be given too broad or unqualified an interpretation. The origin and nature of equity jurisdiction must be borne in mind.[1] While it might well seem

---

[1] See Chapter 1.

153

proper that the jurisprudence of any civilized country should make available to an injured party the specific performance of the contract obligations of the refractory party, if the injured party should choose to seek that relief,[2] it must be remembered that in Anglo-American jurisprudence, equitable relief is not available if it can be said that the legal remedy, damages in short, is plain, adequate, and complete.[3]   Thus, the availability of relief by way of specific performance of a contract is limited, with us, to situations in which relief by way of damages alone does not provide as plain, adequate, and complete a remedy as specific performance.[4]   For instance, a contract for the payment of money will not be enforced by a court of equity, since it can do no more than a court of law, give a decree for the amount due.[5]   But if some affirmative act by the defendant is involved, in addition to the payment of money, which will provide relief to the plaintiff not obtainable at law, the payment of the money as well as the performance of the affirmative act is properly compellable in equity.[6]

There are also situations, of course, in which it is not practicable to compel specific performance.   Such a situation may be that in which it is not feasible or within the court's ability to supervise and see to a proper performance,[7] although it is well worthy of note that modern equity courts have considerably broadened their

---

2 See Szladits, "Concept of Specific Performance in Civil Law," 4 *Am. J. Comp. Law* 208 (1955).

3 See Secs. 5, 18.

4 In Louisiana, by virtue of code provisions, specific performance of a contract is available only when no adequate compensation can be awarded in damages. See Tri-State Transit Co. v. Sunshine Bus Lines, 181 La. 779, 160 So. 411 (1935). See also Jackson, "Specific Performance of Contracts in Louisiana," 24 *Tulane L. Rev.* 401 (1950).

5 See, *e.g.*, Morrison v. Land, 169 Cal. 580, 147 P. 259 (1915).

6 Where defendant has contracted to pay a certain sum of money for realty owned by plaintiff, the plaintiff's resort to equity is not alone for a decree for the payment of the money but also to compel acceptance of the realty by the defendant, in short the performance or completion of the contract as a whole or in full.   And see Sec. 70, *infra*.

7 In contracts to build or repair, see *infra*, Sec. 74; in contracts to arbitrate, see *infra*, Sec. 75.

Some courts take the view that if the contract calls for a succession of acts over a long period of time so that enforcement of performance would require protracted supervision, it is not practicable or feasible or possible for the court to see to enforcement.   See, *e.g.*, Long Beach Drug Co. v. United Drug Co., 13 Cal.2d 158, 88 P.2d 698, 98 P.2d 386 (1939); Edelen v. Samuels, 126 Ky. 295, 103 S.W. 360 (1907); Henderson v. Coon, 244 Ala. 324, 13 So.2d 564 (1943).   Exception is frequently made in this rule by such courts where the public interest would

viewpoint as to what is practicable or feasible.[8]   Or the situation may be one affecting personal relationships or personal services which should not, according to our concepts, be enforced against a party, aside from any question of practicability of enforcement. In this latter regard, courts of equity will not, regardless of any inadequacy of a legal remedy, enforce a contract to marry,[9] or, as a usual rule, to enter into a partnership,[10] or to render personal services.[11]

The basis, then, of equity's jurisdiction to enforce specific per-

---

suffer if specific performance were not ordered. See Edison Illuminating Co. v. Eastern Pennsylvania Power Co., 253 Pa. 457, 98 A. 652 (1916).

In class action by employees for specific performance to compel employer to continue a pension plan, relief was denied on ground there was no contractual duty on employer to do so and no promissory estoppel against employer, Hughes v. Encyclopaedia Brittanica, 1 Ill.App.2d 514, 117 N.E.2d 880, 42 A.L.R.2d 456.

[8] In contracts to arbitrate, see *infra*, Sec. 75; in contracts to build or repair, see *infra*, Sec. 74; specific performance of collective bargaining agreement, see note, 37 *Va. L. Rev.* 739 (1951).

It is also noticeable as to contracts that call for continued acts over a long period of time. Continued performance ordered of the defendant is frequently conditioned on continuance of performance by the plaintiff. See Montgomery Traction Co. v. Montgomery Light & Water Co., 229 F. 672 (1916); Prospect Park & Coney Island R. Co. v. Coney Island & Brooklyn R. Co., 144 N.Y. 152, 39 N.E. 17 (1894). It must be noticed that the fact that the public interest is involved usually induces the courts to overlook the "difficulties" of protracted supervision.

Conflicting views in the same jurisdiction on the subject of supposed difficulties of supervision are pointed out by Professor Simpson, "Equity," *1947 Annual Review of American Law.*

[9] See Merwin, *Principles of Equity* (1895) 396.

"If cases could be found, which we doubt, it would be unnecessary to cite them to support the principle that a suit for specific performance will not lie to compel one to marry another. It is abhorrent to public policy to force a man or woman, under penalty of contempt of court, to enter into a marriage that is objectionable." Wilson v. Nelson, 130 Neb. 1, 262 N.W. 433 (1935).

So far as concerns legal actions for breach of contract to marry, the modern legislative trend is to abolish such actions.

[10] Karrick v. Hannaman, 168 U.S. 328, 18 S.Ct. 135, 42 L. Ed. 484 (1897) pointing out that continuous supervision of partnership would be required to see that plaintiff was treated as partner by defendant; Denson v. Mapes, 71 F. Supp. 503 (1947), (criticized by Simpson, "Equity," *1947 Annual Survey of American Law*); Morris v. Peckham, 51 Conn. 128 (1883), where contract was dissolvable at the will of either party, oral in violation of Statute of Frauds, and terms vague and indefinite: Clark v. Truitt, 183 Ill. 239, 55 N.E. 683 (1899), presenting as reasons that the partnership contract called for personal services and was for an indefinite period so as to be dissolvable at will.

If the terms of the agreement to enter into a contract entitle a party to an interest in property which is to be the subject of the partnership, a court of equity will enforce the agreement so far as may be necessary to insure securing to the party the interest in the property. See Whitworth v. Harris, 40 Miss. 483 (1866).

[11] See *infra*, Sec. 73.

formance of contracts is that damages do not or cannot afford an adequate substitute for the particular thing which was contracted for. Nothing less than acquisition of the particular thing contracted for will satisfy the needs of the plaintiff or do him complete justice.

In this regard, it may be asked to what extent insolvency of the defendant affects the adequacy of the remedy at law. The two conflicting views as to whether insolvency renders the remedy at law inadequate have been discussed already in relation to equitable relief against torts.[12] The discussion there is equally applicable to the contract cases, but with the probability that the majority of the contract cases deny that insolvency alone renders the remedy at law inadequate.[13]

Sec. 68.   Penalty or liquidated damages.

An additional matter which must be noticed is that of the contract with a sum annexed, either as a penalty or as liquidated damages, to secure performance of the contract. If the contract provides for imposition of a penalty or liquidation of damages for its breach, the innocent party may rest satisfied with the recovery of such penalty or damages or waive them and resort to equity for specific performance.[14] But where the provision for penalty

---

[12] See *supra*, Sec. 22.

[13] See Walsh, *Treatise on Equity* (1930) Sec. 63; McClintock, "Adequacy of Ineffective Remedy at Law," 16 *Minn. L. Rev.* 233 (1932).

Insolvency of defendant rendering remedy at law inadequate so as to warrant specific performance. Parker v. Garrison, 61 Ill. 250 (1871).

Insolvency of defendant not in itself ground for compelling specific performance of contract. Geo. E. Warren Co. v. A. L. Black Coal Co., 85 W.Va. 684, 102 S.E. 672, 15 A.L.R. 1083 (1920); Dills v. Doebler, 62 Conn. 366, 26 A. 398, 36 Am.St.Rep. 345, 20 L.R.A. 432 (1892).

Application of statute that no court shall refuse to enforce specific performance of a contract on mere ground that there is an adequate remedy in damages, unless defendant shall satisfactorily show possession of property from which such damages may be made or shall give bond to perform the contract or to pay costs and damages. Baltimore Process Co. v. My-Coca Co., 144 Md. 439, 125 A. 179 (1924), noted 9 *Minn. L. Rev.* 156 (1925).

[14] Glock v. Howard & Wilson Colony Co., 123 Cal. 1, 55 P. 713, 43 L.R.A. 199, 69 Am.St.Rep. 17 (1898).

As a result of the excess of demand over supply in the case of new automobiles after World War II, many reputable dealers sought to prevent newly purchased automobiles from falling into the hands of so-called used car dealers by inserting into the contract of sale a provision that if the purchaser desired to re-sell within

or damages is in the form of an option or alternative to a party, in that he may pay such sum of money in lieu of performance of certain acts, equity will not decree specific performance of such acts, upon election of the party, having the option, to pay such sum.[15] To be distinguished from the foregoing is the contract which provides for a penalty or liquidated damages for delay in performance. Not only may specific performance be compelled but the penalty or damages may be recovered also. Even in the absence of such a provision, a suit for specific performance involves not only the question of such performance but also all claims for compensation and damage on account of the delay in performance.[16]

Sec. 69. Form, definiteness, and certainty of contracts.

It is not the intention to enter into an extended discussion of matters relating to the form and contents of contracts. Such matters are fully covered in the standard texts on Contracts.[17] We consider here, briefly, what is required in the way of these matters to permit of the specific enforcement of a contract.

Contracts may be oral except where required by statute to be in writing. The commonly existent Statutes of Frauds, however, provide variously that to be valid or enforceable certain agreements or contracts must be evidenced by or contained in some note or memorandum in writing, signed by the party to be bound or by his properly authorized agent.[18] Such agreements or contracts include, among others, those not to be performed within a year from the making thereof, those for the leasing for longer than one year or for the sale of realty or an interest therein, and those which are not to be performed within the lifetime of the promisor or those to devise or bequeath any property. Contracts for the sale of goods or choses in action of a certain value are sometimes required

---

a certain period, usually six months, the dealer had the option to re-purchase and that the purchaser was liable in a set sum as liquidated damages if he sold to another. That such a recovery was upheld, see note, Sec. 78.

[15] Davis v. Isenstein, 257 Ill. 260, 100 N.E. 940, 45 L.R.A.N.S. 52 (1913).

[16] Damages in addition to specific performance, see *infra*, Sec. 99.

[17] See, *e.g.*, Williston, *Contracts*, Secs. 567–590.

[18] See Pomeroy, Specific Performance (3d Ed. 1926), Sec. 70; note, 14 *Cornell L.Q.* 102 (1928).

by statute to be in writing to be enforceable.[19]   Accordingly,
equity will not enforce performance of oral contracts which are
required to be in writing, except where the intention is to reduce
the agreement or contract to writing and such intention is prevented by fraud or death,[20] or where the situation falls within the
so-called "part performance" rule.[21]

It is said to be elementary that a contract that is incomplete,
uncertain, or indefinite in its material terms will not be specifically
enforced in equity and that the degree of certainty required in an
equity suit is much greater than that required in an action at law.[22]
The contract, whether permissibly oral or required to be in
writing, must show who are the parties to the contract.   They
must be identified by name or description.[23]   The price to be paid
or consideration to be furnished or performed must be stated in
the contract or the means of ascertaining it must be furnished by
the contract.[24]   The subject matter of the contract must be clearly
and definitely described so that there can be no uncertainty or

---

[19] See Uniform Sales Act, Sec. 4, in force in many states.   The Uniform Act
sets the minimum value at $500 as requiring a written contract, but that amount
has been varied in some states.

[20] See Finucane v. Kearney, Freeman Ch. Rep. (Miss.) 65 (1839).

[21] Equity recognizes situations wherein there has been such "part performance"
by the promisee as will take the case out of the statute of frauds and permit of
enforcement, but this matter is dealt with subsequently.   See *infra*, Sec. 84.

[22] Jannssen v. Davis, 219 Cal. 783, 29 P.2d 196 (1934).   See also Humble, "Certainty in Contracts," 20 *Ky. L.J.* 121 (1932); note, "Certainty of terms required
for specific performance," 36 *Cal. L. Rev.* 120 (1948).

"An action at law is based upon a mere nonperformance by a defendant, and
this negative conclusion can often be established without determining all the terms
of the agreement with exactness.   The suit in equity is wholly an affirmative
proceeding.   The mere fact of nonperformance is not enough; its object is to
procure a performance by the defendant, and this demands a clear, definite, and
precise understanding of all the terms; they must be exactly ascertained before
the performance can be enforced."   Pascoe v. Morrison, 219 Cal. 54, 25 P.2d 9
(1933).

Damages determined by court of equity in lieu of specific performance, see
Gulbenkian v. Gulbenkian, 147 F.2d 173, 158 A.L.R. 990 (1945), noted 31 *Va. L.
Rev.* 705 (1945), and *infra*, Sec. 99.

[23] Irvmor Corp. v. Rodewald, 253 N.Y. 472, 171 N.E. 747 (1930).

[24] Westphal v. Buenger, 324 Ill. 77, 154 N.E. 426 (1926), noted 40 *Harv. L. Rev.*
1019 (1927).

Purchase at "reasonable price," see *infra*, this section.

Written contract for sale of realty requiring purchaser to erect "first-class theater" was sufficiently definite and certain to allow specific performance.   Bettan-
court v. Gilroy Theatre Co., 120 Cal. App.2d 364, 261 P.2d 351 (1953).

ambiguity in identifying it.[25] Certainly in the case of contracts required to be in writing, parol evidence is inadmissible to supply a want in the sufficiency of the description. It is competent, however, to identify the subject matter by parol evidence where the subject matter is so fully described as to permit easily such identification.[26] The various terms of the contract must be set out with certainty, such as those relating to time or times of performance, and the number and amount of payments,[27] and the like.

In regard to the foregoing discussion in this section, we are faced with the situation so common in equity. The principles or rules seem to be clearly delineated but the application of them by various courts to somewhat similar states of facts produces what appear to be conflicting results. On the one hand we find courts declaring that the terms or provisions of the contract are not certain and definite enough to permit of specific enforcement and that any effort on the part of the court to clarify the contract would amount to the court writing a contract for the parties.[28] On the

---

[25] Federated Income Property v. Hart, 84 Cal.App.2d 663, 191 P.2d 59 (1948).

No indication as to what property was intended to constitute agreed security for deed of trust, see Laughurn v. Bryant, 5 Cal.App.2d 721, 43 P.2d 312 (1935).

[26] "It has long been settled that an agreement to sell 'my house and lot' in a certain street or in a certain town, if it appear that the vendor was the owner of only one such house and lot, is sufficient. If he owned several such estates, then the description would clearly be insufficient, because the agreement does not determine which of the several houses was meant." Merwin, *Principles of Equity* (1895) 400.

[27] Purchase price agreed on but not terms of payment, which were left open. Ansorge v. Kane, 244 N.Y. 395, 155 N.E. 683 (1927).

Where contract for sale of realty set out amount of purchase price and amount of down payment and provided that "Balance to be paid at $20 per month," it was not so uncertain as to defeat specific performance because number of monthly payments was not specified. See Mahanay v. Lynde, 48 Cal.App.2d 79, 119 P.2d 430 (1941).

Contracts for sale of automobiles too indefinite as to time of performance, see Kirsch v. Zubalsky, 139 N.J. Eq. 22, 49 A.2d 773 (1946); Cohen v. Rosenstock Motors, Inc., 188 Misc. 426, 65 N.Y.S.2d 481 (1946), noted 33 *Cornell L.Q.* 432 (1948); Goodman v. Henry Caplin, Inc., 65 N.Y.S.2d 576 (1946). Contra, see De Moss v. Conart Motor Sales Co., (1947; Ohio C. P.) 72 N.E.2d 158, noted 36 *Geo. L.J.* 460 (1948), 26 *Tex. L. Rev.* 351 (1948), where contract called for delivery "as soon as possible" and reasonable time for performance was held to have elapsed after eleven months.

[28] See, generally, cases cited in preceding notes.

Where plaintiff conveyed land to defendant railroad for a sum of money and on condition that defendant would build a depot on the land, suitable for the

other hand, we find courts holding, as sufficiently definite and certain, provisions for such things as a "reasonable time," a "reasonable price," or holding that a lack of specifications calls for performance "in the usual manner." [29]   The latter results might well be expected when we consider that the nature of equity is to disregard technicalities and harshnesses generally and, instead, to attempt to afford a just relief to the injured party against the refractory party.

Sec. 70.   Contracts for sale of realty, or for interests therein.

Land has always been a favored subject of Anglo-American law and each parcel or piece of land is assumed to have a peculiar value.   Accordingly, in agreements for the purchase of real property or the acquisition of interests therein the presumption is that only the acquisition of the realty or interest bargained for will give the party exactly what he is entitled to.[30]   No remedy at law is so adequate, complete, and efficacious as this acquisition.[31]   The "presumption" referred to has, accordingly, in the course of the centuries become virtually conclusive, with the result that "When all is fair, and the parties deal on equal terms, it is a universal

---

convenience of the public, etc., it was held that there was nothing definite enough as to the plan, shape, size, materials, or arrangement of the building or its cost to permit enforcement. Blanchard v. Detroit, L. & L. M. R. Co., 31 Mich. 43 (1875).

[29] Open price option to purchase by lessee enforceable at reasonable price, see Shayeb v. Holland, 321 Mass. 429, 73 N.E.2d 731 (1947), noted 61 *Harv. L. Rev.* 372 (1948).

Reasonable time in contract for sale of automobile, see De Moss v. Conart Motor Sales Co., *supra*, note 27.

Where plaintiff conveyed land to defendant railroad for its right of way and the railroad covenanted to build a switch or sidetrack upon the land for the plaintiff's benefit, the court said "It is true that the contract does not specify the length of the switch or sidetrack. In our view, that is not necessary. It is a well-established rule that where a party agrees to do a certain thing, and does not specify how it shall be done, the law implies a promise on his part to do it in the usual manner, and that it shall be complete and effectual for the use to which the same kind of thing is generally applied. The contract contemplated a sidetrack or switch capable of being used for the loading or unloading of cars as the same is usually done at country sidings." Lane v. Pacific & I. N. R. Co., 8 Idaho 230, 67 P. 656 (1901).

[30] Kitchen v. Herring, 42 N.C. 190 (1851).

[31] Losee v. Morey, 57 Barb. (N.Y.) 561 (1865).

rule in equity, to enforce contracts for the sale of lands specifically, at the demand of either the vendor or the vendee; and in such case it is as much the duty of the court to decree specific performance of the contract as it is to give damages for its breach." [32]

It will be noticed that in the foregoing quotation it is said that the contract is enforceable by the vendor as well as by the vendee or purchaser.   Although this right of the vendor to specific performance is probably traceable to affirmative application of the mutuality of remedy rule, that the plaintiff is equitably entitled to specific performance where the defendant would have been if he were the complaining party,[33] the vendor's right has come to be accepted as the uniform rule on the ground that his remedy by way of damages is inadequate,[34] although even so one may note exceptions.[35]

The motive of the party in seeking the acquisition of the realty or interest therein is usually immaterial,[36] as is the quality or quan-

---

[32] Losee v. Morey, 57 Barb. (N.Y.) 561 (1865).

See *Rest. Contracts*, Sec. 360; Cox, "Specific Performance of Contracts to Sell Land," 16 *Ky. L.J.* 338 (1928).

[33] See *infra*, Sec. 79.

[34] "In the action at law for the breach of the contract the plaintiff could only recover the excess, if any, of the sum agreed to be paid for the land above its market value when the contract was to be performed. Such a remedy is manifestly inadequate, and courts of equity, therefore, hold, as a general rule, that when a contract for the sale of real estate has been fairly entered into, the party contracting to sell, as well as the party contracting to buy, is entitled to have it specifically performed. The cases on this question are all one way. It is true courts of equity have, in the exercise of their discretion, refused to apply the rule in certain cases where it would be productive of hardship or inconvenience." Hodges v. Kowing, 58 Conn. 12, 18 A. 979, 7 L.R.A. 87 (1889).

That an action at law for the purchase price will lie if the deed has been tendered, see Fairlawn Heights Co. v. Theis, 133 Ohio St. 387, 14 N.E.2d 1 (1938), noted 5 *Ohio S.U.L.J.* 222 (1939).

[35] See, *e.g.*, Porter v. Frenchman's Bay & Mt. Desert Land & Water Co., 84 Me. 195, 24 A. 814 (1892).

[36] One exception, in a minority of jurisdictions, has existed where the purchaser has contracted to re-sell the realty at a profit to another, as in Hazelton v. Miller, 25 App. D. C. 337 (1905), noted 5 *Col. L. Rev.* 473 (1905), 18 *Harv. L. Rev.* 625 (1905), where the measure of damages is considered to be the lost profit and that its recovery at law is an adequate remedy. However, even in such a situation, the usual view is that the purpose or motive for the acquisition of the realty is immaterial and that the only adequate remedy is such acquisition through specific performance. Mier v. Hadden, 148 Mich. 488, 111 N.W. 1040 (1907); McVoy v. Baumann, 93 N.J. Eq. 360, 117 A. 717 (1922); Bittrick v. Consol. Imp. Co., 51 Wash. 469, 99 P. 303 (1909). And see Cox, "Specific Performance of Contracts to Sell Land," 16 *Ky. L.J.* 338 (1928).

tity of the realty or the interest.[37]   Aside from the fact that equity will not concern itself with trivialities, contracts for interests in realty, however slight, are enforceable in equity, as where the contract is to make or assign a leasehold estate [38] or to grant an easement in gross as distinguished from a mere license.[39]

Sec. 71.   Contracts for sale of personal property.

As already indicated in the discussion of possessory actions to recover personalty,[40] the general rule is that specific performance of contracts for the sale of personalty will not be enforced, on the ground that there is an adequate remedy at law by obtaining personalty of like kind and quality on the open market, and recovering any damages incurred from having to do so or by suing the refractory party for the value of the personalty and with the damages so obtained purchasing similar personalty on the open market.[41]   But where personalty of like kind and quality is not obtainable on the open market or is obtainable only at great trouble and expense or subject to damaging delay, the remedy at law is certainly not so adequate, speedy and efficacious as that in equity by way of specific performance and the equity court will compel specific performance.   The personalty may be of a special and peculiar nature and value to the purchaser, whose needs nothing else will satisfy, or his damages from not obtaining the personalty contracted for may be so conjectural or speculative as not to provide a basis for adequate relief by way of damages.

Illustrations of the foregoing are provided by a canner's contract for certain farm produce which was not obtainable elsewhere

---

[37] Kitchen v. Herring, 42 N.C. 190 (1851).

Contract for sale of growing timber as contract for interest in or part of realty, see Stuart v. Pennis, 91 Va. 688, 22 S.E. 509 (1895); Dells Paper Co. v. Willow River Lumber Co., 170 Wis. 19, 173 N.W. 317 (1919); Walsh, *Treatise on Equity* (1930) Sec. 59.

[38] See Clark v. Clark, 49 Cal. 586 (1875).

[39] Baseball Pub. Co. v. Bruton, 302 Mass. 54, 18 N.E.2d 362, 119 A.L.R. 1518 (1938), noted 17 *Tex. L. Rev.* 490 (1939).

[40] See *supra*, Sec. 66.

[41] Gallagher v. Studebaker Corp., 236 Mich. 195, 210 N.W. 233 (1926), noted 25 *Mich. L. Rev.* 546 (1927).

A somewhat unusual case as to subject matter is Dunner v. Hoover, 43 Cal.App.2d 753, 111 P.2d 737 (1941), which involved a contract for the sale of a milk route for breach of which there was said to be an adequate remedy at law.

within the customary canning period;[42] a farmer's contract for water vital for irrigation purposes and which was not obtainable elsewhere within the period it was needed,[43] a gas company's contract for coal tar essential to its operation and which if obtainable was obtainable at a distance at great additional labor and expense,[44] a contract to convey a patent right or to supply articles manufactured under a patent.[45] Another situation is one in which delivery of goods and payment of the purchase price are to be made in installments over a considerable period of time. This particularly presents the problem of damages being speculative or conjectural since their estimation may rest at least partly upon future events. The difficulty of obtaining proper compensatory damages at law renders specific performance of the contract an appropriate relief.[46] In this situation, though, it is necessary to recognize that equitable relief would not be obtainable in those jurisdictions wherein the courts hold that it is not feasible or practicable for them to see to the enforcement of contracts for a succession of acts over a considerable period of time requiring protracted supervision by the court.[47]

Another illustration of a situation in which the remedy at law is considered inadequate is one of somewhat common occurrence, a contract for the purchase of shares of corporate stock where such stock is not available on the open market or not frequently offered for sale and then only in varying amounts and at varying prices, so that its availability elsewhere is doubtful and its market value unascertainable or uncertain.[48] The need for equitable relief is frequently strengthened by the fact that the stock contracted for has a special value to the purchaser in that it will insure him control of the corporation.[49]

---

42 Curtice Bros. Co. v. Catts, 72 N.J. Eq. 831, 66 A. 935 (1907).

43 Bay City Irr. Co. v. Sweeney, (1904; Tex. Civ. App.) 81 S.W. 545.

44 Equitable Gas Light Co. v. Baltimore Coal Tar Co., 63 Md. 285 (1884).

45 Hercules Glue Co. v. Littooy, 25 Cal.App.2d 182, 76 P.2d 700 (1938); Adams v. Messinger, 147 Mass. 185, 17 N.E. 491 (1888).

46 See Eastern Rolling Mill Co. v. Michlovitz, 157 Md. 51, 145 A. 378 (1929).

47 See, e.g., Long Beach Drug Co. v. United Drug Co., 13 Cal.2d 158, 88 P.2d 698, 89 P.2d 386 (1939); Edelen v. Samuels, 126 Ky. 295, 103 S.W. 360 (1907).

48 General Sec. Corp. v. Welton, 223 Ala. 299, 135 So. 329 (1931); Gilfallan v. Gilfallan, 168 Cal. 23, 141 P. 623 (1914); New England Trust Co. v. Abbott, 162 Mass. 148, 38 N.E. 432 (1894).

49 Waddle v. Cabana, 220 N.Y. 18, 114 N.E. 1054 (1917).

It is of some interest to notice that articles which at one period are easily obtainable on the open market may not be so at another period, due to some change of economic conditions. For instance, the unavailability of new passenger automobiles for purchase by the general public during the period of World War II resulted, immediately after that war, in the pyramiding of a tremendous demand for such automobiles which the manufacturers and dealers were not at once able to satisfy. Considerable litigation resulted by reason of contracts for the sale and delivery of new automobiles where undue lapses of time in delivery occurred or where dealers gave preference in delivery to purchasers subsequent in point of time. In one such case, specific performance of a contract for the sale of a new automobile was decreed where the contract called for delivery "as soon as possible." Reasonable time for performance was determined to have elapsed where eleven months had passed since the making of the contract, and there was said to be no adequate remedy at law, due to the fact that new automobiles were difficult to obtain on the open market.[50] However, in another case where delivery was to be made in 30 to 45 days of a car of specified color and model, specific performance was denied on the ground that damages at law provided an adequate remedy.[51] The cases became surprisingly numerous[52] and provide valuable authority on the question of unavailability of par-

---

Stock available on market but stock needed to secure control, see First Nat. Bank v. Securities Co., 128 Minn. 341, 150 N.W. 1084 (1915).

[50] Heidner v. Hewitt Chevrolet Co., 166 Kan. 11, 199 P.2d 481 (1948), noted 47 *Mich. L. Rev.* 1032 (1949); De Moss v. Conart Motor Sales Co., (1947; Ohio C. P.) 72 N.E.2d 158, aff'd on other grounds 149 Ohio St. 299, 78 N.E.2d 675 (1948), noted 36 *Geo. L.J.* 460 (1948), 26 *Tex. L. Rev.* 351 (1948).

Decision went against the purchaser in other cases of a similar nature, but on the ground that the contract was too indefinite as to time of performance and description of the automobile to permit of specific performance. See Kelley v. Creston Buick Sales Co., 239 Iowa 1236, 34 N.W.2d 598 (1948); Kirsch v. Zubalsky, 139 N.J. Eq. 22, 49 A.2d 773 (1946); Cohen v. Rosenstock Motors, 188 Misc. 426, 65 N.Y.S.2d 481 (1946), noted 33 *Cornell L.Q.* 432 (1948); Goodman v. Henry Caplin, Inc., 65 N.Y.S.2d 576 (1946).

[51] Poltorak v. Jackson Chevrolet Co., 322 Mass. 699, 79 N.E.2d 285 (1948), criticized 62 *Harv. L. Rev.* 149 (1948). And see Pugh v. Tidwell, 52 N.M. 386, 199 P.2d 1001 (1948); Welch v. Chippewa Sales Co., 252 Wis. 166, 31 N.W.2d 170 (1948).

[52] For very comprehensive collection of cases, see Note, 24 *Notre Dame Law.* 415 (1949).

ticular goods on the open market as rendering the remedy at law inadequate.

Sec. 72. —Effect of Uniform Sales Act.

Some question seems to have arisen in recent years as to whether the Uniform Sales Act has affected or changed in any way the general rule that equity will not enforce contracts for sale of personalty where there is an adequate remedy at law.[53] In Section 68 of the Act it is provided that where the seller has broken a contract to deliver specific or ascertained goods, a court having the powers of a court of equity may, if it thinks fit, on the application of the buyer, direct specific performance by the seller.   In the first place, it must be borne in mind that the Act applies only to sales of goods and not to other kinds of personal property.   And in the second place, even as to sales of goods, notice that the Act provides that specific performance may be directed "if the court thinks fit."   This leaves the matter entirely in the discretion of the court.   While the court may conceivably, if it thinks fit, direct specific performance even where there is an adequate remedy at law,[54] in the majority of the cases which have been decided under this section of the Act, the courts seem to have interpreted the discretion given them as sanction to continue to refuse equitable relief when the damages provide an adequate remedy.[55]

Sec. 73. Contracts for personal services.

As a general rule, equity will not enforce specific performance of contracts for personal services.[56] The execution of such con-

---

[53] Uncertainty of present California rule, due to changes in pertinent statutes, is suggested by Witkin, *Summary of California Law.*

[54] See Hunt Foods, Inc. v. O'Disho (1951: N.D. Cal.), 98 F. Supp. 267, where contract for delivery of peaches for four years by grower to canner was specifically enforced under Uniform Sales Act without mention of necessity of inadequacy of remedy at law. Of course, this is a type of situation which is almost uniformly considered not to present an adequate remedy at law.

[55] See comment, [1946] *Wis. L. Rev.* 461.

Comment on specific performance under Uniform Revised Sales Act, see note, "Remedies for Total Breach of Contract Under Uniform Revised Sales Act," 57 *Yale L.J.* 1360, 1379 (1948).

[56] See Parks, "Equitable Relief in Contracts Involving Personal Services," 66 *U. Pa. L. Rev.* 251 (1918); *Rest. Contracts*, Sec. 379.

tracts depends upon the skill, volition, and fidelity of the person who has engaged to perform them and it is impracticable, if not impossible, for a court to supervise their proper execution or to secure their faithful performance.[57] Additionally, some courts also declare that to order performance of the personal services by an unwilling party would amount to involuntary servitude, and so against public policy.[58]

In any event it may be argued that if the services are such as require only ordinary skill and ability, the injured party may, without undue trouble or burden, employ, or contract with, someone else of similar skill and ability to render the services and sue the refractory party at law for such damages as have been entailed by the breach.[59] However, it does not always follow, even here, that the remedy at law is adequate, although such lack will not warrant any equitable relief.[60]

If the services to be rendered are of an unusual or unique nature, as by one possessing special, peculiar, or extraordinary ability or reputation in some intellectual, professional, or physical field, the situation becomes more clearly one in which no adequate remedy at law exists. Is any reason existent why some form of equitable relief should be available? In this situation there has developed the rule, generally traced to the English case of *Lumley v. Wagner*,[61] that where a contract for such services contains a negative covenant by the one to render the services that he will not render like services for anyone else, during the contract term, equity will enjoin the breach of this negative covenant. In other words, it will enjoin the breaching party from rendering such services for another.[62] Indeed, the other employer may be the

---

[57] De Rivafinoli v. Corsetti, 4 Paige (N.Y.) 264 (1883). See Merwin, *Principles of Equity* (1895) 419.

[58] Wakeham v. Barker, 82 Cal. 46, 22 P. 1131 (1889). See also Deuerling v. City Baking Co., 155 Md. 280, 141 A. 542, 67 A.L.R. 993 (1928).

[59] See Parks, "Equitable Relief in Contracts Involving Personal Services," 66 *U. Pa. L. Rev.* 251 (1918).

[60] See Wakeham v. Barker, 82 Cal. 46, 22 P. 1131 (1889); Kessler Co. v. Chappelle, 73 App. Div. 447, 77 N.Y.S. 285 (1902).

[61] (1852) 1 De G., M. & G. 604, 42 Eng. Rep. 687, affirming (1852) 1 De G. & Sm. 485, 64 Eng. Rep. 1209.

[62] Tribune Ass'n v. Simonds, — N.J. Eq. —, 104 A. 386 (1918), noted 32 *Harv. L. Rev.* 176 (1918), 17 *Mich. L. Rev.* 97 (1918). See Parks, "Equitable Relief in Contracts Involving Personal Services," 66 *U. Pa. L. Rev.* 251 (1918); Stevens,

subject of injunction to prevent him availing himself of such services, where he knew of such contract and attempts to profit by its breach or seeks to induce its breach.

To warrant injunctive relief against the one who is to render or is in course of rendering such services, some courts insist that the negative covenant must be expressly stated in the contract,[63] but others will enjoin if the obligation not to work for another can reasonably be implied from the contract.[64] It is undoubted that to support injunction against the breach of negative covenant, the contract must be fair and valid, imposing equality of obligation on both sides.[65] The courts are not always in agreement, however, as to what is a fair contract equally binding or obligatory on both sides.[66]

What are services of an unusual, unique, or extraordinary nature is a question upon which, naturally, the courts are not always in agreement.[67] It may be stated, with some cynicism perhaps, that too often it appears to be merely confined to cases in which the

---

"Involuntary Servitude by Injunction," 6 *Cornell L.Q.* 235 (1921); annotations, Validity and enforceability of restrictive covenant in contract of employment, 9 A.L.R. 1456, 20 A.L.R. 861, 29 A.L.R. 1331, 52 A.L.R. 1362, 67 A.L.R. 1002, 98 A.L.R. 964; Cal. Civ. Code Sec. 3423 (5).

[63] Carlson v. Koerner, (1907) 226 Ill. 15, 80 N.E. 562.

In the English case of Whitwood Chemical Co. v. Hardman, L. R. [1891] 2 Ch. 416, the existence of an express negative covenant was required as a basis for injunction, alleging that Lord St. Leonards, in Lumley v. Wagner, had been very clear and explicit on that point. Although an express negative covenant was present, actually Lord St. Leonards observed that "I am of opinion, that if she had attempted, even in the absence of any negative stipulation, to perform at another theatre, she would have broken the spirit and true meaning of the contract. . . ." And see Clark, "Implications of Lumley v. Wagner," 17 *Col. L. Rev.* 687 (1917).

[64] Harry Rogers Theatrical Enterprises v. Comstock, 225 App. Div. 34, 232 N.Y.S. 1 (1918).

[65] While not precisely in point, see Byram v. Vaughn, 68 F. Supp. 981 (1946), where employee's breach of negative covenant not to solicit employer's customers during his employment or for one year thereafter was not enjoined where contract of employment was merely at will and did not obligate employer to continue employment for any specified term. Similarly, see note 36 *Geo. L.J.* 268 (1948).

[66] Consider Philadelphia Ball Club v. Lajoie, 202 Pa. 210, 51 A. 973, 58 L.R.A. 257, 90 Am.St.Rep. 627 (1902).

With reference to contracts of professional baseball players, see "Baseball and the Law," 32 *Va.. L. Rev.* 1164 (1946).

[67] Difficulty of determination, see Strobridge Lithographing Co. v. Crane, 58 Hun 611, 12 N.Y.S. 898, 20 Civ. Proc. R. 24, 35 N. Y. St. R. 473 (1890).

Listing of cases of various personal services of unusual or unique nature, see Chafee & Simpson, *Cases on Equity* (1st Ed.) 471.

name of the person involved has publicity value or is describable as newsworthy.[68] Even in the case of services of ordinary skill and ability, it does not always follow that there is an adequate remedy at law, but nevertheless the rule is settled that in such cases injunctive relief will not lie although a negative covenant is expressly stated in the contract.[69]

What about the other side of this situation? Can the one who has contracted to render the personal services compel the other party to perform by accepting the services for the period of the contract? The answer is that he cannot, according to the usual view, on the ground that he has an adequate remedy at law for damages.[70] Nor, ordinarily can he obtain relief in a negative sense, by enjoining the other party from discharging him or from otherwise dispensing with his services, sometimes on the ground that there is an adequate remedy at law for damages, or sometimes on the ground of the now generally discredited doctrine of lack of mutuality of remedy, in that the defendant would not have available an equivalent remedy in his favor.[71] An exception to the rule against granting an injunction is said to exist where the employment is coupled with some interest in the business from which it is sought to discharge him or where irreparable injury would result to him from such discharge.[72]

Just what will constitute irreparable injury is not too well settled, since the cases are not numerous.[73] That one with an

---

[68] See note, 90 Am.St.Rep. 634 (1903), to Philadelphia Ball Club v. Lajoie, 202 Pa. 210, 51 A. 973, 58 L.R.A. 257, 90 Am.St.Rep. 627 (1902), wherein baseball player cases are compared to show that "reputation" was determinative rather than ability. And compare Tribune Ass'n v. Simonds, — N.J. Eq. —, 104 A. 386 (1918), noted 32 *Harv. L. Rev.* 176 (1918), 17 *Mich. L. Rev.* 97 (1918), with Kennerly v. Simonds, 247 F. 822 (1917).

[69] See Kessler Co. v. Chappelle, 73 App. Div. 447, 77 N.Y.S. 285 (1902).

[70] Seiler v. Fairfax, 23 La. Ann. 397 (1871). See also, *e.g.*, Cal. Civ. Code Sec. 3390 (2).

[71] Hewitt v. Magic City Furniture & Mfg. Co., 214 Ala. 265, 107 So. 745, 44 A.L.R. 1441 (1926). See annotation, Injunction against discharge of employee, 44 A.L.R. 1443.

Mutuality of remedy, see *infra*, Sec. 79.

[72] See annotation, Injunction against discharge of employee, 44 A.L.R. 1443.

[73] Cases in the labor union field are not dealt with here, although reference may be made to Dubinsky v. Blue Dale Dress Co., 162 Misc. 177, 292 N.Y.S. 898 (1936), noted 50 *Harv. L. Rev.* 700 (1936), 14 *N.Y.U. L. Q.* 401 (1936), wherein employer entered into contract with labor union for three years and within that period moved its plant to another state.

established reputation in his field or profession might well suffer irreparable injury might well be argued.[74] It might also be argued that where there is a negative covenant in the contract, or one reasonably to be implied, that the employer will not employ the services of anyone else for the contract period, that he might be enjoined from breaching that covenant.[75]

The right of veterans of World War II, under the Federal Selective Training and Service Act of 1940, as amended, to compel their re-employment by their former employers, has been frequently upheld in the federal courts. Such an action is essentially equitable in nature, of course, as is the relief granted.[76]

Sec. 74. Contracts to build or repair.

Contracts to build or to repair have not as a general rule in the past in this country, been enforced in equity.[77] This has been variously put upon the ground that it is not practicable or feasible for the court of equity to enforce performance of a contract for continuous services, requiring skill and experience to perform them as well as skill and experience to determine whether or not they have been properly performed,[78] or upon the ground of uncertainty as methods, details, specifications, and cost of the thing to be done.[79]

Where, however, the building is to be done on land owned by the defendant so that the plaintiff is not able to do the work himself or have another do it, specific performance by the vendor

---

[74] See discussion by Parks, 66 *U. Pa. L. Rev.* 251 (1918). Compare the Hewitt Case, *supra*, where plaintiff argued that he would be deprived of the opportunity to establish a reputation.

[75] See Parks, "Equitable Relief in Contracts Involving Personal Services," 66 *U. Pa. L. Rev.* 251 (1918); annotation, Injunction against discharge of employee, 44 A.L.R. 1443.

[76] See annotation, Re-employment of discharged servicemen, 167 A.L.R. 124.

[77] This rule seems to have become fixed in this country at an early date, although many writers have pointed out that early English cases did not hesitate to order specific performance by the defendant. See Walsh, *Treatise on Equity* (1930) Sec. 65; Glenn & Redden, *Cases and Materials on Equity* (1946) 462. Pomeroy declared in 1926 that it was "now well settled" that this is the general rule. Pomeroy, *Specific Performance* (3d Ed.) Sec. 23. And see Oleck, "Specific performance of builders' contracts," 21 *Fordh. L. Rev.* 156 (1952).

[78] Beck v. Allison, 56 N.Y. 366 (1874).

[79] Blanchard v. Detroit, L. & L. M. R. Co., 31 Mich. 43 (1875).
In regard to definiteness and certainty of contract, see also *supra*, Sec. 66.

has usually been considered the only adequate remedy.[80] Similarly, where the purchaser has engaged to build upon land conveyed to him something essential or beneficial to the adjoining land retained by the vendor, specific performance has frequently been decreed,[81] although it has also been not uncommon to deny specific performance on one or the other of the grounds mentioned above.[82]

Even in the past there were cases which refused to subscribe to the reasons given for denying specific performance,[83] and under present-day criticism of validity of those reasons,[84] the tendency is to take a broader view of the situation.[85] It is recognized that the need of detailed supervision, dependent on skill and experience not possessed by the court, is not always a present consideration. The court can order a performance of the contract, assuming that the remedy at law is not adequate, and leave it to the plaintiff to call it to the court's attention if there has been a lack of proper performance. If necessary the court can appoint a master or other appropriate officer, with the requisite skill to determine whether there has been a proper compliance with the terms of the contract. And the objection on the ground of indefiniteness or uncertainty of the contract as to details, materials, cost, etc., of construction can equally well be met in many instances by requiring construction of what is customary for reasonable use in the particular case. This, again, may be determined by an officer of the requisite skill and experience appointed by the court.[86] Indeed, the late Justice Holmes remarked that if, in an action at law, a jury could determine whether what was done or left undone

---

[80] Zygmunt Avenue Realty Co., 108 N.J. Eq. 462, 155 A. 544 (1931), noted 6 *Temple L.Q.* 126 (1932); Strauss v. Estates of Long Beach, 187 App. Div. 876, 176 N.Y.S. 447 (1919).

[81] This is declared to be the tendency of the English courts by Merwin, *Principles of Equity* (1895) 420; Pomeroy, *Specific Performance* (3d Ed.) Sec. 23.

[82] Blanchard v. Detroit, L. & L. M. R. Co., 31 Mich 43 (1875).

[83] Jones v. Parker, 163 Mass. 564, 40 N.E. 1044, 47 Am.St.Rep. 485 (1895), per Holmes, J., with regard to covenant to install heating and lighting equipment.

[84] Professor Walsh describes the impracticability of specific performance because of difficulty of superintendence as "an exploded doctrine." Walsh, *Treatise on Equity* (1930) 328.

[85] Equity jurisdiction must be regulated so as to meet the requirements of ever-changing conditions, see Edison Illuminating Co. v. Eastern Pennsylvania Power Co., 253 Pa. 457, 98 A. 652 (1916).

[86] Lane v. Pacific, etc., R. Co., 8 Idaho 230, 67 P. 656 (1901).

amounted to a failure to make a reasonable compliance so as to base damages thereon, a judge sitting without a jury would find no more difficulty. And, he added, "We do not doubt that an expert would find it easy to frame a scheme for doing the work." [87]

It must be conceded that in many instances there is an adequate remedy at law, as by engaging another to do the work that the defendant has failed to do and recovering any resultant damages,[88] but where the remedy at law is definitely not as adequate as that equity can offer, specific performance should not be denied on the basis of reasons now recognized as having little validity.[89]

Sec. 75.   Contracts to arbitrate.

Where a contract to arbitrate has been carried out and an award made, equity has not hesitated to enforce the award in situations where contracts of the same nature as the award are proper subjects of specific performance. But so far as concerns the enforcement of the agreement to arbitrate, courts both in England and this country were long disinclined to grant such relief. Courts have refused to compel a party to appoint an arbitrator or to compel arbitrators, once appointed, to act.[90] The chief reasons given by the equity courts have been that a court of equity has not the time or ability to supervise the proper performance of such an agreement so as to make its decree effective[91] and that to

---

[87] Jones v. Parker, 163 Mass. 564, 40 N.E. 1044, 47 Am.St.Rep. 485 (1895).

Notice that as far back as 1716 in England, in Vane v. Lord Barnard, 2 Vern. 738, 23 Eng. Rep. 1082, in which the court ordered the defendant to repair his acts of waste by restoring the building to its former condition, "a commission was to issue to ascertain what ought to be repaired, and a master to see it done at the expense and charge of the defendant."

[88] Where contract is executory on both sides, plaintiff may have adequate remedy in obtaining another to do the work and recover any damages resulting. See Pacific Elec. R. Co. v. Campbell-Johnson, 153 Cal. 106, 94 P. 623 (1908).

[89] Where plaintiff had paid for a house to be built by defendant on land conveyed by defendant to plaintiff, the burden imposed upon the plaintiff by having to finance the building by another rendered specific performance by the defendant the proper relief. Brummel v. Clifton Realty Co., 146 Md. 56, 125 A. 905 (1924), noted 25 Col. L. Rev. 348 (1925), 10 Cornell L.Q. 69 (1924). In any event, there is no reason why this burden of financing the building of the house by another should be thrown on the plaintiff. See Williams v. Lowe, 79 N.J. Eq. 173, 81 A. 760 (1911).

[90] See, especially, Simpson, "Specific Enforcement of Arbitration Contracts," 83 U. Pa. L. Rev. 160 (1934).

[91] Miles v. Schmidt, 168 Mass. 339, 47 N.E. 115 (1897).

Criticism of this viewpoint, see Walsh, Treatise on Equity (1930) Sec. 64.

compel arbitration results in the substitution of another tribunal for the court, contrary to public policy.[92] The appointment of arbitrators by the court has been denied as imposing something upon the parties to which they had not agreed.

This attitude of the courts has been subjected to frequent criticism; [93] and growing realization of the advantages of arbitration has resulted in the enactment of statutes in many states providing for specific enforcement of agreements to arbitrate.[94] It is interesting to note that, with the enactment of these statutes, the courts suddenly find it feasible and practicable to do that which they formerly contended was not feasible or practicable.[95]

Even in the absence of statutory authorization, many courts have tended to modify the former view. This has frequently been accomplished by distinguishing between cases where the method of arbitration is said to be of the essence of the contract and cases where the method is not of the essence but merely provides a means of reaching a fair valuation through the use of appraisers of an otherwise valid and enforceable contract. Thus it has been said that "Where in a contract of sale of real estate at a price to be fixed by appraisers chosen by the parties, the stipulation for the valuers is not a condition nor the essence of the agreement, but is subsidiary or auxiliary to its main purpose and scope, and the parties may not be left or placed in statu quo by a refusal to enforce

---

[92] Miles v. Schmidt, 168 Mass. 339, 47 N.E. 115 (1897).

[93] See Walsh, *Treatise on Equity* (1930) Sec. 64; Simpson, "Specific Enforcement of Arbitration Contracts," 83 *U. Pa. L. Rev.* 160 (1934).

[94] See Kagel, "Labor and Commercial Arbitration under California Arbitration Statute," 38 *Cal. L. Rev.* 799 (1950), at 809 ff.

Such a statute not unconstitutional as ousting the court of jurisdiction, see Snyder v. Superior Court, 24 Cal.App.2d 263, 74 P.2d 782 (1937); Berkovitz v. Arbib & Houlberg, Inc., 230 N.Y. 261, 130 N.E. 288 (1921).

Enforcement of agreement to arbitrate according to law of another jurisdiction, see Gilbert v. Burnstine, 255 N.Y. 348, 174 N.E. 706 (1931); Nippon, etc. Co. v. Ewing-Thomas Co., 313 Pa. 442, 170 A. 286 (1930).

Enforcement of arbitration agreements in federal courts, see Kochery, 39 *Cornell L.Q.* 74 (1953).

Exemption of labor agreements from statute providing for specific enforcement of arbitration agreements, see Local 1111, etc. v. Allen-Bradley Co., 259 Wis. 609, 49 N.W.2d 720 (1951), discussed in 36 *Marquette L. Rev.* 117 (1952).

[95] The New York court explains that the statute merely supplies a remedy that formerly did not exist and points out that the courts themselves might have changed the rule if they had been willing to abandon some early precedents. Berkovitz v. Arbib & Houlberg, Inc., 230 N.Y. 261, 130 N.E. 288 (1921).

the contract, a court of equity may determine the price itself, by its master or by appraisers of its own selection, and may enforce specific performance of the agreement of sale. But where the stipulation for the appraisers is a condition or the essence of the contract of sale, and a refusal to enforce it will leave the parties in their original situations when the agreement was made, a court of equity will not specifically enforce it." [96]

Sec. 76.   Contracts to borrow or lend money, to give security, to indemnify, or exonerate.

A contract merely to borrow or to lend money will not ordinarily be enforced in equity. It is considered that there is an adequate remedy at law both for the borrower and the lender. If the lender breaches his agreement to lend the money, the borrower may obtain the money elsewhere and recover damages from the lender in the amount of any increase of interest the borrower has to pay, as well as damages for any injury suffered in not obtaining the money at the time agreed.[97] If the borrower breaches the agreement, the lender may lend the money elsewhere and recover any corresponding loss resulting from obtaining a lesser interest rate, as well as for any loss from the money lying idle until another investment can be obtained.[98]

---

[96] Castle Creek Water Co. v. City of Aspen, 146 F. 8 (1906).

See Simpson, "Specific Performance of Arbitration Contracts," 83 *U. Pa. L. Rev.* 160 (1934). Specific performance of appraisal contracts as distinguished from arbitration, see note, 33 *Va. L. Rev.* 494 (1947).

Enforcement of contract for sale of property, valuation of which is to be arrived at by appraisers appointed by parties. Depies-Heus Oil Co. v. Sielaff, 246 Wis. 36, 16 N.W.2d 386 (1944), noted *Wis. L. Rev.* 320 (1946).

Specific performance granted of contract to sell assets of corporation although price to be fixed by arbitrators. Texas Co. v. Z. & M. Independent Oil Co., 156 F.2d 862 (1946).

[97] Kenner v. Slidell Sav. & Homestead Ass'n, 170 La. 547, 128 So. 475 (1930); Norwood v. Crowder, 177 N.C. 469, 99 S.E. 345 (1919); Steward v. Bounds, 167 Wash. 554, 9 P.2d 1112 (1932); note 18 *Col. L. Rev.* 491 (1918); annotation, Specific performance of contract to lend or borrow money, 41 A.L.R. 357.

Professor McClintock points out that if the borrower cannot obtain the money elsewhere because his credit is poor, equity would not be justified in compelling the lending of the money because it could not assure the lender of its return. McClintock, *Handbook of Equity* (2d Ed.).

[98] See note, 18 *Col. L. Rev.* 491 (1918); Walsh, *Treatise on Equity* (1930) Sec. 52; annotation, Specific performance of contract to lend or borrow money, 41 A.L.R. 357.

However, some exceptional situation or circumstance may justify specific performance of the agreement to lend.[99] Where the borrower has done acts to his detriment in reliance on the promise to lend and the lender has accepted the promissory note and mortgage securing it executed by the borrower, the lender's agreement to lend the money has been specifically enforced.[100]

Even if the borrower has agreed to give security for the loan, the lender's situation is no different where the borrower breaches his agreement before the money is received by him. Likewise, the borrower's situation is the same where the lender breaches the agreement to lend,[101] unless, as pointed out above, the lender has already accepted the security and the borrower has suffered detriment. But after receipt of the money by the borrower, his failure to give the security is a breach for which no adequate remedy is available at law. The most the lender can get at law is a judgment for the debt whether security is given or not. The security is the specific thing to which he is entitled under the contract, and only equity can grant him this specific relief.[102] Nevertheless, even here, some courts insist that failure to give the security is a breach of contract giving an immediate right of action for which the measure of damages is the amount of the debt. They do concede that if the defendant is insolvent so that a judgment would be more or less worthless, specific performance is proper to compel the giving of the security.[103]

The agreement to give security may exist, of course, in other

---

[99] Enforcing agreement in life insurance policy to lend money to insured or owner of policy, see Caplin v. Penn Mut. L. Ins. Co., 182 App. Div. 269, 169 N.Y.S. 756 (1918), aff'd 229 N.Y. 545, 129 N.E. 908 (1920), noted 18 *Col. L. Rev.* 491 (1918).

[100] Columbus Club v. Simons, 110 Okla. 48, 236 P. 12, 41 A.L.R. 350 (1925).

That the circumstances in the Columbus Club Case warranted an exception to the rule was mentioned approvingly in Steward v. Bounds, 167 Wash. 554, 9 P.2d 1112 (1932).

[101] Kenner v. Slidell Sav. & Homestead Ass'n, 170 La. 547, 128 So. 475 (1930). See Norwood v. Crowder, 177 N.C. 469, 99 S.E. 345 (1919); Walsh, *Treatise on Equity* (1930) Sec. 62.

[102] Bradford, etc., R. Co. v. New York, etc., R. Co., 123 N.Y. 316, 25 N.E. 499 (1890). See annotation, Specific performance of contract to lend or borrow money, 41 A.L.R. 357, 361.

[103] See Steward v. Bounds, 167 Wash. 554, 9 P.2d 1112 (1932); Klitten v. Stewart, 125 Wash. 186, 215 P. 513 (1923).

contracts than those to lend money upon agreed security.[104] Indeed, equity will consider that an equitable mortgage or equitable lien exists in favor of the lender or other upon the property which was to be given as security.[105]

Where the contract of the defendant is that he will indemnify, in the sense of reimbursing, the plaintiff for any loss the latter may have to suffer from meeting some demand or paying some claim, the breach of the agreement to indemnify is adequately remedied by an action and recovery at law of the amount due. But where the contract of the defendant is that he will exonerate the plaintiff, in the sense that he will relieve the plaintiff of the necessity of meeting some demand or paying some claim, the sole purpose of the contract is to relieve the plaintiff of the burden of raising the money to meet the demand or claim. The specific thing, compelling the defendant to pay the demand or claim when it accrues, is the only relief that is adequate. Hence, equitable relief is proper.[106]

Sec. 77. Contracts to make particular testamentary disposition or to execute mutual wills.

It is well settled that a valid contract may be made in writing binding a person to make a particular testamentary disposition of his property. Equity, in a proper case, will enforce such an agreement in favor of the promisee by imposing a constructive trust on the property in the hands of the personal representative or heir or other person to whom the property has been transferred in violation of the agreement. The constructive trustee will be required to transfer the property to the promisee. Of course, the promisee must have given consideration or performed services on his part.[107]

---

104 Contract to give surety bond to protect plaintiff from liability for infringement of a patent, see Bosch Magneto Co. v. Rushmore, 85 N.J. Eq. 93, 95 A. 614 (1915).

Agreement to execute chattel mortgage to secure payment of rent, see Shannon v. Cavanaugh, 12 Cal. App. 434, 107 P. 574 (1910).

105 See Walsh, *Treatise on Equity* (1930) Sec. 62.

106 *Ibid.*

Right of seller of stock against buyers who agreed to "indemnify" him against liability for debts of corporation accruing during period when he was stockholder, see Eva v. Andersen, 166 Cal. 420, 137 P. 16 (1913).

107 See Rheinstein, "Critique: Contract to Make a Will," 2 *N.Y.U. L. Rev.* 1224 (1955); Sparks, "Legal Effect of Contracts to Devise or Bequeath Prior to

Even if the contract is not in writing so that it is unenforceable under the Statute of Frauds, equity may grant relief to a promisee who has so changed his position in reliance on the promise that it would be a fraud on him not to allow him such relief.[108] Part performance in the nature of rendition of services has been sufficient to warrant compelling performance of an oral promise to devise.[109]

A promise to leave money is properly enforceable, if at all, in an action at law since a decree in equity would do no more than provide for the recovery of a sum of money. In this regard, proper cognizance must be taken of statutes requiring the filing of claims with the personal representative and refusal thereof by him as a prerequisite to the bringing of an action.[110]

Likewise, in the case of valid contracts to execute mutual wills, if one of the parties fails to execute his will as agreed, the other may sue him for specific performance or, if the party so failing to

---

Death of Promisor," 53 *Mich. L. Rev.* 1, 215 (1954); Sparks, "Enforcement of Contracts to Devise or Bequeath After the Death of Promisor," 39 *Minn. L. Rev.* 1 (1954).

Where testatrix in writing promised to devise certain real property to the plaintiff if the latter would move from New Hampshire to California and live with the testatrix, and plaintiff sold her home in New Hampshire, moved to California and lived with the testatrix, plaintiff was entitled to specific performance of agreement of testatrix. Jones v. Clark, 19 Cal.2d 156, 119 P.2d 731 (1941).

See also McCrillies v. Sutton, 207 Mich. 58, 173 N.W. 333 (1919), noted 33 *Harv. L. Rev.* 835 (1920); "The Contractual Will and Some Consequences of its Breach," 34 *Va. L. Rev.* 590 (1948). Cf. Spinks v. Rice, 187 Va. 730, 47 S.E.2d 424 (1948), noted 34 *Va. L. Rev.* 741 (1948).

[108] Monarco v. Lo Greco, 36 Cal.2d 621, 220 P.2d 737 (1950).

Performance of oral promise did not take oral contract out of operation of Statute of Frauds where services considered capable of measurement in money and recovery on quantum meruit considered adequate, according to Snyder v. Warde, 151 Ohio St. 426, 86 N.E.2d 489 (1949), noted 48 *Mich. L. Rev.* 1043 (1950), which points out that majority of jurisdictions consider the quantum meruit recovery inadequate, either because plaintiff undergoes real hardship to serve promisor which cannot be compensated adequately in money or services are of unique value to promisor because of peculiar filial or domestic relationship.

Part performance and the Statute of Frauds, see *infra*, Sec. 84.

Sale of a business to the promisor for consideration representing partly cash and partly the promisor's oral agreement to devise all the realty owned by her at the time of her death was such a full performance as to constitute "part performance" taking the case out of the Statute of Frauds. Ayres v. Cook, 140 Ohio St. 281, 43 N.E.2d 287 (1942), comment note 18 *U. Cin. L. Rev.* 329 (1949).

[109] Clark v. Atkins, 188 Va. 668, 51 S.E.2d 222 (1949), noted 35 *Va. L. Rev.* 531 (1949).

[110] Morrison v. Land, 169 Cal. 580, 147 P. 259 (1915).

perform has died, the other obtains specific performance by obtaining the imposition of a constructive trust on the one who has received the property which the plaintiff should have had under the contract.[111] As in the case of the promise to leave property by testamentary disposition, an oral contract which should have been written may nevertheless be enforced where the equities demand it.[112]

Sec. 78. Negative contracts or covenants.

So far, we have been mainly concerned with contracts of an affirmative nature, and the compelling of specific performance of the affirmative acts promised or agreed to be done. Equity has generally frowned on the attempt to enforce affirmative contracts indirectly by enjoining the breach of the contract. But where the contract is negative in form, in that the defendant agrees not to perform certain acts, or, as is more commonly the case, is one wherein the defendant agrees to perform affirmative acts and additionally agrees or covenants that he will not perform certain other acts, courts of equity will usually enjoin a breach of the negative promise or covenant, if there is no adequate remedy at law and the contract is fair and reasonable. Certainly this is true where the breach of the negative involves a damage by itself apart from the breach of the affirmative, in that it has a separate significance.[113]

Consideration has already been given to enjoining breach of the negative covenant in contracts for personal services of an unusual or unique nature.[114] Contracts for employment sometimes include negative covenants of other nature, as that the employee

---

111 Caldwell v. Rosenberg, 47 Cal.App.2d 143, 117 P.2d 366 (1941). Compare Notten v. Mensing, 20 Cal.App.2d 694, 67 P.2d 734 (1937), where court expressed doubt over equality of consideration and existence of agreement seems to have been disproved.

See note, Joint or Mutual Wills, 61 *Harv. L. Rev.* 675, at p. 683 (1948); note, "Contract to Make a Will—Anticipatory Breach," 32 *Minn. L. Rev.* 630 (1948); Eagleton, "Joint and Mutual Wills," 15 *Cornell L.Q.* 358 (1930); annotations, Joint and Mutual Wills, 43 A.L.R. 1020, 57 A.L.R. 607, 60 A.L.R. 627, 102 A.L.R. 491.

112 Wilson v. Starbuck, 116 W.Va. 554, 182 S.E. 539, 102 A.L.R. 485 (1935), where contract was oral and taken out of Statute of Frauds by part performance.

113 See Pound, "Progress of the Law—Equity," 33 *Harv. L. Rev.* 420, 440 (1920).

114 See *supra*, Sec. 73.

will not solicit customers of the employee during his employment or for a period of time after its termination, or that the employee will not engage in a similar business after termination of his employment, or that he will not enter the employment of a competitor of the employer after termination of his employment.[115] While unusual or unique nature of the services is not necessarily a requisite to injunctive relief in these situations,[116] it is to be noted that as a prerequisite to equitable relief it must be made to appear that irreparable injury has resulted or will result with reasonable probability.   Injury of such nature is not shown merely by the employee's breach of his covenant not to enter into a competing business or into the employ of a competitor.   The character of his services must have been such that he or his name has obtained a personal hold upon the good will of his employer's business which he will carry with him or such that he has obtained knowledge of confidential matters such as trade secrets the use of which in a competing business will result in irreparable injury.[117] Moreover, the requirements are strict that the contract be fair and reasonable imposing equality of obligation on both parties,[118] and that the restrictions on the exercise of skill and labor elsewhere contain reasonable limitations as to place and period of time, so as not to interfere with public policy or the public interest.[119]

---

[115] See annotations, Validity and enforceability of restrictive covenant in contract of employment, 9 A.L.R. 1456, 20 A.L.R. 861, 29 A.L.R. 1331, 52 A.L.R. 1362, 67 A.L.R. 1002, 98 A.L.R. 964.

[116] Sarco Co. v. Gulliver, 3 N.J. Misc. 641, 129 A. 399 (1925), aff'd 99 N.J. Eq. 432, 131 A. 923 (1926).

[117] Menter Co. v. Brock, 147 Minn. 407, 180 N.W. 553, 20 A.L.R. 857 (1920). Similarly, see Livingston v. Macher, (1947; Del. Ch.) 54 A.2d 169.

[118] Deuerling v. City Baking Co., 155 Md. 280, 141 A. 542, 67 A.L.R. 993 (1928). Restrictive covenant in employment contract was held unreasonable in Welcome Wagon, Inc. v. Morris, 224 F.2d 693 (1955), noted 31 *Notre Dame Law.* 311 (1956).

The employee's breach of a negative covenant not to solicit customers of the employer during the employment or for one year thereafter will not be enjoined where the contract of employment is merely at will and does not obligate the employer to continue the employment for a specified term.   Byram v. Vaughn, 68 F. Supp. 981 (1946), noted 36 *Geo. L.J.* 268 (1948).

Employer not himself performing his obligation, not entitled to enjoin breach of agreement by employee not to solicit employer's customers, see National Overall Dry Cleaning Co. v. Yavner, 321 Mass. 434, 73 N.E.2d 744 (1947).

[119] Deuerling v. City Bakery Co., 155 Md. 280, 141 A. 542, 67 A.L.R. 993 (1928); Sternberg v. O'Brien, 48 N.J. Eq. 370, 22 A. 348 (1891); Noe v. McDermott,

Somewhat analogous to the employee's contract not to engage in competition is the contract of sale of a business and its good will in which the seller covenants that he will not engage in a similar or competitive business. His breach of this covenant is enjoinable, if the restriction as to place or area or as to period of time is fair and reasonable.[120] Occasionally, the situation has arisen that the seller has a relative who was employed in the business and such relative has been required by the buyer to enter into a negative covenant that he will not engage in a similar or competitive business. Whether such a negative covenant is enforceable against such relative may depend upon whether he has received consideration for his covenant. In the absence of any consideration directly consigned to him, it may become important to determine whether he had any ownership interest in the business sold, so as to be entitled to any part of the consideration paid to the seller.[121]

In some jurisdictions, and Massachusetts is an excellent illustra-

---

228 N.C. 242, 45 S.E.2d 121 (1948), noted 32 *Marquette L. Rev.* 282 (1949) (where plaintiff failed to establish a business commensurate with the area restricted).

Where employee agreed not to compete with employer in certain counties of the state for seven years after termination of the contract of employment, the contract of employment was held invalid on the ground its primary purpose was to prevent the employee from quitting his employment, and because the territorial and time restrictions were unreasonable. Ridley v. Krout, 63 Wyo. 252, 180 P.2d 124 (1947), noted 2 *Wyo. L.J.* 71 (1948).

Validity of agreement between employer and employee that latter would pay a weekly sum of money for two years if engaging in competing business, see Stiles v. Reda, 312 Ky. 562, 228 S.W.2d 455 (1950).

"Early common law held such restrictive covenants void prima facie as a restraint of trade, until the Reynolds case (in 1711) distinguished between total and partial restraints of trade. The latter were permissible if based upon good consideration, not contrary to public policy, and ancillary to sale of business or dissolution of a partnership. Today, negative covenants in restraint of employment are treated as a partial restraint of trade. However, there is a growing tendency in the courts to adopt the English distinction between covenants in partial restraint of trade and those in restraint of employment. The latter the courts are reluctant to enforce." Note, 32 *Marquette L. Rev.* 282 (1949).

[120] Diamond Match Co. v. Roeber, 106 N.Y. 473, 13 N.E. 419, 60 Am. Rep. 464 (1887), where covenant was said to be partial and not general, and although practically unlimited as to time, was limited as to area. See Carpenter, "Validity of Contracts not to Compete," 76 *U. Pa. L. Rev.* 244 (1928).

Effect of sale of good will of business in absence of seller's express covenant not to compete, see note 11 *Va. L. Rev.* 392 (1925).

[121] Domurat v. Mazzaccoli, 138 Conn. 327, 84 A.2d 271 (1951).

See Madison v. La Sene, 44 Wash.2d 546, 268 P.2d 1006 (1954), wherein seller later set up his son in business under old name of business. Son was not party to covenant but knew of it. Seller and son were both enjoined.

tion, the courts have attempted to enforce as much of a covenant as appears practicable and reasonable. Or, as it might otherwise be briefly expressed, they have given a partial enforcement to a restraint unreasonable as a whole.[122]

Another form of negative covenant is that found in contracts giving exclusive agencies or exclusive right to handle the goods or products of another. The one receiving the benefit of the agency or of the right to handle the goods and products may covenant that he will not represent others in the same line of business or handle the goods or products of others in the same line of business.[123] Or the one giving the agency or supplying the goods or products may covenant that he will not grant such an agency or supply his goods or products to others in that neighborhood or area.[124]   In either of these situations the contract, of course, must impose mutuality of obligation [125] and not be unlimited or unreasonable as to the area of performance or the period of time.[126]

---

[122] Ceresia v. Mitchell, — Ky. —, 242 S.W.2d 359 (1951); Metropolitan Ice Co. v. Ducas, 291 Mass. 403, 196 N.E. 856 (1935), noted 22 *Va. L. Rev.* 94 (1935).

[123] Associated Oil Co. v. Myers, 217 Cal. 297, 18 P.2d 668 (1933); Standard Fashion Co. v. Siegel-Cooper Co., 157 N.Y. 60, 51 N.E. 408 (1898).

[124] Cramer v. Lewes Sand Co., 15 Del. Ch. 329, 138 A. 78 (1927), noted 26 *Mich. L. Rev.* 217 (1927), agreement to supply sand to plaintiff and not to any other dealer.

[125] Associated Oil Co. v. Myers, 217 Cal. 297, 18 P.2d 668 (1933).

[126] In Long Beach Drug Co. v. United Drug Co., 13 Cal.2d 158, 88 P.2d 698, 89 P.2d 386 (1939), the contract appears to have set no time limit or period of duration of the contract, although the denial of equitable relief was not based on that ground.

CHAPTER 11.

REQUISITES AND CONDITIONS
OF SPECIFIC PERFORMANCE

Sec. 79. Mutuality of remedy or performance.

According to the general rule, the origination of which is usually credited to Fry, English jurist and legal writer, a contract must possess mutuality of remedy, else equity will not enforce it. By mutuality of remedy is meant that each party has a remedy against the other to enforce the contract by specific performance if the need should arise.   Mutuality of remedy, then, is confined to the remedy of specific performance.

The rule has its affirmative or positive application and its negative application.   Under its affirmative application, the plaintiff who seeks specific performance is entitled thereto on the ground that the defendant, if he had been the injured party, would have been entitled to specific performance.   Although the affirmative application has tended to be abandoned or to fall into disuse,[1] several

---

[1] See comment on rule in California, 28 *Cal. L. Rev.* 492 (1940).

illustrations of its application are still observable in the form of settled propositions which seem taken for granted without the necessity of any expressed reason. Thus, in contracts for the sale of realty or other property of unique or unusual nature, the purchaser has long been considered entitled to specific performance, on the ground that he has no other adequate remedy, since only the delivery of the thing contracted for will do him complete justice.[2] Since he has a right to specific performance, under the affirmative application of the mutuality of remedy doctrine, the vendor is likewise entitled to specific performance, frequently regardless of the fact that he may have an adequate remedy at law by way of damages.[3] In the course of time, it seems to have become accepted that the vendor, as well as the purchaser, is entitled to specific performance of a contract for the sale of realty and the rule is frequently so stated as a matter of course.[4] Another illustration is frequently observable in the case of parol contracts for the sale of realty. Where the purchaser has done acts of part performance that would entitle him to have specific performance, many courts have held that by reason of such acts of part performance by the purchaser, the vendor is unquestionably entitled to specific performance, although he is actually being allowed to rely on the change of position by the other party.[5]

Under the negative application of the mutuality of remedy rule, the plaintiff, regardless of the equities in his favor, is denied specific performance on the ground that the defendant, if he had been the wronged party, would not have been entitled to specific performance but would have had to be satisfied with a legal remedy.[6] A common illustration of this has been the agreement of the plaintiff to render personal services in return for realty or some interest therein. Where the plaintiff has not completed or substantially completed performance of the services he has been denied specific

---

[2] See Sec. 70, *supra*.

[3] Notice application to vendor in contract for sale of a patent. Cogent v. Gibson, (1864) 33 Beav. 557, 55 Eng. Rep. 485.

[4] See Sec. 70, *supra*.
It is not necessarily true, of course, that the vendor's remedy at law is adequate. See Olszewski v. Sardynski, 316 Mass. 715, 56 N.E.2d 607 (1944).

[5] See *infra*, Sec. 85.

[6] See statement of rule in Poultry Producers of Southern California v. Barlow, 189 Cal. 278, 208 P. 93 (1922) (although such rules would not now be applicable to a co-operative marketing contract in California).

performance on the ground that it would not lie against him,[7] and this has been true even where the plaintiff has been willing to complete performance of his services or has been prevented from completion by the wrongful conduct of the defendant.[8]

The rule has also been much modified in some jurisdictions which still profess to follow it.   Thus, although under the doctrine's original form, the mutuality of remedy must exist at the time the contract is entered into,[9] it is now frequently considered sufficient if the mutuality exists at the time the suit is brought,[10] although, more accurately, it would seem that the mutuality should exist at the time for performance.[11]

Since the flat application of the rule or doctrine frequently leads to absurd results and disregard of other equitable principles, it has been subject to frequent exceptions even where followed.[12]   And

---

[7] Personal service contracts unenforceable, see *supra*, Sec. 73.

Agreement to marry in return for conveyances of property, etc., see Wilson v. Nelson, 130 Neb. 1, 262 N.W. 433 (1935).

[8] See Wakeham v. Barker, 82 Cal. 46, 22 P. 1131 (1889), followed in Moklofsky v. Moklofsky, 79 Cal.App.2d 259, 179 P.2d 628 (1947) (wherein lower court had decreed conveyance if promised services were performed).

[9] Norris v. Fox, 45 F. 406 (1891); Bracy v. Miller, 169 Ark. 1115, 278 S.W. 41, 43 A.L.R. 114 (1926).

[10] Cavanna v. Brooks, 97 N.J. Eq. 329, 127 A. 247, 37 A.L.R. 361 (1925); Gottlaub v. Cohen, 139 N.J. Eq. 323, 51 A.2d 254 (1947), noted 21 *Temple L.Q.* 149 (1947). In California, see comment, 28 *Cal. L. Rev.* 492 (1940).

[11] Notice that, in Bracy v. Miller, *supra*, note 9, it is pointed out that mutuality did not exist either at the time of making the contract or at the time for performance.

[12] An important exception is that of a contract for the sale of realty under a Statute of Frauds providing that the contract is valid if signed by the party sought to be charged.   Although the plaintiff had not signed so as to have been subject to suit for specific performance, he may seek to enforce the contract against the defendant who signed.   The reason given is that the plaintiff by bringing the suit adopts the contract and obligates himself under it, and thus makes the remedy mutual.

Another exception is the conditional or optional contract.   If the party to whom the offer is made accepts within the time set, there is a mutual contract which he may then enforce, although he himself could not have been proceeded against for specific performance prior to his acceptance.

Still another exception is that of the infant who enters into a contract.   If he elects to enforce the contract upon reaching his majority, he may do so, according to one view, although he could not have been subjected to specific performance.   A close case of some interest is that of Bracy v. Miller, 169 Ark. 1115, 278 S.W. 41, 43 A.L.R. 114 (1925), in which the infant came of age while his suit for specific performance was pending.   He was, nevertheless, denied specific performance.   But where an infant had performed on his part at time he sued, see Ashberry v. Mitchell, 121 Va. 276, 93 S.E. 638, L.R.A. 1918 A 785 (1917).   Attention must be given in these cases to whether the court requires mutuality at the time the contract is entered into or only at time of suit.

where, the contract being bi-lateral, the plaintiff has fully performed or substantially performed he may obtain specific performance, assuming the equities are in his favor, although prior
to his performance he could not have been compelled to perform.[13]

In many jurisdictions, nowadays, the rule is discredited.[14] As
remarked by one court: "Equity enforces specific performance
where there is no adequate remedy at law. This is the ground
of this branch of equity jurisdiction, and it is not consistent with
the test of mutuality of remedy. . . . The mutuality required is
that which is necessary for creating a contract enforceable on
both sides in some manner, but not necessarily enforceable on
both sides by specific performance."[15] In other words, the mutuality now required is that both parties be mutually obligated
under the contract to perform acts of sufficiently equivalent
weight.[16] So long as there is mutuality of obligation to perform

---

[13] Jones v. Clark, 19 Cal.2d 156, 119 P.2d 731 (1941); Thurber v. Meves, 119 Cal.
35, 40 P. 1063, 51 P. 536 (1897).

[14] See Thomas, "The Inequity of Mutuality of Remedy," 11 *Baylor L. Rev.* 54
(1950).

"If there ever was a rule that mutuality of remedy existing, not merely at the
time of the decree, but at the time of the formation of the contract, is a condition of equitable relief, it has been so qualified by exceptions that, viewed as a
precept of general validity, it has ceased to be a rule today. . . . What equity
exacts today as a condition of relief is the assurance that the decree, if rendered,
will operate without injustice or oppression either to plaintiff or to defendant."
Epstein v. Gluckin, 233 N.Y. 490, 135 N.E. 861 (1922), per Cardozo, J.

See note, "Mutuality of Remedy in Federal Courts," 36 *Geo. L.J.* 220.

[15] Eckstein v. Downing, 64 N.H. 248, 9 A. 626, 10 Am.St.Rep. 404 (1887).

Right to equitable relief of specific performance depends not upon mutuality
of remedy but the inadequacy of the remedy at law. G. W. Baker Machine Co.
v. U. S. Fire Apparatus Co., 11 Del. Ch. 386, 97 A. 613 (1916), noted 15 *Mich. L.
Rev.* 87 (1916).

The *Restatement of Contracts*, Sec. 372 (1), states that fact that remedy of
specific performance is not available to one party is not a sufficient reason for
refusing it to the other party.

[16] There is a definite lack of mutuality of obligation to perform where one party,
upon notice, can terminate the contract while the other continues to be bound
without such option of revocation. If the defendant can so terminate, specific
performance will be denied, since it has little effective purpose. If the plaintiff
can so terminate, it may be inequitable to order the defendant to perform a contract that the plaintiff can terminate upon notice, although, of course, relief
by way of specific performance can be conditioned on continued performance by
the plaintiff if one disregards the fact that this does nothing more than continue
the obligation of the defendant to a contract that may be disavowed by the
plaintiff when he chooses. Certainly, distinction is to be made between contracts
which allow a party to terminate upon a few days notice and contracts where
termination follows only upon three months notice or six months notice or some
such period. In the latter situation the party may be considered to be obligated

on both sides, with an appropriate remedy available to each party, there need not be identity of remedy in the form of specific performance.[17] The plaintiff must have properly performed all acts so far required of him,[18] as well as indicating his good faith in continuing performance of all that is still required of him.[19] If he has not as yet been required to perform, he must show that he is ready, able, and willing to perform his obligation when the time of performance arrives.[20] If the inability of the plaintiff to perform has resulted from the wrongful conduct of the defendant, the defendant should not have available to him any claim of lack of mutuality of performance.[21]

It is commonly considered now that a decree of specific performance may be entered against a defendant, conditioned on the continued performance by the plaintiff of those matters as to which he is obligated,[22] although account must be taken of the

---

to perform for a sufficiently long enough period to be of substantial value and so constitute consideration of equivalent weight for the obligation assumed by the other party. See, *e.g.*, Associated Oil Co. v. Myers, 217 Cal. 297, 18 P.2d 668 (1933).

This definite lack of mutuality of obligation has frequently been held true of professional baseball players' contracts, which bind the player but allow of termination by the employer on short notice. See note, "Baseball and the Law," 32 *Va. L. Rev.* 1164, at 1168 (1946). Compare to the contrary the oft-cited case of Philadelphia Ball Club v. Lajoie, 202 Pa. 210, 51 A. 973 (1902).

Contracts terminable by one party only, see annotation, 8 A.L.R.2d 1208.

Adequacy or inadequacy of consideration, see *infra*, Sec. 95.

[17] Zelleken v. Lynch, 80 Kan. 746, 104 P. 563, 46 L.R.A.N.S. 659 (1909), noted 23 *Harv. L. Rev.* 294 (1910).

[18] Conditions requisite to specific performance, see *infra*, Sec. 80.

Right of purchaser in default under sale of goods contract to recover down payment, see note, 31 *Marquette L. Rev.* 295 (1948).

[19] Partial performance and continued willingness to perform on part of plaintiff seeking to enforce defendant's agreement to support and educate plaintiff's child. Weinberger v. Van Hessen, 260 N.Y. 294, 183 N.E. 429 (1932).

[20] When a vendor sues for specific performance of an executory contract of sale or brings action for the unpaid purchase price (considered the equivalent of suit for specific performance by the majority of courts), he should take proper steps to show his willingness to perform, as by tender of the deed before suit and by deposit of the deed in court upon suit. See Fairlawn Heights Co. v. Theis, 133 Ohio St. 387, 14 N.E. 2d 1 (1938).

[21] Cf. Wakeham v. Barker, 82 Cal. 46, 22 P. 1131 (1889).

[22] See, *e.g.*, Montgomery Traction Co. v. Montgomery Light & Water Co., 229 F. 672 (1916); Weinberger v. Hessen, 260 N.Y. 294, 183 N.E. 429 (1932), noted 46 *Harv. L. Rev.* 724 (1933) (agreement to support and educate infant); Elk Refining Co. v. Falling Rock Cannel Coal Co., 92 W.Va. 479, 115 S.E. 431 (1922).

And see *Rest. Contracts*, Sec. 372. In Sec. 373, it is pointed out that specific performance may be refused if the court is not satisfied that performance by the plaintiff is well secured.

fact that some few jurisdictions still cling to the old view that it is impracticable for an equity court to supervise a continuous series of acts over a considerable period of time.[23]

Sec. 80.   Conditions requisite to performance.

The question of conditions requisite to obtaining specific performance frequently becomes involved in learned discussions of conditions precedent, express conditions, conditions implied in law or fact, constructive conditions, and the like.   A perhaps oversimplified interpretation of the situation boils it down to the question of whether the plaintiff has performed or is performing the obligations imposed on him by the contract so as to be equitably entitled to demand that the defendant perform his obligations under the contract.[24]   Before one party can compel another to perform he must have performed himself all obligations imposed upon him as a prerequisite to performance by the other.[25]   If his obligations are to be performed concurrently with those of the defendant or after performance by the defendant, the complainant must show that he is ready, and able, and willing to carry out his obligations, in other words that he is himself possessed of good faith.[26]

Sec. 81.   —Marketable title.

Under an agreement to convey realty, the law implies, in the absence of any contrary stipulation, that a good title in fee simple is to be conveyed.[27]   By this is meant what is generally termed a marketable title, one free from reasonable doubt, although not one free from every doubt.[28]   Therefore an agreement for the sale of

---

[23] See, *e.g.*, Henderson v. Coon, 244 Ala. 324, 13 So.2d 564 (1943); Long Beach Drug Co. v. United Drug Co., 13 Cal.2d 158, 88 P.2d 698, 89 P.2d 386 (1939); Edelen v. Samuels, 126 Ky. 295, 103 S.W. 360 (1907).

[24] Mutuality of obligation, see *supra*, Sec. 79.

[25] Requirement that vendor to have transferable title by date set or contract to be a nullity, see Baldwin v. McGrath, 90 App. Div. 199, 85 N.Y.S. 735 (1904).

Necessity for compliance with provisions as to exercise of option to obtain renewal of lease, see F. B. Fountain Co. v. Stein, 97 Conn. 619, 118 A. 47, 27 A.L.R. 976 (1922), noted 32 *Yale L.J.* 408 (1923).

[26] See *supra*, Sec. 79.

[27] Easton v. Montgomery, 90 Cal. 307, 27 P. 280 (1891); Wallach v. Riverside Bank, 206 N.Y. 434, 100 N.E. 50 (1912).

[28] Schul v. Clapp, 154 Kan. 372, 118 P.2d 570 (1941); Norwegian Evangelical Free Church v. Milhauser, 252 N.Y. 186, 169 N.E. 134 (1929), per Cardozo, C. J.

realty is not incomplete because it omits to state the nature of the title to be conveyed.[29]   A vendor who fails or refuses to offer a marketable title has not met his obligation under the contract or performed on his part the condition precedent to the right to demand performance by the purchaser.

According to the view in many jurisdictions, a title obtained by adverse possession is not a marketable title,[30] although in other jurisdictions this view has been qualified to require that such a title, to be unmarketable, must depend upon a long and difficult investigation of the facts and that if the facts are sufficiently clear such title must be accepted.[31]   If the title by adverse possession has been confirmed by judicial declaration, as in a suit to quiet title or the like, it would seem to constitute a marketable title.

And according to the better view, the offer of a quitclaim deed to the purchaser is not a sufficient compliance with the contract on the part of the vendor.   However, the agreement by the purchaser to accept a quitclaim deed is an agreement to accept such title as the vendor has and amounts to a stipulation that a marketable title free from reasonable doubt is not expected.[32]   There is authority to the contrary, evidently on the theory that by the quitclaim deed the vendor agrees to convey such title as he has and that to the extent that he has title it is free from reasonable doubt; hence the purchaser is said to have the right to object that a marketable title is not offered even though he has agreed to accept a quitclaim deed.[33]

Since the contract usually provides that on or by a certain date the vendor is to make a conveyance or tender a deed, that is, furnish a marketable title, it is generally said that he has until such "closing day" or "law day" to complete or perfect his title, and that the purchaser may not object until that day that the title is not marketable.[34]   While some courts have at times made a somewhat unbending application of this rule,[35] it is equitably subject

29 Merwin, *Principles of Equity* (1895) 401.

30 Simis v. McElroy, 160 N.Y. 156, 54 N.E. 674 (1899).

31 See Conley v. Finn, 171 Mass. 70, 50 N.E. 460, 68 Am.St.Rep. 399 (1898).

32 See McManus v. Blackmarr, 47 Minn. 331, 50 N.W. 230 (1891).

33 Wallach v. Riverside Bank, 206 N.Y. 434, 100 N.E. 50 (1912).

34 See Walsh, *Treatise on Equity* (1930), Sec. 75.

35 Formerly, this seems to have been true in California. See, *e.g.*, Hanson v. Fox, 155 Cal. 106, 99 P. 489, 132 Am.St.Rep. 72, 20 L.R.A.N.S. 338 (1909).

to a good deal of qualification. For instance, if the defect in the title is one which in the nature of things cannot be removed by any ordinary method of business negotiation, the purchaser need not wait until closing day to object that the vendor does not have marketable title.[36]   Or if the vendor, while the contract is executory and in violation thereof, sells the property to a third person, in view of his wrongful or fraudulent conduct the vendor has no equitable ground for claiming that he has until closing day to perfect his title.   It is not reasonable to suppose that the vendor can go into the open market and repurchase the property before closing day or, in fact, that he has any such intention.[37]

Speaking of fraud, if the vendor misrepresents the nature or extent of his title at the time of negotiating or entering into the contract, he is not equitably entitled to have until closing day to perfect or complete his title.[38]   Of course, it is necessary to distinguish the situation where the purchaser knows of the defect or lack in the vendor's title but enters into the contract on the understanding that the title will be perfected by closing day,[39] as well as the situation where, knowing of the defect or lack, the purchaser nevertheless agrees to purchase such title as the vendor has.

Under the original form of the doctrine of mutuality of remedy, that at the time of entering into the contract a remedy by way of specific performance must exist in favor of the defendant, in order to allow of specific performance in favor of the complainant, it will be seen that if the vendor does not have title at the time of making of the contract, he would be barred by lack of mutuality from himself obtaining specific performance.[40]   However, in jurisdic-

---

[36] Prentice v. Erskine, 164 Cal. 446, 129 P. 585 (1913) (public servitude).

[37] Brimmer v. Salisbury, 167 Cal. 522, 140 P. 30 (1914); Fort Payne, etc., Co. v. Webster, 163 Mass. 134, 39 N.E. 786 (1895).

In the somewhat unusual case of In re Vaughan's Estate, 156 Misc. 577, 282 N.Y.S. 214 (1935), aff'd 248 App. Div. 730, 289 N.Y.S. 825 (1936), noted 49 *Harv. L. Rev.* 651 (1936), the vendor did reacquire title before closing day and tendered such title. Although having knowledge that the vendor had transferred title to another, the purchaser never took any step to disavow the contract on that ground before closing day. Specific performance was granted to the vendor.

[38] See Henderson v. Miller, 119 Wash. 362, 205 P. 1 (1922).

[39] See Caplan v. Buckner, 123 Md. 590, 91 A. 481 (1914); Chappus v. Lucke, 246 Mich. 272, 234 N.W. 232 (1929).

[40] Freeman v. Anders, 103 N.J. Eq. 430, 143 A. 550 (1928).

Mutuality of remedy, see *supra*, Sec. 79.

tions where the doctrine of mutuality of remedy is discredited or modified, this lack of title, where known by the purchaser at the time of entering into the contract, would not in itself defeat specific performance in favor of the vendor.[41]

Although the vendor may reasonably be charged with knowledge of defects in his title and expected to cure or remove them by closing day, it is advisable for the purchaser, upon discovering them before closing day, to call them to the attention of the vendor within a reasonable time, either as a basis of his declaring a rescission or in order to allow their cure or removal. Otherwise, the court may well suspect that the purchaser has saved up his knowledge until closing day to provide himself with a ground for repudiating the contract if he should at that time feel that it is inconvenient to him to carry out the contract.[42] Indeed, it is frequently a principle of law or, at least, a local custom that the purchaser has a duty to give reasonable notice to the vendor of such defects that the purchaser has discovered.[43]

Frequent reference has been made to the right of the purchaser to object to the title offered as being unmarketable. This may take the form of successfully defending against an action for specific performance brought against him by the vendor; [44] or by suit against the vendor to rescind the contract and to recover any consideration so far paid, plus expenses in searching the title; [45] or by treating the contract as rescinded and suing at law to recover any consideration paid by him, plus expenses of searching the title; [46] or by suit against the vendor for specific performance and joining as parties those whose claims or interests render the vendor's title unmarketable, where it is possible to settle or dispose of those

[41] Finks v. Fitzpatrick, (1932; Tex. Com. App.) 48 S.W.2d 593, noted 11 *Tex. L. Rev.* 237.

[42] See Easton v. Montgomery, 90 Cal. 307, 27 P. 280 (1891); Higgins v. Eagleton, 155 N.Y. 466, 50 N.E. 287 (1898).

[43] Bean v. Browne, 202 Ky. 215, 259 S.W. 47 (1924); Moot v. Business Men's Invest. Ass'n, 157 N.Y. 201, 92 N.E. 1 (1898); Groskin v. Knight, 290 Pa. 274, 138 A. 843 (1927), noted 76 *U. Pa. L. Rev.* 760 (1928).

[44] Lynbrook Gardens v. Ullman, 291 N.Y. 472, 53 N.E.2d 353 (1943), noted 57 *Harv. L. Rev.* 575 (1944).

[45] Easton v. Montgomery, 90 Cal. 307, 27 P. 280 (1891).

[46] Moore v. Williams, 115 N.Y. 586, 22 N.E. 233, 12 Am.St.Rep. 844, 5 L.R.A. 654 (1889).

claims and convey to the purchaser a marketable title as a result; [47] or, conceivably, to sue the vendor for specific performance and to require him to institute such litigation as will perfect the title; [48] or to sue the vendor for specific performance to the extent that he can make a conveyance, with an abatement or deduction in the purchase price.[49]   Whether damages, other than return of the consideration paid and the expenses of a title search, are recoverable by the purchaser is a matter of dispute in this country.   Under the so-called English rule, followed in some of our states, no recovery may be had other than the amount of consideration paid and expenses of a title search, so long as the vendor has acted in good faith.   However, in a majority of our states, the operation of the good faith rule is denied and the purchaser may recover damages for the loss of the bargain.[50]

Assuming that the equities favor the vendor, and the court has all indispensable parties before it in a suit by the vendor for specific performance, so that it can determine and settle the rights and claims of all those having an interest in the property, no facts being in dispute, and see that the purchaser gets a marketable title, the court may order specific performance.   But if any persons having an interest under a hostile claim of title are not parties to the action, so that the court's decree cannot affect them, the purchaser will not be compelled to accept the title if such claims subject the title to reasonable doubt.[51]   In this connection, it will be recalled that if the realty is within the court's jurisdiction, it may have jurisdic-

---

[47] Consider Miller v. Dyer, 20 Cal.2d 526, 127 P.2d 901, 141 A.L.R. 1428 (1942).

[48] See Henschke v. Young, 224 Minn. 339, 28 N.W.2d 766 (1947).

Discussion of this means of procedure, see interesting comment, 47 *Mich. L. Rev.* 102 (1948).   The writer points out the somewhat analogous situation that, if the vendor has a contract to buy the land he has contracted to deliver to the purchaser, the purchaser can, in a suit for specific performance, compel him to exercise his right so as to be able to perform.   In this respect, consider Miller v. Dyer, 20 Cal.2d 526, 127 P.2d 901, 141 A.L.R. 1428 (1942).

[49] See *infra*, Sec. 83.

[50] See annotation, Measure of recovery by vendee under executory contract for purchase of real property where vendor is unable or refuses to convey, 48 A.L.R. 12, at p. 36.

Professors Glenn and Redden, in their *Cases and Materials on Equity* (1946) 502, 503, term the English rule the majority rule.   The only exceptions thereto are stated to be where the vendor wilfully defaults or contracts to sell knowing he has imperfect title.

[51] Barger v. Gery, 64 N.J. Eq. 263, 53 A. 483 (1902).

tion to proceed in rem upon service by publication upon indispensable parties.[52]   However, the vendor cannot sue the purchaser for specific performance and therein require him to await the outcome of litigation planned or pending on the vendor's part to clear or perfect his title.   This would make time of performance uncertain and would bind the purchaser without any assurance that the vendor would be successful in his litigation so as to be able to perform.[53]

Sec. 82.   —Time as of the essence of the contract.

The phrase "Time is of the essence of the contract" and its interpretation or application have resulted in much confusion.   As pointed out by one court, it is not always clear what courts and text writers mean who use this phrase.[54] The rule, as worked out by many courts, is that if time is of the essence of the contract, the failure of the party to perform on or by the time set will definitely and arbitrarily deprive him of the right to obtain specific performance.   But if time is not of the essence of the contract, the court may consider the equities of the parties, particularly the equities in favor of the one who did not perform on time, and nevertheless grant him specific performance if it would appear equitable to do so.   This still leaves us with the question of when is time of the essence of the contract and when is it not.   At law, of course, time is always of the essence of the contract.[55]   There is no reason, in one sense, why it is any less so in equity.   It has been pointed out that every part of a contract is of its essence; whenever an act is required to be done within a specified time, time is always of the essence of the contract.[56]   Apparently what is meant by the equity courts which have developed the rule already set out is that if time is not expressly declared to be of the essence, or is not to be implied from the contract to have been so intended, the court may grant or deny specific performance as the equities of the case warrant.

---

[52] See *supra*, Sec. 7.
[53] See comment, 47 *Mich. L. Rev.* 102 (1948).
[54] Richmond v. Robinson, 12 Mich. 193 (1864).
   Discussion of rule in English law, see P. Moerlin Fox, "Time Shall Be of the Essence," 25 *Australian L.J.* 106 (1951).
[55] See Norrington v. Wright, 115 U.S. 188, 29 L. Ed. 366 (1885).
[56] Richmond v. Robinson, 12 Mich. 193 (1864) (suit for specific performance).

But if time is expressly declared to be of the essence of the contract, in those words, or is to be implied as so intended from the contract, by reason thereof specific performance can in no circumstances be granted.[57] Such a strict or literal application of the term may produce a definitely inequitable result.[58]

While some contracts may provide for performance of acts "within a reasonable time" or some equivalent expression,[59] ordinarily contracts provide for performance "on" a certain date or dates or "on or before" a certain date or dates. Should a party to the contract be deprived of specific performance if he has not himself performed on or by a date required of him? Offhand, it might well be said that if he has not himself performed the act or acts required of him on or by the date or dates required, he is not equitably entitled to demand performance from the other party. But arbitrarily to take this view might involve a disregard of the equities in his favor, a thing which a court of equity does not or certainly should not do. If his failure to perform on or by a required date results from circumstances beyond his control or is otherwise excusable, as where he has not been grossly negligent, wilful, or fraudulent in a breach of duty, and he offers performance so soon thereafter that no harm results to the other party or any harm to the other is slight and compensation therefor is offered, it may well produce a harsh and inequitable result to declare a forfeiture or loss of his rights under the contract. Particularly, where the contract is in course of performance or has been substantially performed and he has previously performed properly and has materially committed himself, the result may be harsh and inequitable if consideration is not given to the equities in his favor. From the very nature of equity itself and because equity abhors forfeitures, courts of equity should give considera-

---

[57] A forfeiture provision in the contract, if performance does not occur at the date set therefor, has usually been considered to indicate intention that time shall be of the essence. See Ballantine, "Forfeiture for Breach of Contract," 5 *Minn. L. Rev.* 329 (1921).

[58] See, *e.g.*, Heckard v. Sayre, 34 Ill. 142 (1864), where purchaser had paid two-thirds of the purchase price but was a week late in tendering the final installment. He presented what seems to have been a reasonable excuse and no loss of consequence resulted to the vendor.

[59] Definiteness of such contracts so as to permit of enforceability, see *supra*, Sec. 69.

tion to the foregoing matters. Indeed, such grounds as delay resulting from accident, fraud, surprise, or mistake have been recognized,[60] and even those of mere neglect where the delay has been slight, the loss to the other party small and compensable and compensation is tendered, and not to grant the relief would result in such hardship as to make it unconscionable to enforce literally the provision as to time.[61] If it be found that there is no reasonable excuse for the failure to perform when required or, even though there be a reasonable excuse, to grant specific performance would do an injustice to the party against whom such relief is sought, specific performance should be denied. The majority of modern cases which refuse equitable relief against default are usually those in which the contract is executory at the time of the default and the defaulter has not committed himself to the point where undue hardship results to him from equity's refusal to aid him.[62]

Many courts determine the right to specific performance on the basis of the equities involved.[63] Even courts which subscribe to the rule previously set out will consider the equities where they find that time is not of the essence.[64] Frequently, where time is

---

[60] A perhaps oversimplified illustration is that in which the purchaser is to make a final payment on a certain day. He sets out on that day with the money but is set upon and robbed. On the day following, having recovered sufficiently from his injuries and having raised another sum of money, he tenders it to the vendor and requests performance. The vendor has suffered no loss from the day's delay or his loss is slight and compensable. Would it be equitable to deny the purchaser specific performance?

[61] Notice that while an option to renew a lease may present the situation of time being of the essence, nevertheless the circumstances of the particular lessee may be such that he suffers great hardship if denied relief from an excusable failure or neglect to exercise the option strictly within the time provided. See F. B. Fountain Co. v. Stein, 97 Conn. 619, 118 A. 47, 27 A.L.R. 976 (1922), noted 32 *Yale L.J.* 409 (1923).

[62] See Edgerton v. Peckham, 10 N.J. Eq. 115, 64 Am. Dec. 445 (1854), which presents a good analysis and expresses a "modern" viewpoint; Baldwin v. McGrath, 90 App. Div. 199, 85 N.Y.S. 735 (1904), aff'd 113 App. Div. 902, 98 N.Y.S. 1096 (1906), 188 N.Y. 606, 81 N.E. 1159 (1907).

Even in the case of executory contracts, a technical delay as of one day, for instance, may not in the circumstances warrant a loss of rights under the contract. See, *e.g.*, Breitman v. Gattman, 88 Cal.App.2d 124, 198 P.2d 311 (1948); King v. Connors, 222 Mass. 261, 110 N.E. 289 (1915).

[63] Richmond v. Robinson, 12 Mich. 193 (1864).

[64] Time not expressly stipulated in the contract to be of the essence of the contract and declared by the court not to have been intended to be of the essence. There was only a one-day delay in tendering performance. King v. Connors, 222 Mass. 261, 110 N.E. 289 (1915).

expressly declared to be of the essence but the equities favor the one seeking specific performance, such courts escape an inequitable result by blandly stating that the parties did not really mean what they said in the contract or that, despite what the contract says, time is not of the essence.[65]

It is unfortunate that such an arbitrary rule has been followed, a rule which on its face takes no account of the equities involved. Frequently in cases which deny relief on the ground that time is of the essence and the party seeking relief did not perform on time, an examination of the facts shows a wilful and inexcusable delay.[66] It would certainly be better to put the denial on that ground rather than on the ground that time is of the essence.

It is often stated that although time is not of the essence of a particular contract, it becomes of the essence where there is a failure to perform on time and the other party has overlooked this failure by granting an extension of time in which to perform.[67] Actually what we have is fair and equitable conduct by the party not in default. He makes no effort to take any technical advantage of the default but generously gives an additional time in which to perform. If the defaulting party again fails to perform, within this extension of time, he has little to offer in his own favor from an equitable standpoint. In many states, by statute it is required that the party not in default give written notice to the

---

[65] Steele v. Branch, 40 Cal. 3 (1870).

According to Cal. Civ Code, Sec. 1492, as it qualifies Sec. 3275, equitable relief is available only where time is not of the essence. Nevertheless, even where time is of the essence, it is indicated that in exceptional cases the court may grant relief. Henck v. Lake Hemet Water Co., 9 Cal.2d 136, 69 P.2d 849 (1937).

The effect on the rights of a defaulting vendee and the clarification in California of some of the confusion between statutes and decisions, accomplished by Barkis v. Scott, 34 Cal.2d 116, 208 P.2d 367 (1949), is discussed in 37 *Cal. L. Rev.* 704 (1949).

[66] In vendor's suit to quiet his title, the court declared that where time is stipulated to be of the essence of the contract, such provision will be enforced. However, the facts showed that the purchaser had been in arrears in payments for over two years when the suit was filed. Fresno Irrig. Farms Co. v. Canupis, 39 Cal. App. 134, 178 P. 300 (1918). Similarly, in Glock v. Howard & Wilson Colony Co., 123 Cal. 1, 55 P. 713, 69 Am.St.Rep. 17, 43 L.R.A. 199 (1898), the purchaser, after his first default of 3½ years and more than 6 months after default in final payment due, tendered the money and demanded performance. On the vendor's refusal, he brought action to recover the payments already made. Relief was denied.

[67] Garcin v. Pennsylvania Furnace Co., 186 Mass. 405, 71 N.E. 793 (1904).

defaulting party of his intention to terminate the contract if the defaulting party does not perform within an additional period, set by the statute.[68]

Time is also said to be of the essence of contracts relating to property speculative in character with fluctuating values.[69]   Here again, it can be seen that it is the equities which are involved which really determine the result.

Where a contract is terminated by a default in performance this should not involve a forfeiture of all sums paid prior to the default by the defaulting party.   Even though the contract provides for the retention of all sums paid prior to default, as liquidated damages or the like, it would not seem equitable to allow the other party to retain any amount in excess of the damages he suffers.[70] However, the cases are in conflict on this point and in many jurisdictions it seems accepted that the non-defaulting party is entitled to retain all of the sum paid by the defaulting party, where the contract so provides, or even without the contract expressly providing.[71]

Sec. 83.   Partial performance with abatement or compensation.

A vendor must be able to deliver what he has agreed to sell, or equity will not compel the purchaser to accept it.   Nevertheless, if the vendor can perform substantially what he has agreed to do, failing only in some slight or immaterial matter, equity will enforce the contract against the purchaser if reasonable compensation can be made to him for the deficiency.[72]   Thus, if the con-

---

[68] See Selover, etc., Co. v. Walsh, 226 U.S. 112, 33 S.Ct. 69 (1912); Kryger v. Wilson, 242 U.S. 171, 37 S.Ct. 34 (1916).

[69] Skookum Oil Co. v. Thomas, 162 Cal. 539, 123 P. 363 (1912); Garcin v. Pennsylvania Furnace Co., 186 Mass. 405, 71 N.E. 793 (1912).

[70] See Pierce v. Staub, 78 Conn. 459, 62 A. 760 (1906); Garcin v. Pennsylvania Furnace Co., 186 Mass. 405, 71 N.E. 793 (1904) (where amount to be retained was proper liquidated damages).

Defaulting vendee may recover part payments but only to the extent that he can prove they exceed vendor's damages.   Baffa v. Johnson, 35 Cal.2d 36, 216 P.2d 13 (1950).   And see note, 37 *Cal. L. Rev.* 704 (1949), to Barkis v. Scott, 34 Cal.2d 116, 208 P.2d 367 (1949).

[71] See annotation, Right of vendee in default to recover back money paid on the contract and withheld by vendor as forfeited, 31 A.L.R.2d 8.

[72] In Van Blarcom v. Hopkins, 63 N.J. Eq. 466, 52 A. 147 (1902), the dimensions

tract is for a certain estate and the vendor fails to make out a good title to a very small part of it and that part is not material to the possession and enjoyment of the whole, for the purposes for which the purchaser desires the property, specific performance with compensation or with abatement in the purchase price will be decreed against the purchaser.[73]   However, this has been described as a hazardous doctrine,[74] since it may force upon the purchaser a contract which he never made and amount to a court of equity writing a new contract for him.   Accordingly, the doctrine should not be applied except where it is clear that the variation or difference is slight and that it has no injurious effect upon the purchaser.[75]

Where the variation or difference is describable as substantial, the advantage lies entirely with the purchaser.   He has the election either to rescind the contract and receive back any consideration he has so far parted with [76] or he may compel the vendor to convey such title as he has, with a deduction or abatement in the purchase price, usually on a proportionate basis.[77]   Thus, where

of the lot contracted to be sold were only slightly less than called for by the contract, the purchaser was familiar with the physical lines of the lot, and nothing indicated its insufficiency for his purposes.

[73] Tolchester Beach Imp. Co. v. Boyd, 161 Md. 269, 156 A. 795, 81 A.L.R. 895 (1931).

[74] See Merwin, *Principles of Equity* (1895) 415.

[75] See note, "Specific Performance with Compensation," 40 *Harv. L. Rev.* 476 (1927); annotation, Right of vendor to specific performance with abatement from purchase price where he is unable to perform as to part of property, 81 A.L.R. 900 (1932).

In Friede v. Pool, 217 Minn. 332, 14 N.W.2d 454 (1944), noted 13 *Fordh. L. Rev.* 259 (1944), the deficiency in quantity of the land was slight but the deficiency was such as to seriously interfere with the possession, enjoyment, and use of the land for farming purposes.

[76] Louisville & Nashville R. Co. v. Fuson, 203 Ky. 708, 262 S.W. 186 (1924).

[77] Moore v. Gariglietti, 288 Ill. 143, 81 N.E. 826, 10 Ann. Cas. 560 (1907).

Determining and deducting value of wife's inchoate right of dower from purchase price, see O'Malley v. Miller, 148 Wis. 393, 134 N.W. 840 (1912); note, 9 *Cornell L.Q.* 470 (1924); note, 29 *Minn. L. Rev.* 280 (1945). In some states specific performance will be decreed only upon payment of all the consideration, and no deduction will be made for the value of the wife's inchoate dower right. See Cowan v. Kane, 211 Ill. 572, 71 N.E. 1097 (1904). Modification in New Jersey, see Stein v. Francis, 91 N.J. Eq. 205, 109 A. 737 (1919). In community property states where dower does not exist, no such problem can arise with relation to the vendor's separate property. Since the community property is owned equally by husband and wife, and usually the wife's signature to a conveyance or transfer of community realty is required, no contract to sell signed only by the husband can be enforced, even as to his half of the property. See de Funiak, *Principles of Community Property* (1943) Secs. 113, 117, and Supplement thereto.

Where there is a destruction of improvement on the property, see *infra*, Sec. 93.

there is a material or substantial variation, although the vendor can compel no performance by the purchaser, the purchaser can compel performance by the vendor to the extent that he is able to perform.[78] In those jurisdictions subscribing to the doctrine of mutuality of remedy,[79] this right of the purchaser to performance constitutes a recognized exception to the doctrine.[80]

Usually, the contract price is used to determine the value of that which can be conveyed and the resultant amount of the abatement in or deduction from the purchase price,[81] although the market value has sometimes been used. The Restatement of Contracts recommends either method, at the discretion of the court.[82] Of course, if it is impossible to estimate the value of what can be conveyed, no basis exists for compelling performance with a determinable deduction or abatement. The purchaser must either pay the agreed price for what the vendor can convey or consent to a rescission.[83] The difficulty in determining valuations or amounts usually comes in the contracts for exchange of lands, with a resultant inability to compel any performance without in effect writing a new contract for the parties.[84] Incidentally, the contention that partial performance with abatement would amount to enforcement of a contract the parties never intended is made more frequently than it is accepted by the courts.

A modification of the view as to the purchaser's right to partial performance with abatement or deduction is said to exist in some

---

[78] See note, "Specific Performance with Compensation," 40 *Harv. L. Rev.* 476 (1927); Murphy, Specific Performance with Abatement under Uniform Vendor and Purchaser Risk Act, 11 *Intra. L. Rev.* (N.Y.U.) 79 (1956).

[79] Mutuality of remedy, see *supra*, Sec. 79.

[80] Miller v. Dyer, 20 Cal.2d 526, 127 P.2d 901, 141 A.L.R. 1428 (1942).

[81] As in Moore v. Gariglietti, 288 Ill. 143, 81 N.E. 826, 10 Ann. Cas. 560 (1907).

[82] See *Rest. Contracts*, Sec. 365.

[83] The English case of Rudd v. Lascelles, [1900] 1 Ch. 815, is frequently cited as an illustration of this, but it must be recognized that other factors entered into the court's denial of performance with abatement.

[84] Olson v. Lovell, 91 Cal. 506, 27 P. 765 (1891), although not stated in so many words by the court, is actually an illustration of this. Plaintiff agreed to pay money and transfer land in exchange for land owned by defendant and defendant's cotenant. Defendant signed for himself and his cotenant but it developed that the cotenant had neither consented to a sale nor authorized defendant to act for him. Plaintiff thereupon offered half the money and a half interest in his land to defendant and in return sought to compel a conveyance by defendant of latter's half interest in the land of himself and his cotenant. Such relief was properly denied to plaintiff since the result would have been enforcement of a contract which neither had entered into.

jurisdictions where the vendor in good faith is mistaken as to the extent of his title or as to the area of the property contracted to be sold. Evidently to protect the vendor from the effect of an honest mistake which might impose hardship upon him, he has been allowed to rescind with a restoration to the purchaser of what he may have paid plus necessary disbursements for title search but without any damages for breach of contract. This interpretation would actually seem to fall within the classification that no contract has resulted between the parties because of mistake and should properly be distinguished from a contract capable of performance to the extent that the vendor is able with a deduction in the compensation.[85]

Of course, if the purchaser contracts with full knowledge of any lack or defect, the consideration being based upon such title as the vendor has, the purchaser is not entitled to claim any abatement or deduction in connection with specific performance on the part of the vendor.[86] Where performance in full by the vendor is dependent upon concurrence by others, whether or to what extent the purchaser may compel performance is not always easily solvable and the cases may sometimes appear to be in conflict.[87] Where the intention or agreement between the vendor and purchaser is that the obligation of the vendor is conditioned upon his obtaining the concurrence of others and despite his best efforts in

---

[85] This modification is instanced by Walsh, *Treatise on Equity* (1930) Sec. 76, as the rule in England, New York and some other states.

[86] Cochran v. Blount, 161 U.S. 350, 16 S.Ct. 454 (1896). See Hughes v. Hadley, 96 N.J. Eq. 467, 126 A. 33 (1924).
An opposite view was reached, on the ground of fault of the vendor in the failure of remaining interests to convey, in Jones v. English, — Tex. —, 274 S.W.2d 666 (1955), noted 40 *Minn. L. Rev.* 85 (1955).

[87] "The important question presented by this branch of the case is, shall the husband be decreed to make compensation for the lands of his wife which he cannot convey? The court has power to give compensation, but, like the general power of decreeing or refusing specific compensation, it is discretionary. . . . Compensation is to be awarded, when it appears from a view of all the circumstances of the particular case, it will subserve the ends of justice; and it will be denied, when on a like view, it appears it will produce hardship or injustice to either of the parties. No inflexible rule can be adopted applicable to all cases, but each must be decided on its own special facts." Peeler v. Levy, 26 N.J. Eq. 330 (1875).
Where vendor has equitable title by virtue of a contract with third persons holding legal title, see Miller v. Dyer, 20 Cal.2d 526, 127 P.2d 901, 141 A.L.R. 1428 (1942), and annotation thereto, p. 1432.

good faith, he is unable to obtain this concurrence, no specific performance should be granted against the vendor even as to such title as he possesses. But where it can be said that the vendor commits himself unconditionally as to such title as he has and is to add to it or complete it through the concurrence of others but whose concurrence he is unable to obtain, he should be compellable, at the purchaser's election, to perform to the extent that he is able with a deduction or abatement in the purchase price. While some of the cases lay stress on knowledge by the purchaser that the vendor does not himself have the entire or complete title to what is agreed to be sold and that he must needs obtain the concurrence of others, the real importance of such knowledge is that it may indicate the intention or agreement that the vendor's obligation is conditioned on his obtaining such concurrence.[88]

Sec. 84. Part performance and the Statute of Frauds.

Although the Statute of Frauds requires certain contracts to be in writing to be enforceable,[89] including those for the sale or transfer of realty or interests therein,[90] in equity "part performance" by the purchaser under an oral agreement for the sale of realty or an interest therein will, in most jurisdictions, remove the case from the operation of the Statute of Frauds and entitle him to specific performance by the vendor.[91]

---

[88] In Moore v. Gariglietti, 228 Ill. 143, 81 N.E. 826, 10 Ann. Cas. 560 (1907), the vendor agreed to convey a tract in which she actually owned only a two-fifths interest as a tenant in common with her children, and that she did not own it all was known to the purchaser at the time he contracted for the tract. Nevertheless, the latter was held entitled to a conveyance of the vendor's interest with a deduction of three-fifths from the purchase price. On the other hand, in Peeler v. Levy, 26 N.J. Eq. 330 (1875), the court lays great stress on the purchaser's knowledge that the vendor could perform only with the consent or concurrence of his wife and denies the purchaser any equitable relief, expressing the conviction it was represented to defendant that he would not be bound unless his wife assented.
Concurrent contracts and deeds executed by vendor and by those from whom she in turn was purchasing, see Miller v. Dyer, preceding note.

[89] See *supra*, Sec. 69.

[90] See 2 Williston, *Contracts* (Rev. Ed., 1936) Sec. 531.

[91] See Kepner, "Part Performance in Relation to Parol Contracts for the Sale of Land," 35 *Minn. L. Rev.* 1, 431 (1950–51); Moreland, "Statute of Frauds and Part Performance," 78 *U. Pa. L. Rev.* 51 (1929); Pound, "Part Performance— Theory Underlying," 33 *Harv. L. Rev.* 929 (1920); annotation, Doctrine of part performance in suits for specific performance of parol contract to convey real property, 101 A.L.R. 923 (1936).

"Part performance," in this regard, is a somewhat misleading term and has been described as a misnomer.[92]   It might be assumed from the term that it necessarily means that the purchaser has partly performed specific things which the contract requires him to do.   Although the acts may be those done in pursuance of or in fulfillment of the oral agreement,[93] they need not necessarily be acts which the contract requires him to do but may be acts done by him in reliance on the oral contract or the oral promises of the vendor.[94]   The matter really comes down to the point that the purchaser, through reliance on the vendor's oral promises or agreements, has placed himself in such a position that it would now be a fraud on him if the vendor were not compelled to perform.[95] The purchaser, in other words, has changed his position to his permanent or irreparable injury, to the extent that his status quo cannot be restored, to the extent that his remedy at law is inadequate or indeterminable, so that equitably only specific performance by the vendor provides just and adequate relief.[96]

Properly, then, any acts by the purchaser in reliance on and referable to the oral contract or oral promises which bring him to this pass should come within the meaning of "part performance." But what is sufficient evidence that he has been brought to this pass?   Certain acts may, of course, be strongly evidentiary of the

---

Rule of "part performance" is applied only to contracts for sale of land and hence not to a contract for services having a duration longer than a year.   Cleapor v. Atlanta, B. & C. R. Co., 123 F.2d 374 (1941); Britain v. Rossiter, (1879) 11 Q.B.D. 123.

No acts of part performance which will remove a case from operation of Statute of Frauds are recognized in Kentucky, Mississippi, North Carolina, and Tennessee.   The purchaser may recover any money he has paid and for improvements made while in possession.   See cases, annotation, 101 A.L.R. 923, 944.

[92] See McClintock, *Handbook of Equity* (2d Ed.) Sec. 58, citing *Rest. Contracts*, Sec. 197.   See also Walsh, *Treatise on Equity* (1930), pp. 681, 682.

[93] For instance, the purchaser may have performed in full all that is required of him under the contract, and this might be performance which is a "part performance" within the somewhat technical meaning of that term.   Sometimes the courts describe it as "part performance" which entitles to equitable relief; sometimes they describe it as full or complete performance which entitles to equitable relief.

[94] See Miller v. Ball, 64 N.Y. 286 (1876).

[95] See note, 24 *Va. L. Rev.* 807 (1938).

[96] "Part performance is efficacious only when the vendor has allowed the purchaser to change his condition, in reference to the estate, so that he cannot be restored to his statu quo, or so as equitably to estop the vendor from saying that he has not bound himself to sell."   Merwin, *Principles of Equity* (1895) 404.

fact that he must have so changed his position that a fraud will be practiced on him if he is not granted specific performance. Unfortunately, many courts of equity have come to accept certain evidentiary act or acts as an arbitrary yardstick of part performance. If a certain type of act is done, there is arbitrarily considered to be a part performance, without any real consideration of whether there is an irremediable change of position. If a certain act is not done, arbitrarily there is no part performance, without effort to determine whether the purchaser has, in fact, so changed his position, in reliance on the oral promise, as to impose a fraud on him.[97]

What most courts consider a part performance which will take the case out of the operation of the Statute of Frauds involves the purchaser's taking possession of the realty, by a possession referable to the oral contract.[98] Some view possession alone to be sufficient as part performance.[99] Others require possession plus the doing of some additional act,[100] such as the payment of part or all

---

[97] See Holsz v. Stephen, 362 Ill. 527, 200 N.E. 601, 106 A.L.R. 737 (1936); Pomeroy, *Specific Performance* (3d Ed., 1926) Sec. 108a; note, 24 *Va. L. Rev.* 807 (1938).

[98] There must be a change of possession and the possession must be pursuant to the contract, must be open and visible, and must be exclusive, according to Merwin, *Principles of Equity* (1895) 404, 405. However, exclusiveness of possession, if required, will frequently work inequity, as many courts now recognize. See discussion, *infra*, this section.

Where an oral contract to sell realty is made between lessor and lessee, the lessee's possession is referable to his lease and not to the oral contract of sale. Hawke v. Ellwanger, 108 Cal. App. 105, 291 P. 279 (1930); Andrew v. Babcock, 63 Conn. 109, 26 A. 715 (1893). As to alleged oral contract to renew a lease, see Hotel Candler v. Candler, 198 Ga. 339, 31 S.E.2d 693 (1944).

[99] In Arkansas, California, Connecticut, Delaware, Iowa, Maryland, Minnesota, New Hampshire, New Jersey, North Dakota, Ohio, South Carolina, Washington, and West Virginia, according to the excellent analysis of Professors Chafee and Simpson, *Cases on Equity* (1934) 1111. (Notice that as subsequently stated, by statute in Iowa payment of purchase price or part thereof is alone sufficient to constitute part performance.) In comparison with the list by Professors Chafee and Simpson may be noticed the listing of cases by states in the annotation, 101 A.L.R. 923, at 1003 (1936). Maryland is not included in the latter listing. The following states, not listed above, are included: Alabama (old case), Indiana, Maine, Michigan, Missouri (old case), Montana, Oklahoma, Oregon, Pennsylvania, Virginia (old case), and Wisconsin.

Illustration, see Bradley v. Loveday, 98 Conn. 315, 119 A. 147 (1922). And see article, "Part Performance, Estoppel and the California Statute of Frauds," 3 *Stanford L. Rev.* 281 (1951).

Possession as sufficient part performance to permit of enforcement of oral trust of realty, see Haskell v. First Nat. Bank, 33 Cal.App.2d 399, 91 P.2d 934 (1939).

[100] In the tentative draft of the *Restatement of Contracts*, possession alone

of the purchase price,[101] or the making of valuable and lasting improvements,[102] or the making of improvements of such nature as not to be compensable in money.[103] Reliance on an arbitrary standard of this sort frequently leads to inequitable results, for some courts have given such reliance to possession that they have insisted on technical requirements of possession.[104] Other courts, fortunately, have been willing to dispense with technical or legal requirements of possession. Even to the extent that the requirement is followed that possession is a necessary element of part performance, exclusive possession has not been required [105] or else, in

---

was favored as sufficient to constitute part performance. However, in its final form, in Sec. 197, it favors valuable improvements or possession plus payment of part or all of the consideration. It would seem that to be able to make valuable improvements would imply possession.

[101] In Alabama, Florida, Illinois, Nebraska, New York, Oregon and Vermont, according to Professors Chafee and Simpson, *supra*. They point out that even possession plus the making of valuable and lasting improvements is insufficient, unless accompanied by payment, in Alabama, Illinois, and perhaps Nebraska and Oregon. That Wisconsin was formerly, at least, among this group, see Blanchard v. McDougal, 6 Wis. 167, 70 Am. Dec. 458 (1858).

[102] In Georgia, Kansas, Maine, Michigan, Missouri, Montana, New York, Pennsylvania, Vermont, Virginia, and Wisconsin, according to Professors Chafee and Simpson, *supra*. However, notice, as subsequently pointed out, that in Georgia by statute payment of the purchase price alone will constitute part performance. And as to Wisconsin, see preceding note.

In Brewood v. Cook, — U.S. App. D.C. —, 207 F.2d 439 (1953), noted 42 *Geo. L.J.* 134 (1953), oral agreement to convey land was enforced where it induced making of collateral contract and plaintiff had entered on land and made improvements in the amount of $300 in reliance on oral agreement.

[103] In Massachusetts and probably in Texas, according to Professors Chafee and Simpson, *supra*.

Illustration, see Burns v. Daggett, 141 Mass. 368, 6 N.E. 727 (1886). However, see Andrews v. Charon, 289 Mass. 1, 193 N.E. 737 (1935), where there was no making of such valuable improvements that would take the case out of the Statute of Frauds under the commonly expressed Massachusetts view, but there was payment of the purchase price, assumption of a mortgage, payment of taxes, possession and occupancy for many years and the court concluded that all the facts in combination would result in an unjust and unconscionable injury and loss if relief was denied. Such was reformation of a deed to include part of a tract omitted by mistake.

[104] This might, at first glance, appear to be the result in Burns v. McCormick, 233 N.Y. 230, 135 N.E. 273 (1922), where plaintiff alleged selling of his home and business in another town and moving with his family to promisor's property and performing in full his side of the oral contract. However, it appears that court is definitely not satisfied that the evidence establishes any such oral agreement and may be considered to be looking for reasons to deny enforcement.

[105] Lamb v. Hinman, 46 Mich. 112, 6 N.W. 675 (1881).

Wife taking such possession of realty as her relationship with husband, the promisor, permitted, see Barbour v. Barbour, 48 N.J. Eq. 429, 24 A. 227 (1892).

the circumstances, the possession has been interpreted to be a sufficiently exclusive possession from an equitable standpoint,[106] or, again, possession as a requisite may be ignored entirely.[107] In short, they have really considered whether the acts of the purchaser have been such as to subject him to fraud if the agreement by the vendor is not carried out.[108]

It is the usual equitable rule that the mere payment of part or even all of the purchase money,[109] or the performance of services, where that is the consideration,[110] does not constitute sufficient part performance. The reason given is that the purchaser has a full and adequate remedy at law for the recovery of the money paid,[111] or to recover for the value of services rendered.[112] However, in some jurisdictions statutory enactments have provided that payment of part or all of the purchase price constitutes a sufficient part performance.[113] And where services are rendered, there is fre-

---

Further, where consideration on wife's part was promise to marry promisor, see Peek v. Peek, 77 Cal. 106, 19 P. 106, 11 Am.St.Rep. 244, 1 L.R.A. 185 (1888); Ayoob v. Ayoob, 74 Cal.App.2d 236, 168 P.2d 462 (1946); annotation, What constitutes part performance sufficient to take agreement in consideration of marriage out of statute of frauds, 30 A.L.R.2d 1419.

[106] Bryson v. McShane, 48 W.Va. 126, 35 S.E. 848, 49 L.R.A. 527 (1900).

[107] See Mannix v. Baumgardner, 184 Md. 600, 42 A.2d 124 (1945).

[108] See particularly, Best v. Gralapp, 69 Neb. 811, 96 N.W. 641 (1903), wherein the court said, "Where a man of middle age and the head of a family closes out his business, disposes of his property, presumably at a sacrifice, as is inevitable in such cases, and removes to another state for the purpose of taking charge of the property and person of an aged parent, the entire course of his life is so far changed that it would be impossible to compensate him adequately in damages or to restore him, after a lapse of some years, to his original position. To permit the statute of frauds to be asserted in such a case is to work a fraud upon the promisee." Upon the argument of lack of possession being raised on petition for rehearing, the court took the view that the promisee had sufficient possession to satisfy the equitable principles relating to necessity of possession.

[109] Cases from thirty states are listed in the annotation, 101 A.L.R. 1023, at 1079 (1936), in support of this view.

[110] Cases from sixteen states are listed in the annotation, 101 A.L.R. 1023, at 1093 (1936), in support of this view.

[111] That this may not necessarily be so, see Neatherly v. Ripley, 21 Tex. 434 (1858).

[112] Cordano v. Ferretti, 15 Cal. App. 670, 115 P. 657 (1911).

[113] In Iowa, payment of the purchase price or part thereof, and in Georgia, full payment of the purchase price, is sufficient as a part performance taking the case out of the Statute of Frauds. See Georgia Code, 1933, Sec. 20–402; Iowa Code, 1939, Sec. 11286; Wright, "The Iowa 'Purchase Money' Doctrine," 19 *Iowa L. Rev.* 54 (1933).

Effect of judicial decision in Delaware, see Com'rs of Lewes v. Breakwater Fisheries Co., 13 Del. Ch. 234, 117 A. 823 (1922).

quent consideration that if the services are of such a personal and peculiar character that it is impossible to estimate their value by any pecuniary standard, and it is evident that the parties did not intend so to measure them, and if the plaintiff after rendering the services cannot be restored to his former situation, it is such a part performance as will take the case out of the statute.[114]

Sec. 85.   —Specific performance by purchaser.

So far we have considered the right of the purchaser to have specific performance of an oral contract to sell realty. Can the vendor compel specific performance of such a contract on the part of the purchaser? Certainly, where he has done acts in reliance on the promises or representations of the purchaser so that it will be a fraud on him if he does not obtain specific performance. he is as much entitled to equitable relief as would be the purchaser in such a situation. However, the cases relating to the vendor's right to specific performance are in considerable conflict.[115] Undoubtedly, many of the cases have been decided under the doctrine of mutuality of remedy, whereby the plaintiff's right to specific performance is dependent upon whether or not the defendant would be entitled to such remedy if he were the complainant.[116] Thus, where the purchaser has met the requirements of his jurisdiction as to part performance, whether those be possession or possession plus payment or possession plus improvements or the like, so that he would be entitled to specific performance,

---

114 See Monarco v. Lo Greco, 35 Cal.2d 621, 220 P.2d 737 (1950); Jones v. Davis, 165 Kan. 626, 197 P.2d 932 (1948); Best v. Gralapp (Neb.), *supra*, footnote 108. Compare Burns v. McCormick (N.Y.), *supra*, footnote 104. And see Jones, "Performance of Services as Taking Oral Contract out of Statute of Frauds," 19 *Ky. L.J.* 169 (1930).

Services were considered capable of measurement in money and recovery on quantum meruit adequate, in Snyder v. Warde, 151 Ohio St. 426, 86 N.E.2d 489 (1949), but note thereto in 48 *Mich. L. Rev.* 1043 (1950), points out majority of jurisdictions consider quantum meruit inadequate, either because plaintiff undergoes hardship to serve promisor which hardship cannot be compensated adequately in money or because services are of unique value to promisor because of filial or domestic relationship.

115 A great number of cases are set out in the annotation, 101 A.L.R. 923, at 973 ff. (1936), but the discussion is lacking in analysis of the reasons behind the decisions.

116 Mutuality of remedy, see *supra*, Sec. 79.

the vendor has been granted specific performance under the doctrine of mutuality of remedy.[117]

But where such doctrine is discredited, it provides no basis for granting a vendor specific performance.[118] The vendor cannot rely merely on acts of part performance by the purchaser to take the case out of the Statute of Frauds,[119] but must stand or fall according to the strength of his own equitable position. If legal remedies will return him the realty substantially unchanged and will allow him recovery of proper damages for any injuries incurred, his legal remedies may be termed adequate. He does not need specific performance to save him from having a fraud perpetrated upon him or to save him from unconscionable or irreparable wrong. However, if the acts of part performance by the purchaser have been such as materially to change the nature or substance of the property so that it cannot be returned to the vendor in its original condition, the equities may so favor the vendor as to entitle him to specific performance as the only adequate remedy.[120]

Of course, where the transaction has proceeded to the point where the vendor has executed and delivered a conveyance to the purchaser, his acceptance thereof and the possession thereby given him constitute grounds for the vendor to maintain an action for and recover the purchase money on the purchaser's oral promise to pay, according to the commonly accepted view. Not only has the vendor performed in full but the purchaser has so far acted as to estop him to deny the contract.[121] A somewhat similar situation occurs in the case of oral contracts to exchange realty. Where the plaintiff has executed and delivered a conveyance of his realty to the defendant, his acceptance thereof and the posses-

---

[117] Pearson v. Gardner, 202 Mich. 360, 168 N.W. 485 (1918), noted 17 *Mich. L. Rev.* 193 (1918).

[118] See Walter v. Hoffman, 267 N.Y. 365, 196 N.E. 291, 101 A.L.R. 919 (1935), noted 35 *Col. L. Rev.* 1324 (1935), 3 *U. Chi. L. Rev.* 510 (1936).

[119] Palumbo v. James, 266 Mass. 1, 164 N.E. 466 (1929), noted and criticized, 13 *Minn. L. Rev.* 519 (1929), 38 *Yale L.J.* 821 (1929).

[120] Walter v. Hoffman, 267 N.Y. 365, 196 N.E. 291, 101 A.L.R. 919 (1935), noted 35 *Col. L. Rev.* 1324 (1935), 3 *U. Chi. L. Rev.* 510 (1936).

[121] See rule as stated by *Rest. Contracts*, Sec. 193 (3); 1 Williston, *Contracts*, Sec. 493.

sion thereby given him usually are considered to create a situation where the plaintiff is equitably entitled to specific performance of the defendant's agreement. The plaintiff's performance in full removes the case from the operation of the Statute of Frauds.[122] The receipt of possession of the defendant's realty by the plaintiff is not a requisite. However, if such possession has been received, the plaintiff's position is that much stronger. This is no doubt of importance in jurisdictions which tend to ignore the fact of performance in full by the plaintiff and estoppel on the part of the defendant and look rather to see if the plaintiff has fulfilled the requirements as to part performance, such as taking possession, demanded of a purchaser.[123]

Sec. 86.   —Oral gifts of or oral promises to give realty.

As in the case of parol contracts to sell realty, equity will lend its aid to enforce a parol gift or the parol promise to make a gift of realty, if it considers that a fraud or unconscionable wrong would otherwise be perpetrated upon the promisee. However, it seems to be a uniform requirement that the promisee must have gone into possession of the realty and made valuable improvements thereon under the inducement of the promise.[124] This requirement exists even in a jurisdiction which, as to a parol promise to sell realty, considers that possession alone is sufficient to take the case out of the operation of the Statute of Frauds.[125]

In a few jurisdictions, a variation has appeared. Although the rule stated above has been followed in the case of a present gift, as to a gift in futuro the improvements made must exceed in amount the rental value of the realty in order to entitle the promisee to the aid of equity.[126]

---

[122] Bigelow v. Armes, 108 U.S. 10, S.Ct. 83, 27 L. Ed. 631 (1882); Pearsall v. Henry, 153 Cal. 314, 95 P. 154 (1907).

[123] Texas requirement that exchange of possession is not sufficient, see Wells v. Carter, (1935; Tex. Civ. App.) 78 S.W.2d 678.

[124] Freeman v. Freeman, 43 N.Y. 34, 3 Am. Rep. 657 (1870).

Statutory prohibition against enforcement of parol gifts or parol promises of gifts of realty, see Va. Code (Michie, 1942), Sec. 5141 (enacted 1887).

[125] Burlingame v. Rowland, 77 Cal. 315, 19 P. 526 (1888); Seavey v. Drake, 62 N.H. 393 (1882).

[126] Burris v. Landers, 114 Cal. 310, 46 P. 162 (1896), followed in Green v. Brown, 37 Cal.2d 391, 232, P.2d 487 (1951).

CHAPTER 12

THE VENDOR AND PURCHASER RELATIONSHIP

Sec. 87. Relationship generally—Equitable conversion.

The vendor-purchaser relationship may be said to turn primarily upon the so-called doctrine of equitable conversion, whereby in the eyes of the equity court the purchaser of realty, under the contract of sale and purchase, becomes the equitable or real owner, despite the fact that title has not yet been transferred to him. The title is considered to be withheld by the vendor merely as a means of security for the payment of the rest of the purchase price and is held in trust for the benefit of the purchaser, subject to his fulfillment of his obligations.[1] The contract must, of course, be one that will permit of enforcement by specific performance, other-

---

[1] Millville Aerie v. Weatherby, 82 N.J. Eq. 455, 88 A. 847 (1913).

Compare In re Kuhn's Estate, 132 Wash. 678, 233 P. 293 (1925), holding that a contract of purchase which is executory and forfeitable upon default in performance gives neither legal nor equitable title or interest. This view by the Washington court would seem to be overruled or qualified in view of such cases as In re Binge's Estate, 5 Wash.2d 446, 105 P.2d 689 (1940). See also comment, 6 *Wash. L. Rev.* 42 (1931).

Criticism of equitable conversion theory, see Stone, "Equitable Conversion by Contract," 15 *Col. L. Rev.* 256 (1913).

wise no equitable conversion takes place.[2]   Some jurisdictions require that the purchaser shall have received possession of the realty in order to bring about equitable conversion,[3] but this requirement does not exist in most jurisdictions.[4]

Since the purchaser now equitably owns realty, upon his death his rights in the property are realty and descend to those entitled to his realty, subject to the rights of the vendor under the contract.[5] The vendor, on the other hand, now owns personalty, a chose in action for the payment of the rest of the purchase price, and on his death, those who take his personalty would succeed to the right to the payment of the rest of the purchase price.[6]   So far as concerns the legal title which he still holds as security and as a trustee, it passes to those who would succeed to his realty but they take it in turn as trustees, with the duty to transfer it to the contract purchaser at the time for performance of the contract.[7] However, if the vendor has reserved the right to possession of the property, those succeeding to his realty would be entitled to the use and enjoyment or rents, issues, and profits of the property in the meantime.[8]

The question of who are necessary parties to suits for specific performance necessarily arises where one of the parties to the contract has previously died.   Varied aspects of this situation may come into question.   Where the purchaser dies and specific performance is sought against the vendor, the purchaser's heirs or

---

[2] As where vendor lacks the title he has contracted to convey, see Amundson v. Severson, 41 S.D. 377, 170 N.W. 633 (1919).

[3] See Ingraham v. Chandler, 179 Iowa 304, 161 N.W. 434, L.R.A. 1917 D 713 (1917).

[4] Possession of property, see *infra*, Sec. 89.

[5] House v. Dexter, 9 Mich. 246 (1861).

In Siesel v. Mandeville, 140 N.J. Eq. 490, 55 A.2d 167 (1947), noted 61 *Harv. L. Rev.* 718 (1948), husband and wife contracted to buy land and to give a purchase money mortgage.   The husband died and the wife sued for specific performance. It was held that the wife, by equitable conversion, became a tenant by entirety with the husband and was now sole owner of the equitable right and could specifically enforce the contract and compel the vendor to accept a mortgage executed by her alone.

[6] Coles v. Feeney, 52 N.J. Eq. 493, 29 A. 172 (1894).

[7] This is true whether they take realty of the decedent by intestacy or by devise.

[8] See Eddington v. Turner, 27 Del. Ch. 411, 38 A.2d 738, 155 A.L.R. 562 (1944), noted 93 *U. Pa. L. Rev.* 216 (1944).

Possession, see *infra*, Sec. 89.

devisees are the ones entitled to have deed of conveyance executed to them but any unpaid portion of the purchase price must come from assets in the hands of the executor or administrator. They would all seem, accordingly to be indispensable parties.[9] Similarly, where it is the purchaser who has died but specific performance is sought by the vendor, the heirs or devisees to whom a deed will be executed should be named as defendants but certainly the purchaser's executor or administrator who may have to make the payment from assets in his hands should be named a defendant. Where the vendor has died and specific performance is sought against the purchaser, the vendor's executor or administrator and the heirs or devisees of the vendor should properly be parties. The purchase price, as personalty, passes into the hands of the executor or administrator but since the heirs or devisees have the technical legal title they must execute the necessary deed of conveyance to the purchaser.[10] Conversely, where the vendor has died but the purchaser is the one who seeks specific performance, both the executor or administrator and the heirs or devisees of the vendor should be named as defendants. The former would be entitled to receive any purchase money due and the latter must execute the deed of conveyance.[11] Statutory provisions, especially of local probate codes, frequently take into account such situations and should be examined for the reader's local law. These enactments may provide for the executor or administrator suing or being sued alone or for the executor or administrator of a deceased vendor being authorized to execute any necessary deed of conveyance.[12]

---

[9] Where purchaser died, his heirs as proper parties to seek deed, see House v. Dexter, 9 Mich. 246 (1861), where bill by purchaser's administrator alone was dismissed, even though leave was asked to amend to make purchaser's heirs parties; Downing v. Risley, 15 N.J. Eq. 93 (1862), where bill brought by purchaser's heirs was defective because his administrator not made a party.

[10] Where vendor died and his executors sought specific performance against purchaser, the bill was held defective in not making devisees of the vendor parties. Coles v. Feeney, 52 N.J. Eq. 493, 29 A. 172 (1894). And see Shimoff, "Equitable Conversion Where Purchaser Defaults after Death of Vendor," 10 *Intra. L. Rev.* (N.Y.U.) 124 (1955).

[11] See Haar v. Schloss, 168 N.C. 97, 83 S.E. 306 (1914).

[12] See, *e.g.*, Griffith v. Stewart, 31 App. D.C. 29 (1908), aff'd 217 U.S. 323, 30 S.Ct. 528, 54 L. Ed. 782, 19 Ann. Cas. 639 (1909).

See Simpson, "Legislative Changes in the Law of Equitable Conversion," 44 *Yale L.J.* 559, 754 (1935).

Although the contrary view has been developed in England,[13] in this country where there is a lease of property with an option in the lessee to purchase and the lessor dies before the option is exercised, there has as yet been no equitable conversion and the property descends as realty subject to the option, whereupon those entitled to the realty take the purchase price.[14] Where it is the lessee who dies, before exercising the option, the option has been considered not to pass as realty to his heirs. It has been considered personalty of which the executor or administrator may dispose in the administration of the estate.[15]

Sec. 88.   —Effect of breaches on equitable conversion.

Another matter of difficulty arises where there is a right to enforce the contract or to rescind it, as for default on the other side, and the party having the right to elect dies before any election has been made. Is the vendor and purchaser relationship in effect at the time of death, despite the breach by the other party, so as to affect the nature of the interest which passes? Who has the right to enforce or to rescind the contract?

For example, where a purchaser breaches and the vendor dies before electing to enforce or to rescind, if the breach has terminated the vendor-purchaser relation the realty passes to the heirs or devisees of the vendor. It may be assumed that they would much prefer this and would naturally object to any waiver of the breach, if permissible, by the personal representative of the vendor. Certainly, it seems reasonable to find that a breach by the purchaser after the vendor's death is one which may be enforced or waived by the vendor's personal representative, on the ground that per-

---

13 The English view and its repudiation generally in this country is discussed at length in Eddington v. Turner, 27 Del. Ch. 411, 38 A.2d 738, 155 A.L.R. 562 (1944), noted 93 *U. Pa. L. Rev.* 216 (1944).

14 Rockfort-Rockland Lime Co. v. Leary, 203 N.Y. 469, 97 N.E. 43, Ann. Cas. 1913 B 62, L.R.A. 1916 F 352 (1911); Smith v. Loewenstein, 50 Ohio St. 346, 134 N.E. 159 (1923).

In Eddington v. Turner, 27 Del. Ch. 411, 38 A.2d 738, 155 A.L.R. 562 (1944), noted 93 *U. Pa. L. Rev.* 216 (1944), testator died owning realty subject to a purchase option which was exercised after testator's death. Testator's sister was given, by testator's will, a life interest in the property. Held: that she was entitled to a life interest in the proceeds of the sale.

15 See Gustin v. Union School Dist., 94 Mich. 502 54 N.W. 156, 34 Am.St.Rep. 361 (1893).

sonalty passed to the personal representative and nothing to heirs and devisees except the bare legal title in trust.[16] Even if the breaches by the purchaser take place before the vendor's death, it is argued that the equitable interest of the purchaser cannot be considered to disappear and reappear as he breaches and as the vendor expressly or impliedly waives such breaches.[17]

Similarly, where the vendor has breached and the purchaser has the choice of rescinding or enforcing the contract (probably with the right of abatement in the purchase price),[18] the right to choose and to receive the property is said to be in the personal representative of the purchaser, for otherwise the heirs or devisees of the purchaser would always choose to take the land, leaving the personal representative to pay the purchase price or certainly some part of it.[19] Of course, it may well be argued that, if the vendor had no title or an extremely defective one, no equitable interest ever arose by conversion.[20]

Actually, there may not be too much uniformity in the case results in such situations, as the results may vary considerably as the courts attempt to reach what each court considers an equitable result.

Sec. 89. Possession of property.

Where there is nothing express or implied as to possession in a contract for the sale of realty, the right to possession of the property and its benefits while the contract is executory remains in the vendor.[21] However, the purchaser is entitled to possession and the benefit of the property where the contract expressly or impliedly entitles him thereto. The one entitled to the possession

---

16 See Williams v. Haddock, 145 N.Y. 144, 39 N.E. 825 (1895).

17 See Walsh, *Equity* (1930) 419. Compare Pickens v. Campbell, 104 Kan. 425, 179 Pac. 343 (1919), where vendor-purchaser relation held not to exist at time of vendor's death, by reason of purchaser's prior breach.

18 See Sec. 83.

19 See McClintock, *Equity* (2d Ed.) 293; Walsh, *Equity* (1930) 419.

20 See Thomas v. Howell, 34 Ch. Div. 166, (1886), criticized by Walsh, *Equity* (1930) 420, as being out of accord with principles of specific performance with abatement or compensation.

21 Iowa Railroad Land Co. v. Boyle, 154 Iowa 249, 134 N.W. 590, 38 L.R.A.N.S. 420 (1912).

Purchaser's possession as referable to lease and not to contract of sale, see Barrell v. Britton, 244 Mass. 273, 138 N.E. 579 (1923).

and benefits of the property has the burden of taxes and the like, in the absence of any contract provision relative thereto,[22] and is responsible for the proper care and maintenance of the property. Failure to care for and maintain the property may subject the one in possession to liability for waste at the suit of the other party.[23]

The one in possession may properly maintain action against those causing injury to the property.[24]

Sec. 90.   Liens and other remedies.

It is well recognized in most American jurisdictions that the vendor has what is termed a vendor's lien upon the property to secure the payment to him of the purchase price due.[25]   Upon default by the purchaser he may seek foreclosure of this lien and the sale of the property under the control of the equity court to obtain the remainder of the price due him.[26]   The vendor, of course, has a variety of other remedies available to him upon default by the purchaser.   It will be found that the remedy or remedies availed of frequently vary from one jurisdiction to another, sometimes by reason of law, sometimes by reason of custom which favors some particular remedy or other.[27]   These remedies have variously included suit to rescind the contract,[28] to quiet title,[29]

---

[22] See Miller v. Corey, 15 Iowa 166 (1863).

[23] Waste, see *supra*, Sec. 26.

Purchaser in possession committing acts, *i.e.*, by felling timber, which impaired the value of the vendor's security.   Moses Bros. v. Johnson, 88 Ala. 517, 7 So. 146, 16 Am.St.Rep. 58 (1889).

Waste by vendor, see note 48 *Harv. L. Rev.* 821 (1935).

[24] See Krakow v. Wille, 125 Wis. 284, 103 N.W. 1121 (1905).

[25] As distinguished from the so-called grantor's lien where title has been conveyed to the purchaser.

[26] See Merwin, *Principles of Equity* (1895) 144, 145; Walsh, *Treatise on Equity* (1930) Sec. 92.

[27] Reference to the cases of one's own state will demonstrate this.   And see Walsh, *Treatise on Equity* (1930) Sec. 91.

[28] Which would involve a settlement of the equities between the parties, as to such matters as value of improvements, rental value, depreciation, etc.

[29] This has seemed favored in California, since it obtains a cancellation of any rights of the purchaser under the contract, without requiring the vendor to offer an extension of time in which to pay, as is essentially the case in a suit for strict foreclosure, or without requiring any offer to return payments so far made to the extent that they may exceed rental value, depreciation, etc. See, *e.g.*, Glock v. Howard & Wilson Colony Co., 123 Cal. 1, 55 P. 713, 69 Am.St.Rep. 17, 43 L.R.A. 199 (1898).   But compare Barkis v. Scott, 34 Cal.2d 116, 208 P.2d 367 (1949), noted 37 *Cal. L. Rev.* 704 (1949).

for so-called strict foreclosure,[30] for damages for breach of contract, which is an action at law, of course, or to recover the unpaid remainder of the purchase price, that is for specific performance.[31] Frequently, it will be found that the vendor is actually combining pleas for several of these remedies in his complaint.[32]

In jurisdictions recognizing a vendor's lien, the purchaser is also deemed to have a lien upon the property to secure his payments so far made or to secure the value of the improvements he may have made or to protect other special equities in his favor. In other words, in situations where he is entitled to the recovery of such payments or the value of improvements made or where he is entitled to deductions because of the vendor's inability to perform in full, he may secure himself in such matters by foreclosure of his lien and the sale of the property or of so much of it as the vendor has title to, and recovery from the proceeds thereof.[33] While a minority view has been expressed that it is inconsistent for a purchaser to ask for rescission of the contract on the ground of the vendor's default and also to ask for foreclosure of his lien,[34] the usual view is that there is no inconsistency and that the purchaser's lien is an equitable means of protection existent in his favor, even where he asks for rescission of the contract.[35]

---

[30] Sheehan v. McKinstry, 105 Ore. 473, 210 P. 167 (1922).
Generally this remedy is not available unless no payments or only relatively small payments have been made on the purchase price.
[31] Amaranth Land Co. v. Corey, 182 Cal. 66, 186 P. 765 (1920).
[32] In White v. Sage, 149 Cal. 613, 87 P. 193 (1906), the suit was for specific performance, but alleged the vendor's lien and asked judgment for any unpaid balance, that a reasonable time be given defendant in which to pay (an element of strict foreclosure) and in default of such payment that defendant's interest in the land be sold, the proceeds applied to the amount due and defendant's rights in the land foreclosed. A demurrer was sustained to this complaint on the ground that adequacy of consideration was not shown as required in California.
In Strauss v. Bendheim, 32 Misc. 179, 66 N.Y.S. 247 (1900), the vendor obtained a decree of specific performance but with a provision therein that if the purchaser could not perform, then the property to be sold and the vendor paid from the proceeds (i.e., foreclosure of his vendor's lien), with a deficiency judgment against the purchaser, if necessary.
[33] "We find no well-considered case in any state that denies a lien to the vendee, even if payment is the only ground therefor, except such as withhold a lien from the vendor also." Elterman v. Hyman, 192 N.Y. 113, 84 N.E. 937, 127 Am.St.Rep. 862, 15 Ann. Cas. 819 (1908).
[34] Davis v. William Rosenzweig Realty Operating Co., 192 N.Y. 128, 84 N.E. 943, 127 Am.St.Rep. 890, 20 L.R.A.N.S. 175 (1908).
[35] McCall v. Superior Court, 1 Cal.2d 527, 36 P.2d 642 (1934); White v. Hobolth,

While the right to possession is sometimes required in order to give rise to the lien, especially for a purchaser's lien, more generally the liens exist independent of possession.[36]

Sec. 91.   Transfers and assignments.

Where the vendor transfers to another any promissory notes or purchase money bonds executed to him by a purchaser under a contract for the purchase of realty, the transferee takes them accompanied by the security of the realty for their payment.   As in the case of the transfer of negotiable instruments secured by a mortgage, the vendor's lien on the realty benefits the transferee of the negotiable instruments.[37]

Where the contract vendor conveys the property to a third person in violation of the contract, the contract purchaser may not recover the property from such third person if the latter qualifies as a bona fide purchaser,[38] although the contract purchaser may impose a constructive trust upon the proceeds of that sale in the hands of the vendor.   If such proceeds exceed in value the amount of the damage to the contract purchaser or exceed the market value of the property, which would constitute the measure of recovery at law by the contract purchaser, the equitable remedy of imposing a constructive trust on the proceeds prevents the vendor from profiting from his wrongful act and gives such benefit to the one more equitably entitled thereto.[39]

If the third person is not a bona fide purchaser, in that he purchased from the vendor with knowledge or notice of the prior agreement, he may be compelled by the contract purchaser to reconvey the property.[40]

---

224 Mich. 286, 195 N.W. 82 (1923).   See Walsh, *Treatise on Equity* (1930) 504; comment, "The Vendee's Lien on Land and Chattels," 33 *Mich. L. Rev.* 108 (1934).

[36] This is sometimes provided by statute. See, *e.g.*, Cal. Civ. Code, Secs. 3046, 3050.

[37] See Graham v. McCampbell, Meigs (Tenn.) 52, 33 Am. Dec. 126 (1838).

[38] See Haughwout v. Murphy, 22 N.J. Eq. 531 (1871).

[39] Taylor v. Kelly, 3 Jones Eq. (N.C.) 240 (1857).

In the case of shares of stock, see Falk v. Hoffman, 233 N.Y. 199, 135, N.E. 243 (1922).

[40] Recording acts may be available to permit of recordation and thus of notice of the contract of sale. Possession by the contract purchaser is, in some states, *e.g.*, California, notice to the third person or puts him on inquiry. Consult local statutes and decisions.

In the situation where the third person has paid part of the purchase price to the vendor before obtaining notice of the prior contract, three views prevail, according to Professor Scott. The first is that the third person qualifies as a bona fide purchaser; the second is that he is not in any respect a bona fide purchaser and must surrender the property to the contract purchaser and look to the vendor for recovery of anything paid him; and third, that the third person is protected to the extent that he has paid part of the price to the vendor, in that the prior contract purchaser must reimburse the third person for what he has so far paid, before the contract purchaser may obtain the property from the third person. This last view is the majority view in this country.[41]

Where a judgment creditor of the vendor levies on the realty which is the subject of the contract of sale and has it sold at a judicial sale, the purchaser takes it subject to the contract purchaser's rights if the purchaser at the judicial sale has knowledge or notice of the contract. In other words, he succeeds to the vendor's rights to payment of the rest of the purchase money, from the time he notifies the contract purchaser, and has the obligation of conveying title to the contract purchaser upon completion of payment of the purchase price.[42] However, if a purchaser at the judicial sale takes without any knowledge or notice of the prior agreement, he takes as bona fide purchaser, not subject to any rights of the contract purchaser,[43] and this has been so held even in the case of the judgment creditor who purchases the property at the judicial sale without any notice at all of the prior agreement, although the latter has been recognized as a disputed point.[44]

Mortgage of land by vendor as subordinate to prior contract of sale and as amounting to assignment of balance due under contract, see Jaeger v. Hardy, 48 Ohio St. 335, 27 N.E. 863 (1898). Consider effect of Recording Acts in such situations.

See Stone, "Equitable Rights and Liabilities of Strangers to a Contract," 19 *Col. L. Rev.* 177.

[41] 2 Scott, *Trusts*, Sec. 303. See also Haughwout v. Murphy, 22 N.J. Eq. 531 (1871).

[42] Judgment creditor himself buying at judicial sale with notice of prior agreement, see Moyer v. Hinman, 13 N.Y. 180 (1855); May v. Emerson, 52 Ore. 262, 96 P. 454, 1065 (1908).

[43] 2 Scott, *Trusts*, Sec. 309.1.

[44] Riley v. Martinelli, 97 Cal. 575, 32 P. 579, 33 Am.St.Rep. 209, 21 L.R.A. 33 (1893).

But on this latter point there is authority to the contrary.[45]

Subject to such restrictions as may be validly imposed,[46] a contract purchaser may sell or assign his rights under the contract,[47] or his equitable interest may be reached by his creditors.[48] The assignee of the purchaser's rights succeeds to the purchaser's position as equitable owner,[49] and may enforce specific performance against the vendor, provided the assignee has complied with the obligations imposed by the contract upon the purchaser.[50] No assignment or sale to another on different terms than those comprised in the original agreement gives the purchaser's transferee any right to specific performance against the original vendor.[51] However, on the basis that the contract purchaser has acquired an equitable interest in the property, his transferee may seek to obtain

---

[45] Professor Bogert, in his *Handbook of the Law of Trusts* (2d Ed. 1942) 546, cites authorities to the effect that the judgment creditor cannot be a bona fide purchaser in the absence of statute.

[46] Express provisions in a contract against assignment by the purchaser may, according to some views, amount to restrictions on the right of alienation and so be invalid. In any event, restrictive provisions will be strictly construed. One method of evading possible effects of invalidity, sometimes used, is to provide for termination of the contract in the event of an attempted assignment. Discussion, see Goddard, "Non-Assignment Provisions in Land Contracts," 31 *Mich. L. Rev.* 1 (1932).

[47] Merwin, *Principles of Equity* (1895) 416, 417.

[48] See Higgins v. McConnell, 130 N.Y. 482, 29 N.E. 978 (1892).

Notice that the manner or methods of doing so may vary from state to state. Consider particularly the matter of the so-called code states.

[49] Lenman v. Jones, 222 U.S. 51, 32 S.Ct. 18, 56 L. Ed. 89 (1911); Epstein v. Gluckin, 233 N.Y. 490, 135 N.E. 861 (1922).

[50] Merely by reason of receiving the assignment from the purchaser, the assignee does not become obligated to the vendor to perform. However, by act or conduct sufficient to show that he has obligated himself under the contract, he satisfies the requirements of the rules of mutuality of remedy or of mutuality of obligation to perform, whichever is followed, so as to allow him to resort to specific performance against the vendor. Under either rule, his bringing suit for specific performance against the vendor is considered an adoption or confirmation of the contract on his part so as to satisfy the respective rule. See Epstein v. Gluckin, 233 N.Y. 490, 135 N.E. 861 (1922).

Whether assignee may offer his own purchase money obligations in place of those of his assignor, in absence of any contract provision relative thereto, is a matter of dispute. Compare Montgomery v. De Picot, 153 Cal. 509, 96 P. 305, 126 Am.St.Rep. 84 (1908) and Lojo Realty Co. v. Johnson's Estate, 227 App. Div. 292, 237 N.Y.S. 460 (1929), aff'd 253 N.Y. 579, 171 N.E. 791 (1931).

Acceptance of assignment by assignee as prima facie a promise to assignor to assume performance of his duties, see *Rest. Contracts*, Sec. 164 (2). In Langel v. Betz, 250 N.Y. 159, 164 N.E. 890 (1928), this was disapproved.

[51] See Bittrick v. Cons. Imp. Co., 51 Wash. 469, 99 P. 303 (1909).

from him such title as he can transfer, his equitable interest, and may even join the original vendor as a party defendant and seek to have the contract purchaser enforce his rights against the original vendor.[52]

Sec. 92.   Lis pendens.

The equitable doctrine of lis pendens is that a suit in equity concerning the title to realty is notice to all the world of the title of the respective parties to the suit.   Whoever buys of either party pending the suit is charged with notice of the title set up by the other party and will be bound by any decree affecting the title which may be rendered in the suit.   Thus, a suit for specific performance of a contract for the sale of realty is notice to all the world and whoever then buys the property takes it with notice of the other party's claim of title.   He may be compelled to convey the realty to the successful party pursuant to the original agreement.[53]   However, in many states nowadays, this equitable doctrine of lis pendens is modified by statute which provides, in effect, that no pending suit relating to realty shall be notice to third persons until a memorandum or other notice of the pendency of the action is filed with the recorder or register of deeds or other proper official in the county where the realty lies.[54]

Sec. 93.   Risk of loss.

In the situation where a contract for the sale of property has been entered into and the property is totally or partially destroyed by fire or other cause, without fault, before title has passed to the purchaser, who bears the burden or risk of the loss?   In the case of sales of realty, where there is destruction of buildings or injury

---

[52] See, especially, Miller v. Dyer, 20 Cal.2d 526, 127 P.2d 901, 141 A.L.R. 1428 (1942) and annotation thereto, p. 1432; *supra*, Sec. 81.

Right of subpurchaser of portion of realty to specific performance, see notes, 40 *Geo. L.J.* 335 (1952); 4 *Stanford L. Rev.* 443 (1952).   Latter points out that majority rule is that subpurchaser of the whole can obtain specific performance of both contracts by joining parties to original contract as defendants, but subpurchaser of part should not be entitled to specific performance against original vendor unless latter gets full performance of all conditions to which he is entitled.

[53] See Merwin, *Principles of Equity* (1895) 417 ff.

[54] Consult local statutes. See also Haughwout v. Murphy, 22 N.J. Eq. 531 (1871).

to the land from superior force, the so-called majority view has been that the risk or burden falls on the purchaser. This has frequently been placed on the ground that, under the doctrine of equitable conversion, he has become the equitable owner of the property and must shoulder the loss. It is, accordingly, obligatory upon him to complete the payment of any part of the purchase price remaining unpaid and accept title to the damaged or injured property.[55]   Under the so-called minority view, the risk or burden of the loss falls upon the vendor. This is usually based on the ground that there is a failure of consideration, by reason of which the purchaser is entitled to rescind the transaction and recover back any consideration he has so far paid.[56]   It seems immaterial, under either view, which party has been in possession of the property at the time of the loss or destruction.[57]

A third view was developed originally in California by judicial decision [58] and has been made the subject of the Uniform Vendor and Purchaser Risk Act which has been adopted in a number of

---

[55] Sewell v. Underhill, 197 N.Y. 168, 90 N.E. 430 (1910).

It is necessary to distinguish, however, that even in jurisdictions following the majority rule, the contract may relieve the purchaser from the risk or burden by requiring that the property be conveyed to him in its original condition. See, e.g., Marks v. Tichenor, 85 Ky. 536, 4 S.W. 225 (1887); Brownell v. Bd. of Education, 239 N.Y. 369, 146 N.E. 630 (1925), noted 10 Cornell L.Q. 379 (1925).

Recent criticism of the "numerical but dwindling majority" rule, see Hirschler & Fleischer, "Risk of Loss in Executory Contracts for Purchase of Lands," 34 Va. L. Rev. 965 (1948). See also 4 Williston, Contracts (1936) Sec. 929; Stone, "Equitable Conversion by Contract," 13 Col. L. Rev. 369 (1913).

[56] Anderson v. Yaworski, 120 Conn. 390, 181 A. 205, 101 A.L.R. 1232 (1935), noted 49 Harv. L. Rev. 497 (1936), 30 Ill. L. Rev. 809 (1936), N.Y.U. L.Q. 492 (1936); Libman v. Levenson, 236 Mass. 221, 128 N.E. 13, 22 A.L.R. 560 (1920); Wilson v. Clark, 60 N.H. 352 (1880); Good v. Jarrard, 93 S.C. 229, 76 S.E. 698 (1912).

But notice that under this view there must be a substantial failure of consideration. Change in value, from the fire or other cause, which is not so great as to be considered material will not justify rescission of the contract. See Hawkes v. Kehoe, 193 Mass. 419, 79 N.E. 766, 9 Ann. Cas. 1053, 10 L.R.A.N.S. 125 (1907).

[57] Collection of cases on who must bear risk of loss, see annotation, 101 A.L.R. 1241, and preceding annotations cited therein.

[58] See Smith v. Phoenix Ins. Co., 91 Cal. 323, 27 P. 738, 25 Am.St.Rep. 191, 13 L.R.A. 475 (1891); Conlon v. Osborn, 161 Cal. 659, 120 P. 755 (1911); Kelly v. Smith, 218 Cal. 543, 24 P.2d 471 (1933), noted 7 So. Calif. L. Rev. 475. But some of the decisions of the intermediate courts of appeal have ignored these decisions and placed the risk of loss on the vendor on the ground of failure of consideration.

states,[59] including California.[60] The gist of this statutory rule is that the risk or burden of substantial or material loss is placed on the party who is in possession of the property at the time of the destruction or loss. This presumably proceeds on the theory that the one in possession has the burden of taking due care of the property and guarding against loss by appropriate forms of insurance.[61] This statutory provision becomes an integral part of the contract, according to the statute, "unless the contract expressly provides otherwise." [62] It is necessary to keep in mind that decisions approving or applying the so-called majority or minority rules may no longer be authority in the particular jurisdiction, by reason of enactment of the Uniform Act, unless to the extent that the loss is not "substantial" or "material." [63]

Under modern business practice, it is probable that any contract relating to the sale of realty or interests therein will provide as to who has the burden of insuring the property and to what extent.[64] In the absence of any such provision, two conflicting rules have prevailed. The first and more equitable is that whichever party

[59] See Uniform Laws Annotated. With minor changes the Act is in force in Hawaii, Michigan, New York, South Dakota, and Wisconsin and now, as well, in California, as mentioned in the text and note following. And see Diller, "Legislation and Risk of Loss Cases," 5 *U. Chi. L. Rev.* 860 (1938); Simpson, "Legislative Changes in Law of Equitable Conversion by Contract," 44 *Yale L.J.* 754 (1935).

[60] See comment, 21 *So. Calif. L. Rev.* 177 (1948).

[61] See Murphy, "Specific Performance with Abatement under Uniform Vendor and Purchaser Risk Act, 11 *Intra. L. Rev.* (N.Y.U.) 79 (1956).
Statutory liability for failure to extinguish forest fire as imposed on purchased, both by reason of being the beneficial owner and the one entitled to possession, see First State Bank v. United States, (1937; 9 Cir.) 92 F.2d 132, noted 26 *Geo. L.J.* 494 (1938).

[62] As to what sort of agreement between vendor and purchaser prevents the statute from becoming an integral part of the contract, see World Exhibit Corp. v. City Bank Farmers Trust Co., 270 App. Div. 654, 61 N.Y.S.2d 889 (1946), aff'd 296 N.Y. 586, 68 N.E.2d 876 (1946), criticized by Simpson, "Equity," *1946 Annual Survey of American Law.*

[63] If the loss is not "substantial or material," is the former judicial rule of the jurisdiction still applicable? Consider World Exhibit Corp. v. City Bank Farmers Trust Co., 270 App. Div. 654, 61 N.Y.S.2d 889 (1946), aff'd 296 N.Y. 586, 68 N.E.2d 876 (1946).

[64] See, *e.g.,* Kelly v. Smith, 218 Cal. 543, 24 P.2d 471 (1933), noted 7 *So. Calif. L. Rev.* 475.
Agreement as to right to insurance proceeds, see Bruce v. Jennings, 190 Ga. 618, 10 S.E.2d 56 (1940).

carries the insurance does so for the benefit of the party who must bear the risk of loss. Where the insurance is carried by the party other than the one having to bear the risk of loss, the proceeds are held in trust for the benefit of the latter party.[65] The other view has determined that the proceeds are the result of a personal contract with the insurer and inure entirely to the benefit of the one who took out the insurance.[66] But even in jurisdictions which have approved this latter view, this may have been negatived by legislation to the contrary.[67]

---

[65] Smith v. Phoenix Ins. Co., 91 Cal. 323, 27 P. 738, 25 Am.St.Rep. 191, 13 L.R.A. 475 (1891); Millville Aerie v. Weatherby, 82 N.J. Eq. 455, 88 A. 847 (1913); Dubin Paper Co. v. Insurance Co. of North America, 361 Pa. 68, 63 A.2d 85 (1949), noted 98 *U. Pa. L. Rev.* 766 (1950); Beattie v. Gay's Express, Inc., 112 Vt. 13, 22 A.2d 169 (1941). And see annotation, 40 A.L.R. 607 (1925); note, 10 *Intra. L. Rev.* (N.Y.U.) 236 (1955).

[66] Brownell v. Bd. of Education, 239 N.Y. 369, 146 N.E. 630 (1925), noted 10 *Cornell L.Q.* 379 (1925).

[67] As in New York.

CHAPTER 13.

DEFENSES TO SPECIFIC PERFORMANCE— DAMAGES

Sec. 94. Nature of defenses.

Much of what has been previously discussed covers matters which constitute defenses to specific performance. Herein, we take up the principles that govern and consideration of matters of defense not previously dealt with under other specific heads.

The specific performance of a contract is not a matter of strict legal right. It is always a matter within the discretion of the court, to be granted or refused according to all the equities in the case.[1] Considerable criticism has been made of the expression or statement that the granting of equitable relief lies in the discretion of the court. Such discretion cannot, of course, be arbitrarily or capriciously exercised. The discretion may be said to exist in relation to determining in whose favor the equities exist, since what one person may consider fair another may not. Once the equities have been determined to exist in favor of one party or the other, the court must then either grant or deny the relief sought.[2]

---

[1] See Merwin, *Principles of Equity* (1895) 406.

[2] "In my judgment, his honour the Chancellor is correct in saying that it is not a matter of course, in all cases, to decree specific performance of contracts. . . .

221

Sec. 95. Hardship and inadequacy of consideration.

Accordingly, although a valid contract has been made, a court of equity will not enforce it if it is a harsh or unconscionable contract. The parties will be left to their remedy and defenses at law.[3] It is also sometimes said that if, without fault of either party, by reason of subsequent events or collateral circumstances, its enforcement would work hardship or injustice to either of the parties, equity will not enforce it,[4] or will enforce it only upon condition that the hardship on the other party be cured or softened by the one in whose favor specific performance is granted.[5] Equally well, however, it has been said that, absent misrepresentation, undue influence or the like, equity will not relieve one from the consequences of a bad bargain since that is a risk that is taken in the making of any contract and that equity cannot act as the guardian of mankind.[6] It is difficult to establish any uniform

---

It requires the exercise of a sound discretion upon a view of all the circumstances. That discretion must, indeed, not be arbitrary and capricious. It must be regulated upon grounds that will make it judicial. . . . If the contract has been entered into by a competent party, and is, in its nature and circumstances, unobjectionable, it is as much a matter of course to decree specific performance, as it is to give damages at law." Seymour v. Delancey, 3 Cow. (N.Y.) 445 (1824).

And see Pomeroy, *Specific Performance* (3d Ed. 1926) Sec. 46.

[3] Campbell Soup Co. v. Wentz, 172 F.2d 80 (1949); Quan v. Kraseman, 84 Cal.App.2d 550, 191 P.2d 16 (1948); Friend v. Lamb, 152 Pa. 529, 25 A. 529, 25 A. 577, 34 Am.St.Rep. 672 (1893).

See note, "Specific Performance of Crop Contracts," [1949] *Wis. L. Rev.* 800.

[4] Speer v. Erie R. Co., 68 N.J. Eq. 615, 60 A. 197 (1904). See Merwin, *Principles of Equity* (1895) 406.

Zoning ordinance enacted after making of contract which prevents purchaser from using property for purposes intended by him is a hardship which may defeat specific performance. Anderson v. Steinway & Sons, 178 App. Div. 507, 165 N.Y.S. 608 (1917), aff'd 221 N.Y. 639, 117 N.E. 575 (1917); Clay v. Landreth, 187 Va. 169, 45 S.E.2d 875, 175 A.L.R. 1047 (1948), and annotation thereto, p. 1055.

[5] Watters v. Ryan, 31 S.D. 536, 141 N.W. 359 (1913), conditioning any relief on consent of plaintiff to modification of contract; Fontaine v. Brown County Motors Co., 251 Wis. 433, 29 N.W.2d 744 (1947), noted 46 *Mich. L. Rev.* 981 (1948), requiring payment of appreciation in value as condition.

[6] See Fox v. Spokane International R. Co., 26 Idaho 60, 140 P. 1103 (1914); Knott v. Cutler, 224 N.C. 427, 31 S.E.2d 359 (1944); Lawrence, *Equity Jurisprudence* (1929) Sec. 258.

Hardship does not excuse vendor from performing contract to sell land. Smith v. Farmers State Bank, 390 Ill. 374, 61 N.E.2d 557 (1945), noted U. Chi. L. Rev. 211 (1946).

measure applicable to every instance, since in each case the court will be influenced in reaching its decision by what it conceives to be the equities present in the individual case.[7]   Frequently, where severe hardship develops by reason of subsequent events, the court by the exercise of hindsight will declare that the contract in its inception was a harsh and unconscionable one.[8]

However, mere change in value while the contract is executory does not warrant refusal of performance, since adequacy or fairness of consideration is determined as of the date the contract was made.[9]   And even in determining adequacy or fairness of consideration as of that date, actual value may not be conclusive.   Equity considers the circumstances under which the contract was made and gives due weight to such things as love and affection, which may influence the fixing of a price or value actually inconsistent with actual value.[10]   Inadequacy of consideration as a defense will usually be found to exist in connection with other matters, such as fraud or undue influence or taking advantage of dire necessity.[11] Indeed, it has been held that mere inadequacy of consideration alone, merely in the sense that the situation is describable as a bad bargain, is not a defense.   It must appear that the contract was unfairly procured by overreaching or the like on the part of the plaintiff or the consideration must be so inadequate as to amount to evidence of fraud.[12]   However, in some jurisdictions inadequacy of consideration alone is described as a defense to specific performance, and if it is determined that inadequacy of consideration

---

[7] In Lawrence, *Equity Jurisprudence* (1929) Sec. 258, the author remarks on the vagueness of the language frequently employed and states that the facts disclosed in each case in which specific performance is denied invariably reveal well established equitable grounds for such refusal.   And see Glenn, "Oppressive Bargains," 19 *Va. L. Rev.* 594 (1932).

[8] See, *e.g.*, Jacklich v. Baer, 57 Cal.App.2d 684, 135 P.2d 179 (1943), involving Max Baer, former prizefighter.

[9] O'Connell v. Lampe, 206 Cal. 282, 274 P. 336 (1929).

[10] See Pound, "Consideration in Equity," 13 *Ill. L. Rev.* 667 (1919), setting out certain established situations in which agreements or promises are enforceable despite an absence of consideration, including declarations of trust and parol gifts of land where donee has taken possession and acted on the gift.

[11] See Woolums v. Horsley, 93 Ky. 582, 20 S.W. 781 (1892).

Mental weakness and lack of business experience of defendant.   Wilson v. Bergman, 112 Neb. 145, 198 N.W. 671 (1924).

[12] Knott v. Cutler, 224 N.C. 427, 31 S.E.2d 359 (1944).

existed at the time of executing the contract, equity will refuse specific performance.[13]

In the case of an option to purchase, it is generally considered that such option may be supported by any valuable consideration, however small. Of course, once there is an election to exercise the option, the consideration for the property itself must be adequate to support the contract.[14]

Sec. 96. Fraud, undue influence, and mistake.

Fraud and undue influence in themselves, of course, will constitute defenses to specific performance.[15] Indeed, fraud in equity does not require scienter as in law.[16] And unfair conduct, although not sufficiently extreme to qualify as fraud to warrant an equitable suit to rescind a contract, may be sufficiently inequitable to constitute a defense to a suit for specific performance.[17]

Mistake may also constitute a defense to a suit for specific performance. This does not mean mistake of the type wherein the instrument designed to express the intention of the parties does not express their intention or does not express it accurately. The proper remedy there is reformation of the instrument to accord

---

[13] O'Hara v. Wattson, 172 Cal. 525, 157 P. 608 (1916), noted 15 *Mich. L. Rev.* 183 (1917).

See notes, "Inadequacy of Consideration Alone as Defense to Suits for Specific Performance," 25 *Va. L. Rev.* 834 (1939); "Inadequacy of Consideration as Defense in Suit for Specific Performance," 42 *Cal. L. Rev.* 345 (1954).

[14] See, *e.g.,* Marsh v. Lott, 8 Cal. App. 384, 97 P. 163 (1908).

[15] Although the fraud does not injure the defendant but instead one not a party to the contract, equity will refuse to give its aid to enforce performance in the plaintiff's favor. Kelly v. Central P. R. Co., 74 Cal. 557, 16 P. 386, 5 Am.St.Rep. 470 (1888). It may be noticed that the defense of unclean hands may also be advanced in this situation.

[16] See New York Life Ins. Co. v. Marotta, (1932; 3 Cir.) 32 F.2d 1038, that fraud in the equitable sense was properly allowable to be set up in defense of an action to recover on life insurance policies, in effect, of course, an action for performance by the defendant insurer.

[17] Woolums v. Horsley, 93 Ky. 582, 20 S.W. 781 (1892); Banaghan v. Malaney, 200 Mass. 46, 85 N.E. 839, 128 Am.St.Rep. 378, 19 L.R.A.N.S. 871 (1908) (nondisclosure, lack of business experience, and prevention of obtaining advice). See also Cathcart v. Robinson, 5 Pet. (U.S.) 264, 8 L. Ed. 120 (1831), per Marshall, C. J.; Knott v. Cutler, 224 N.C. 427, 31 S.E.2d 359 (1944).

One making honest but false representations declared to come into court with unclean hands. Wisherd v. Bollinger, 293 Ill. 357, 127 N.E. 657 (1920).

Non-disclosure not sufficient to defeat specific performance. Standard Steel Car Co. v. Stamm, 207 Pa. 419, 56 A. 954 (1904).

with their intention and its enforcement as so reformed.[17a]   In a sense, specific performance is defeated, but only of the terms of the inaccurate instrument.[18]   Rather the mistake is of a type or nature which defeats entirely a suit for specific performance.   This may be on the ground that the minds of the parties have not met so as to create a contract,[19] or that they entered into the contract in unconscious ignorance or forgetfulness of a fact, past or present, material to the contract,[20] or in the belief either in the present or past existence of a thing material to the contract which does not or has not existed.[21]   Where there is no fraud or misrepresentation, the terms of the contract are not ambiguous, and the defendant is a mature man of at least ordinary intelligence and business experience, the defendant cannot defeat performance on the ground of mistake in that he did not understand the meaning of the contract.[22]

It may be observed, briefly, that where an honest but false representation induces entry into a contract, which would not have been entered into except for such representation, the situation may be described as fraud in equity as well as mistake.[23]

Sec. 97.   Illegality or impossibility.

A contract will not be enforced, of course, if it goes upon an illegal consideration or would result in violation of law or its tendency is contrary to the design of public policy.[24]   In some situations in which the court of equity has assumed jurisdiction because the case has appeared to be one proper for the exercise of

---

17a See *infra* Sec. 101.

18 See Born v. Schrenkeisen, 110 N.Y. 55, 17 N.E. 339 (1888).

19 Burkhalter v. Jones, 32 Kan. 5 (1884).

Valuable building site not intended to be included by defendant vendor whose sale price was based on its exclusion from property sold.   Mansfield v. Sherman, 81 Me. 365, 17 A. 300 (1889).   Similarly, see Chute v. Quincy, 156 Mass. 189, 30 N.E. 550 (1892).

Criticism, see Chafee and Simpson, *Cases on Equity* (2d Ed. 1946) 676.

20 See Printz v. McLeod, 128 Va. 471, 104 S.E. 818 (1920).

21 See Smith v. Zimbalist, 2 Cal.App.2d 324, 38 P.2d 170 (1934), noted 10 *Tulane L. Rev.* 147 (1935), 9 *So. Calif. L. Rev.* 169 (1935).

22 Caldwell v. Depew, 40 Minn. 528, 42 N.W. 479 (1889).

23 A situation of frequent occurrence is that wherein the vendor honestly but falsely, in other words, mistakenly, represents that the tract of land is greater in quantity than it actually is and the price is based thereon.

24 Kreamer v. Earl, 91 Cal. 112, 27 P. 735 (1891).

equity jurisdiction, it develops that specific performance is impracticable or impossible. Although equity will retain jurisdiction to render such relief as is possible, as by determination and award of damages, this impracticability or impossibility of performance may be described as being a defense.[25] Performance may be impossible, for instance, because it is discovered that before or pending suit, the defendant has conveyed the property in question to a bona fide purchaser from whom it may not be recovered.[26] Or it may develop that the defendant never had the property or never obtained the property which he contracted to convey.[27] Performance may also be impossible due to war or economic conditions, under the so-called doctrine of frustration or commercial frustration. The performance may merely be temporarily impossible, in which case performance may be compelled after the removal of the frustrating cause. On the other hand, the delay may have been such as to render performance impossible after removal of the frustrating cause because of changed circumstances which impose hardship or would require performance on terms never originally contemplated or intended.[28]

Sec. 98.   Unclean hands, laches, and limitation of actions.

Certain of the defenses of an equitable nature, such as laches and unclean hands, discussed previously with reference to suits to enjoin torts, will lie equally in suits for specific performance of contracts. Since the principles are the same in either kind of suit, it is unnecessary to discuss these defenses again.[29] Where statutes of limita-

---

[25] Damages in lieu of specific performance, see *infra*, Sec. 99.

[26] See, *e.g.*, Haughwout v. Murphy, 22 N.J. Eq. 531 (1871); Flackhamer v. Himes, 24 R.I. 306, 53 A. 46 (1902).

Seller of stock who does not own stock he has contracted to sell, see annotation, 22 A.L.R. 1072.

[27] Situation where vendor has equitable interest under contract of purchase which he, in turn, has with another, see Miller v. Dyer, 20 Cal.2d 526, 127 P.2d 901, 141 A.L.R. 1428 (1942), and annotation thereto, p. 1432.

Partial performance with compensation, see *supra*, Sec. 83.

[28] See Village of Minnesota v. Fairbanks, Morse & Co., 226 Minn. 1, 31 N.W.2d 920 (1948), noted 47 *Mich. L. Rev.* 117 (1948).

See note, 19 *So. Calif. L. Rev.* 439 (1947), as to temporary or complete impossibility of performance; Shelton, "Contract Performance and Temporary Impossibility," 5 *S.W.L.J.* 462 (1951).

Frustration of leases, see comment note, 33 *Va. L. Rev.* 488 (1937).

[29] See *supra*, Sec. 24.

tion apply expressly or by implication to equitable suits to enforce contracts, the running of the period of limitations may constitute a defense.[30]

Sec. 99. Damages in addition to or in lieu of specific performance.

Formerly, where law and equity were administered in separate courts, a bill or petition filed in equity was dismissed where the court determined that an adequate remedy at law existed. Under modern code merger of law and equity jurisdiction in the same court and in one form of civil action, dismissal does not result from the determination of the court that the case is not one properly calling for the exercise of equity jurisdiction because of the adequacy of a remedy at law in damages. Amendment of the complaint to seek purely legal relief is sometimes required, but even this should be unnecessary under code provisions authorizing the court to grant any relief consistent with the case made by the complaint and embraced within the issue developed by the complaint and answer.[31] The point is that the action becomes one at law for damages with a jury impaneled, where a jury is requested by the defendant.[32]

Discussion of unclean hands doctrine, see Chafee, "Coming Into Equity with Unclean Hands," 47 *Mich. L. Rev.* 877, 891 (1949).

Illustration of laches in specific performance suit, see Cook v. Stafford, 86 Mich. 163, 48 N.W. 785 (1891). Detailed discussion of laches, see Maguire v. Hibernia Sav. & L. Soc., 23 Cal.2d 719, 146 P.2d 673, 151 A.L.R. 1062 (1944).

[30] See Peixouto v. Peixouto, 40 Cal. App. 782, 181 P. 830 (1919) (where statute had not run).

See also, *supra,* Sec. 24.

[31] Walsh v. Macaire, 102 Cal.App.2d 435, 277 P.2d 517 (1951).

See Helvestine v. Helvestine, 67 App. D. C. 121, 89 F.2d 970 (1937), that "It is settled law that 'if the plaintiff should mistake the relief, to which he is entitled in special prayer, the court may yet afford him the relief, to which he has a right, under the prayer of general relief, provided it is such relief as is agreeable to the case made by the bill.' "

In Jackson v. Strong, 222 N.Y. 149, 118 N.E. 512 (1917), the court declared that "the weight of authority is that where some ground of equitable jurisdiction is alleged in a complaint but fails of proof in its entire scope on the trial, and it appears that there never was any substantial cause for equitable interference, the court will not retain the action and grant purely legal relief, but will dismiss the complaint." This may very well be true where the plaintiff's case is so lacking in merit as not to entitle him to any relief. But that was far from true in the instant case.

[32] See, *e.g.*, Pugh v. Tidwell, 52 N.M. 386, 199 P.2d 1001 (1948).

However, if the court has determined that no adequate remedy at law exists and assumes equity jurisdiction of the cause and then discovers that specific performance of the contract is not practicable or possible, it retains the case in equity and determines and awards such relief in the way of damages as the merits of the plaintiff's case call for.[33]   This result may follow even where the plaintiff voluntarily abandons his request for equitable relief and merely asks for damages, provided the suit was brought in good faith.[34]   The foregoing matters are frequently true even where law and equity are administered in separate courts.[35]   This is pursuant to application of the equitable maxim or principle that once equity has assumed jurisdiction, it will retain jurisdiction to give complete relief or at least such relief as is possible, thus saving the plaintiff the necessity of additional litigation.   It is true, however, that some courts, in code states, have been confused in this situation and have considered the situation to be the same as that in which it is originally determined that the cause is properly one for law instead of equity and, accordingly, have tried the question of damages as

---

In Barlow v. Scott, 24 N.Y. 40 (1861), the complaint, seeking specific performance, showed in itself that performance was impossible. It was held competent for the court to grant any relief consistent with the case made by the complaint and embraced within the issue. To the objection of the defendant, on appeal, that it was error for the trial court to determine and award damages itself, without a jury, it was said that there was nothing in the record to show that the action was so tried without the defendant's consent, and that no objection was made at the trial.

[33] "Where, through no fault of the plaintiff, specific performance cannot be decreed, the court having obtained jurisdiction of the subject matter, properly within its cognizance, may grant monetary relief which in an action at law would be by way of damages." Engasser v. Jones, 88 Cal.App.2d 171, 198 P.2d 546 (1948), where a contract for the sale of land was oral but there had been sufficient part performance by the plaintiff to entitle him to specific performance, if feasible.

Where contract for sale of preferred stock was not specific enough in all its terms so as to warrant specific performance, the court could try the issue of and award damages. Gulbenkian v. Gulbenkian, 147 F.2d 173, 158 A.L.R. 990 (1945), noted 31 *Va. L. Rev.* 705 (1945).

And see Levin, "Equitable Clean-Up and the Jury: A Suggested Orientation," 100 *U. Pa. L. Rev.* 320 (1951).

[34] Mantell v. International Plastic Harmonica Corp., 141 N.J. Eq. 379, 55 A.2d 250 (1947), noted 33 *Minn. L. Rev.* 77 (1948).

[35] See note, 31 *Va. L. Rev.* 705 (1945); Durfee, *Cases on Equity* (1928) 94, 95.

In jurisdictions where formerly law and equity were separately administered, see Milkman v. Ordway, 106 Mass. 232 (1870); Mantell v. International Plastic Harmonica Corp. (N.J.), *supra*.

at law, with a jury.   It must be recognized, of course, that where the contract is not proved or where equitable reasons exist for refusing the plaintiff the aid of equity, the court will not retain the case for the purpose of awarding damages.[36]

Where the cause is not only one proper for the exercise of equity jurisdiction but specific performance is practicable, upon the equities being determined to be in the plaintiff's favor, the court may also award damages as supplementary to the equitable relief.[37] This is true both in code states [38] and in jurisdictions where law and equity are administered in separate courts.[39] This, again, is pursuant to application of the equitable maxim or principle that once equity has assumed jurisdiction, it will retain jurisdiction to give complete relief, thus saving the plaintiff from the necessity of additional litigation.   It has been said, however, that equity will not award damages in addition to equitable relief in situations where no action for such damages would lie in a court of law.[40] This is undoubtedly describable as an application of the maxim that "Equity follows the law."

Damages are ordinarily measured as at law, according to the plaintiff's loss.[41]   In the case of specific performance, it will be

---

[36] Failure to prove contract, see Brauer v. Laughlin, 235 Ill. 265, 85 N.E. 283 (1908).

Where specific performance refused because of plaintiff's default, see Findley v. Koch, 126 Iowa 131, 101 N.W. 766 (1904).   But see Bullock v. Adams' Ex'rs, 20 N.J. Eq. 367 (1869).

Where plaintiff knew of inability of defendant to perform, at time he filed suit, see Crouser v. Boice, 51 Cal.App.2d 198, 124 P.2d 358 (1942) (dictum); Kempshall v. Stone, 5 Johns. Ch. (N.Y.) 193 (1821).   But see Barlow v. Scott, 24 N.Y. 40 (1861).

[37] See *Rest. Contracts*, Sec. 365, Comment d.

[38] See Abbott v. The 76 Land & Water Co., 161 Cal. 42, 118 P. 422 (1911), in which, however, plaintiff first sought and obtained specific performance and thereafter brought another action to recover damages alleged to have been suffered through depreciation in value of the property during the first litigation.

Specific performance and award of damages for that part of contract not specifically enforceable, see Walsh v. Macaire, 102 Cal.App.2d 435, 227 P.2d 517 (1951), pointing out power of equity court to award complete relief without necessity of amendment of complaint.

[39] Where law and equity formerly separately administered, see Keppel v. Lehigh Coal & Nav. Co., 200 Pa. 649, 50 A. 302 (1901).

[40] Draper v. J. B. & R. E. Walker, Inc., 115 Utah 358, 204 P.2d 826 (1949) (suit to quiet title).

[41] Measure of recovery by purchaser where vendor unable or refuses to convey, see annotation, 48 A.L.R. 12.

noted that since the specific performance gives the plaintiff exactly what he bargained for, his only actual damage is that resulting from the delay in receiving or obtaining the performance.[42]

Where a plaintiff has elected to accept partial performance, such performance as the defendant can make, with compensation for the part that cannot be performed, the compensation is such as will give the plaintiff a precise equivalent for that which he lost by reason of the defendant's inability to perform in full.[43]

---

[42] Reasonable rental value as legal measure of damages which purchaser suffers from vendor's delay in performance, see Lifton v. Harshman, 90 Cal.App.2d 180, 202 P.2d 858 (1949).

[43] Harsha v. Reid, 45 N.Y. 415 (1871).

Chapter 14.

REFORMATION AND RESCISSION

Sec. 100. In general.
Sec. 101. Reformation.
Sec. 102. Rescission or cancellation.

Sec. 100.   In general.

In the original edition of this work there was no discussion of the equitable remedies of reformation and rescission, since those remedies constitute a large field and are usually the subject matter of independent treatment.   Nor in this edition is it intended to give any detailed and extensive coverage of those remedies.   However, since it is probable that some definition and identification of them may be helpful to the reader, they are referred to briefly at this point.

The terms "reformation" and "rescission" must be distinguished from each other, since they relate to different situations and are not usually alternate remedies as to which a petitioner may choose.[1] They may well be termed mutually exclusive remedies, for if the situation is one warranting the use of one of the remedies, it will usually be the case that the other is not appropriate or available. And while in a broad sense the same grounds, as for instance mistake and fraud, may appear as bases for relief in either remedy, distinction must be made as to their application.   For instance, mistake as to the existence or the quality of the subject matter of a contract (entitling to rescission) must be distinguished from mis-

---

[1] See *infra*, Secs. 101, 102.

take in reducing to writing the agreement or intention of the parties which is fully understood by them (entitling to reformation).[2] And fraud in bringing about the execution of a written instrument or contract (entitling to rescission) should be distinguished from fraud in drafting the instrument or contract whereby it does not express correctly the agreement of the parties (entitling to reformation).[3] Indeed, in the field of fraud, account may have to be taken of the classical common law distinction between fraud in the inducement and fraud in the factum.[4] That the former is ground for rescission seems more or less the uniform view, but whether the latter warranted rescission or warranted reformation has brought about differences of interpretation and application.[5] However, these are not matters which can be pursued further in this work.

Sec. 101. Reformation.

Since the common law did not take notice of the mistakes and omissions that so frequently arise in business affairs and so provided no means of altering or correcting mistakes in written contracts or other written instruments, resort had to be to equity for relief.[6] This brought about the development and existence of the remedy in equity of the suit to reform written contracts or other written instruments so as to make them conform with what the parties thereto had agreed upon,[7] and their enforcement as so reformed.[8]

---

[2] Professor Merwin pointed out that the definition and the true character of mistake is twofold, that it is either "(1) excusable ignorance of some material matter of law or fact by which a party has been led to part with some right or to assume some obligation, or (2) it is an accidental error or omission in a written instrument whereby the instrument fails to express the actual agreement of the parties." Merwin, *Principles of Equity* (1895) 232.

[3] See *infra*, Secs, 101, 102.

[4] In the classical common law practice, fraud in the inducement was defined as misrepresentation concerning the consideration or collateral matters while fraud in the factum was defined as misrepresentation of the character of the instrument itself. See also note, 33 *Va. L. Rev.* 210 (1947).

[5] See Whipple v. Brown Bros. Co., 225 N.Y. 237, 121 N.E. 748 (1919), noted 19 *Col. L. Rev.* 145 (1919).

[6] See *supra*, Sec. 3. In Louisiana, see Diaz, "Reformation of Instruments in Louisiana," 30 *Tulane L. Rev.* 486 (1956).

[7] See Lundborg v. Wolbrink, 331 Mich. 596, 50 N.W.2d 168 (1951), pointing out that a court of equity can, that a court of law cannot, grant relief by reformation of a written instrument on ground of fraud or mutual mistake.

[8] In other words, specific performance of the contract shown to have been agreed to. Notice also that in the code state, in an action at law for money,

The necessity for such relief usually results from mistake in reducing the agreement of the parties to the writing intended to effectuate their agreement,[9] although there have also been situations in which fraudulent conduct of one of the parties has resulted in the writing not properly representing the agreement or intention of the parties.[10]

It must be borne in mind that where the evidence does not establish what the parties originally agreed upon and they are in conflict or dispute as to what their agreement is, there can be no reformation, since to make the writing conform with what one party insists on will be to force on the other party something that the evidence does not establish that he agreed to.[11]

Sec. 102.   Rescission or cancellation.

When we consider the term "rescission," we find involved with it the term "cancellation." Formerly, at least, these terms had somewhat differing meanings although both were applicable to abrogation of an instrument or contract. Rescission was frequently applied to an abrogation by act of the parties and cancellation to abrogation by decree of the court,[12] but in modern practice it seems customary to apply the term rescission to suits to abrogate a transaction or contract.[13]

Equity provides relief by way of a suit to rescind or cancel a written instrument or contract where such instrument has been executed or such contract has been entered into due to fraud, mistake, undue influence or duress, or where the contract is harsh and

---

allegedly based on a contract right, the defendant may present as an equitable defense mistake requiring reformation of the contract, which reformation may then affect the outcome of the action. See Cook, "Equitable Defenses," 32 *Yale L.J.* 645 (1923).

9 Willett v. Stewart, 227 Wis. 303, 277 N.W. 665 (1938).

"To reform an instrument in equity is to make a decree that a deed or other agreement shall be made or construed as it was originally intended by the parties, when an error or mistake as to a fact has been committed." Moore, *Cyc. Law Dict.* (3d Ed.) "Reform."

10 Cleghorn v. Zumwalt, 83 Cal. 155, 23 P. 294 (1890); Holbeck v. Williamson, 255 Mich. 430, 238 N.W. 269 (1931).

11 See Donald Freedman & Co. v. Newman, 255 N.Y. 340, 174 N.E. 703, 73 A.L.R. 95 (1931), noted 16 *Cornell L.Q.* 390, 44 *Harv. L. Rev.* 866, 40 *Yale L.J.* 795.

12 See Moore, *Cyc. Law Dict.* (3d Ed.) "Rescission of Contracts."

13 See, *e.g., Callaghan's Wis. Pl. & Pr.* (3d Ed.) de Funiak & Williams, Section 80.02.

inequitable or the like.[14]   This is to be distinguished from the so-called legal rescission in which the plaintiff has supposedly already rescinded by restoring or offering to restore the consideration he had received and is now suing at law to recover the money or the value of the consideration he gave to the other party and which the latter is now wrongfully withholding.   In the equity suit, the plaintiff has not himself rescinded but petitions the court to order rescission and the restoration to him of what he has parted with.[15] Of course, in equity also, restitution to the opposite party is required as a usual condition of relief to the plaintiff [16] but circumstances may make a formal tender unnecessary prior to filing suit,[17] and indeed it is frequently considered that bringing the suit in equity is in effect a tender [18] or else that tender is unnecessary because the decree in equity can be conditioned on restitution.[19]

In the field of mistake, where that is the ground of relief, much importance is usually attached to whether the mistake is one of fact or of law [20] and whether the mistake is describable as mutual or unilateral.[21]   It has been customary to state as a rule that equity does not give relief from a mistake of law,[22] but in actuality there have been numerous exceptions to such rule [23] and in some jurisdictions by reason of statute relief is as much available for mistake of

---

[14] Kelley v. Tomahawk Motor Co., 206 Wis. 568, 240 N.W. 141 (1932).

[15] See Mueller v. Michels, 184 Wis. 342, 197 N.W. 201, 199 N.W. 380 (1924). Rescission at law and in equity, see also comment, 36 *Cal. L. Rev.* 606 (1948).

[16] Kundel v. Portz, 301 Mich. 195, 3 N.W.2d 61 (1942).

[17] Actual restoration in specie may be impossible. This is of no moment since all that is necessary is that one party shall be placed in substantially his original position and that the other shall derive no unconscionable advantage from his conduct. Bayse v. Paola Refining Co., 79 Kan. 755, 101 P. 658 (1909).

[18] Touma v. Holly Lumber & Supply Co., 294 Mich. 96, 292 N.W. 576 (1940).

[19] De Blouw v. Ramm & Co., 284 Mich. 589, 279 N.W. 919 (1938).

[20] Mistake of law has been defined as an erroneous conclusion as to the legal effect of known facts. See Moore, *Cyc. Law Dict.* (3d Ed.).

[21] Mutual mistake has been defined in equity as a mistake common to all the parties to a written contract or instrument. See Moore, *Cyc. Law Dict.* (3d Ed.). Unilateral mistake, of course, is mistake by one party only. It is to be noticed that mistake on one side only and fraud on the other side is equivalent to mutual mistake.

[22] Numerous writers have called attention to this. See, *e.g.*, Lawrence, *Equity Jurisprudence* (1929), Secs. 105, 106, 304, 305; McClintock, *Principles of Equity* (2d Ed.) 248 ff.

[23] See preceding note. Evasion of or escape from effect of the rule is common among American courts. See, *e.g.*, Bronson v. Leibold, 87 Conn. 293, 87 A. 979 (1913); Reggio v. Warren, 207 Mass. 525, 93 N.E. 805 (1911).

law as for mistake of fact.[24]   Somewhat similarly, while it has been common to state that equity relieves only in the case of a mutual mistake,[25] there actually are frequent exceptions to this.[26]

In the field of fraud, what is fraud in equity must be distinguished from fraud at law.   Fraud has a broader meaning in equity and intention to defraud or to misrepresent is not a necessary element.   The primary matter is whether one has been misled to his injury in respect of a material matter, having a right to rely on the representation.[27]

---

[24] Hannah v. Steinman, 159 Cal. 142, 112 P. 1094 (1911).

[25] Mistake must be mutual, material, and not induced by negligence, see Cleghorn v. Zumwalt, 83 Cal. 155, 23 P. 294 (1890).

[26] Mistake said not to be mutual but both parties "separately" mistaken, see Page v. Higgins, 150 Mass. 27, 22 N.E. 63 (1889); Crowe v. Lewin, 95 N.Y. 423 (1884). Rescission where mistake described as unilateral, see St. Nicholas Church v. Kropp, 135 Minn. 115, 160 N.W. 500 (1916). And see discussions, McClintock, 28 *Minn. L. Rev.* 460 (1944); Abbot, 23 *Harv. L. Rev.* 608 (1910); Patterson, 28 *Col. L. Rev.* 859 (1928).

[27] See, *e.g.*, McClintock, *Principles of Equity* (2d Ed.) 216; 2 Pomeroy, *Equity Jurisprudence*, Sec. 887; Walsh, *Treatise on Equity* (1930) 493 ff.

Liability and remedies for innocent misrepresentation, see note, 46 *Mich. L. Rev.* 810 (1948).

CHAPTER 15.

OTHER EQUITABLE REMEDIES OR
FORMS OF RELIEF

Sec. 103. In general.

Equitable remedies to prevent injury, to compel performance of contracts, and to correct or cancel written instruments have already been given attention. Occasion for and pursuit of such remedies constitute the bulk of equity's exercise of jurisdiction, although not, of course, including all of the remedies peculiar to a court of equity. There are, as may be surmised, many remedies of a special and limited character, developed to provide relief in situations where no adequate remedy at law exists.

Such equitable remedies have included such matters as the bill or proceeding to discover evidence,[1] suits for an accounting,[2] suits

---

[1] The so-called bill of discovery has been described as a proceeding brought to obtain from the defendant a disclosure of material facts or documents to be used as evidence in another suit between the same parties. This may also include use of the bill by a creditor against a debtor for discovery of assets and for relief where the creditor has exhausted his remedy at law. Merwin, *Principles of Equity* (1895) 474 ff. See also James, "Discovery," 38 *Yale L.J.* 746 (1929); Freedman, "Discovery as an Instrument of Justice," 22 *Temple L.Q.* 174 (1948); Speck, "Use of Discovery in United States District Courts," 60 *Yale L.J.* 132 (1951).

[2] Suit in equity for accounting lies where there is some special and substantial

for contribution,[3] or subrogation,[4] the so-called creditor's bill or suit,[5] the bill or suit to remove a cloud upon the title to property or to quiet title to property,[6] the bill quia timet,[7] the bill of peace,[8] the bill of interpleader,[9] and others.[10] Because of their special or particular nature or application, many of these equitable remedies are dealt with in the law schools and in the legal encyclopedias under other headings than equity, particularly at the present day. Nevertheless, to give the reader some indication of the extent and variety of the equitable remedies, some of these special and particular remedies are briefly defined or explained in this section and the sections following.

Sec. 104.   Contribution.

Where two or more parties have assumed, in company with each other, the whole of a liability, as where two or more are co-sureties for a principal, and one of these parties has paid the whole

---

ground for equity jurisdiction and the remedy at law is inadequate. Some of the grounds for equity jurisdiction are existence of a fiduciary or trust relationship, the need of discovery, or the complicated character of the accounts. Oconto County v. Carey, 183 Wis. 420, 198 N.W. 590 (1924). See also Merwin, *Principles of Equity* (1895) 311 ff.

3 See *infra*, Sec. 104.

4 See *infra*, Sec. 105.

5 "Whenever a creditor has obtained a judgment at law, and execution issued upon the judgment has been returned unsatisfied for want of property which can be seized at law, equity will assist the creditor to reach and apply to his debt any other property of the debtor not attachable at law; and this it does by what is called a creditor's bill." Merwin, *Principles of Equity* (1895) 387. Further as to such matter, see courses and treatises dealing with creditors' rights.

6 At the present day such remedies are customarily treated in courses and treatises relating to real property. Discussion, see Howard, "Bills to Remove Cloud from Title," 25 *W. Va. L.Q.* 4 (1917).

7 See *infra*, Sec. 106.

8 See *infra*, Sec. 107.

9 See *infra*, Sec. 108.

10 For example, "marshalling assets," which relates to this type of situation: Creditor *A* has the right to resort to either of two distinct funds while creditor *B* has the right to resort to only one specific fund; *A* will be required to resort to the fund which is not subject to *B* and is not permitted to resort primarily to the fund which is subject to *B*, thus leaving *B* an opportunity of settling his claim.

Many of the present-day casebooks and treatises on equity list among the miscellaneous equitable remedies the declaratory judgment. This is actually a statutory remedy but in a broad way may be classed as equitable in nature since its purpose is really to prevent future difficulties or losses. See Borchard, *Declaratory Judgments;* Clark, *Code Pleading* (2d Ed.) 333 ff.; Cyc. Fed. Proc. (3d Ed.) Ch. 90.

of the debt or more than his share of it, he has a right to recover from the others their proportionate share of the amount so paid by him. His right to receive and their duty to pay such share are comprehended within the term "contribution."[11] It has been said that this right of contribution does not depend upon agreement among those jointly obligated but is an equitable right growing out of the relation of the parties and that the law attaches the duty and implies the promise to contribute.[12] Other language is to the effect that contribution in equity does not depend upon joint liability or upon an implied agreement but is founded on the principle that equality of burden as to a common right is equity.[13]

Inasmuch as it has been said that the duty to contribute is attached to or implied by law and the recovery sought is the payment of money, it may well be asked if there is not an adequate remedy at law which makes the interposition of equity unnecessary. However, the enforcement of the principle of contribution seems to be considered particularly a matter for equity and it is said that the mere fact that there is a remedy at law does not take away the right to contribution in equity.[14] It must be noted that when law and equity are administered in separate courts, at law the action has to be against each joint obligor separately for his aliquot part only. In equity, the one paying may unite all those who ought to contribute and, moreover, if one or more of the joint obligors or co-contractors are insolvent, full recovery can be apportioned against and had from the solvent ones.[15] Similarly, if some of the joint obligors or co-contractors are out of the state, recovery can be apportioned against and had from the solvent ones within the

---

[11] Merwin, *Principles of Equity* (1895) 321. Likewise, see Moore, *Cyc. Law Dict.* (3d Ed.), "Contribution"; Lawrence, *Equity Jurisprudence* (1939) Sec. 742 ff.; Bispham, *Principles of Equity* (10th Ed.) Sec. 328 ff.

One paying more than his share of a joint obligation may recover contribution from his joint obligor. Lorimer v. Julius Knack Coal Co., 246 Mich. 214, 224 N.W. 362 (1929).

[12] Lawrence, *Equity Jurisprudence* (1929) Sec. 743; Merwin, *Principles of Equity* (1895) 321.

Oral agreement between joint obligors as to extent of liability inter se, see annotation, 65 A.L.R. 822.

[13] Lex v. Selway Steel Corp., 203 Iowa 792, 206 N.W. 586 (1925).

[14] Peter (Werborn's Adm'r) v. Kahn, 93 Ala. 201, 9 So. 729 (1890).

[15] Lorimer v. Julius Knack Coal Co., 246 Mich. 214, 224 N.W. 362 (1929); Merwin, *Principles of Equity* (1895) 323.

Proportion of obligation enforceable by way of contribution between joint obligors, see annotation, 64 A.L.R. 213.

state.[16] Certainly, at the present day, where the code or statutes of a state have provided for one form of action and merged legal and equitable powers in one court, there would seem to be no reason why the one who has paid may not sue all the solvent ones in an action at law and recover of them as if they were all those who were bound.[17]

Since the application of this principle of contribution may arise among partners, joint executors or administrators, joint owners of property, sureties and indorsers, and in many other relationships, it will be noticed that it will recur in a number of courses or topics. The question of contribution among joint tortfeasors is customarily dealt with under the head of "Torts" and so is not treated here.[18]

Sec. 105. Subrogation.

The doctrine or right of subrogation has been defined as follows: One who has been obliged to pay the debt of another is in equity entitled to succeed to the protection of all the securities held by the creditor for the payment of such debt. This may apply to the situation in which one has paid the debt of another as his surety or because the payer's own property is subject to some prior lien or encumbrance for the debt.[19] While this principle of subrogation is of equitable origin and exists to bring about equitable results independent of any agreement,[20] the right of subrogation may also be based upon an agreement therefor, known as "conventional (i.e., contractual) subrogation."[21] At the present day, particularly in the so-called code states, the right of subrogation may be recognized in law as well as in equity.[22]

---

[16] Merwin, *Principles of Equity* (1895) 323.

[17] Faurot v. Gates, 86 Wis. 569, 57 N.W. 294 (1893).

[18] Contributions among joint tortfeasors, see annotation, 1 N.C.C.A. (N.S.) 373; Prosser, *Torts* (2d Ed.).

[19] Merwin, *Principles of Equity* (1895) 324 ff. See also Bispham, *Principles of Equity* (10th Ed.) Sec. 338 ff.; Lawrence, *Equity Jurisprudence* (1929) Sec. 621 ff., Moore, *Cyc. Law Dict.* (3d Ed.), "Subrogation."

[20] Smith v. Sprague, 244 Mich. 577, 222 N.W. 207 (1929).

Use of subrogation to bring about marshalling of assets or securities, see Bispham, *Principles of Equity* (10th Ed.) Sec. 341.

[21] Home Owners' Loan Corp. v. Rupe, 225 Iowa 1044, 283 N.W. 108 (1938).

[22] Black v. Chicago Great Western R. Co., 187 Iowa 904, 174 N.W. 774 (1919); Plate Glass, etc., Co. v. Ridgewood Realty Co., 219 Mo. App. 186, 269 S.W. 659 (1925).

The nature and kind of debts and liens subject to subrogation and the persons in various relationships who are entitled to subrogation are matters which may be pursued more at length in treatises on the subject of subrogation.[23]

Sec. 106. Bill quia timet.

The bill quia timet (in the Latin, "because he fears") has been the subject of somewhat varying explanation among the writers. For instance, the late Professor Walsh, in his discussion, puts more stress on it as a remedy needed and used where law and equity are administered in separate courts, in the following situation. The plaintiff seeking the equitable relief has, in the eyes of equity, a valid defense to a right of action at law which the equity defendant has filed at law or will do so but which defense the court of law will not allow to be introduced.[24]   Presently, in the modern code state, where there is but one form of civil action and legal and equitable procedure and powers are merged, an equitable defense can be availed of in an action at law.[25]   Hence the necessity of the bill quia timet, in the sense of a separate suit or proceeding, becomes somewhat rare.[26]

Discussion by other writers, such as Bispham, is on the broad basis that the bill quia timet is a remedy to protect rights against future possible injuries or impairment.[27]   Such a broad consideration of remedies where there is reasonable probability of irreparable injury in the future may well include bills to remove clouds from title to property,[28] bills of interpleader,[29] and other such instances.[30]

---

[23] See, *e.g.*, Title Guarantee & Trust Co. v. Haven, 196 N.Y. 487, 89 N.E. 1082, 25 L.R.A.N.S. 1308 (1909), 17 Ann. Cas. 1131 (discharge of tax lien through mistake).

[24] Walsh, *Treatise on Equity* (1930) Sec. 116.

Illustrative case, see Fuller v. Percival, 126 Mass. 381 (1879), described by Professor John Cribbet as one of the best examples of a bill quia timet.

[25] See Hinton, "Equitable Defenses under Modern Codes," 18 *Mich. L. Rev.* 717 (1920).   Merger in United States, see *supra*, Sec. 4.

[26] See, *e.g.*, McHenry v. Hazard, 45 N.Y. 580 (1871).

[27] See Bispham, *Equity Jurisprudence* (10th Ed.) Sec. 588 ff.; Moore, *Cyc. Law Dict.* (3d Ed.), "Bill Quia Timet."

Illustrative case, see well-known case of Vanderbilt v. Mitchell, 72 N.J. Eq. 910, 67 A. 97, 14 L.R.A.N.S. 304 (1907), noted 7 *Col. L. Rev.* 533 (1907), 21 *Harv. L. Rev.* 54 (1907).

[28] See *supra*, Sec. 103.

[29] See *infra*, Sec. 108.

[30] Surrender and cancellation of contracts, see Chafee, *Cases on Equitable Remedies* (1939) Ch. III.

Sec. 107. Bill of peace.

Another ground of equitable jurisdiction, said to be closely related to the subject of interpleader, is the prevention of multiplicity of suits.[31] Thus, the so-called bill of peace originated as a means or remedy of seeking to enjoin repeated attempts to litigate the same right.[32] While there has been dispute as to the extent or application of equity jurisdiction in this regard,[33] the bill of peace has been described as falling into two classifications; one, to enjoin actions by members of a class, each insisting upon the same right, and, two, to enjoin a succession of actions by the same individual upon the same or virtually the same claim.[34]

There is no doubt that development of the equitable principle of preventing multiplicity of actions or suits has presently outgrown the original scope of the bill of peace [35] and the term "bill of peace" is itself rarely used at the present time, particularly in the so-called code states. Discussion is usually in terms of preventing multiplicity of actions or suits.[36]

Sec. 108. Bill of interpleader.

The bill of interpleader is the remedy developed in equity to aid the person innocently in the position of what is called a stakeholder. He is one who owes a debt or holds a certain fund or other personal property and is willing and eager to pay it or hand it over to the creditor or owner entitled to it but there are several claimants, each asserting it is his. The common law offered the stake-

---

[31] Merwin, *Principles of Equity* (1895) 506.

Multiplicity of actions at law, see also *supra*, Sec. 20.

[32] See Moore, *Cyc. Law Dict.* (3d Ed.), "Bill of Peace"; Chafee, *Cases on Equitable Remedies* (1939) Ch. II.

[33] See discussion, American Lead Corp. v. Davis, 111 Ind. App. 242, 38 N.E.2d 281 (1941).

See also Chafee, "Bills of Peace with Multiple Parties," 45 *Harv. L. Rev.* 1297 (1932); Fletcher, "Jurisdiction of Equity Relating to Multiplicity of Suits," 24 *Yale L.J.* 642 (1915).

[34] Bispham, *Principles of Equity* (10th Ed.) Sec. 415.

Use of bills of peace against recurrence of vexatious litigation, whether by numerous class insisting on the same right or by individual reiterating an unsuccessful claim, see State Mut. Rodded Fire Ins. Co. v. Engel, 269 Mich. 348, 257 N.W. 839 (1934).

Multiplicity of tort actions, see note, 25 *Va. L. Rev.* 925 (1938).

[35] Lawrence, *Principles of Equity* (1929) Sec. 1022.

[36] Enjoining multiplicity of actions at law, see *supra*, Sec. 20.

holder no relief, in that if he paid in good faith to one claimant, he might nevertheless be sued by and required to pay another claimant.   And a judgment at law in favor of one claimant against the stakeholder was no defense to an action against the stakeholder by another claimant.   However, in equity the bill or suit of interpleader offers him a remedy in that he may interplead (bring) into one action all of the claimants, turn the money or property over to the court, be himself dismissed from the proceeding, and have the court decide which of the claimants is entitled to the fund or property, as well as ordering or commanding the other claimants not to seek to litigate or enforce their claims against the stakeholder.[37]

To support the strict or true bill of interpleader, the petitioner must himself not set up or claim any interest in the fund or property.   However, equity has developed the bill in the nature of a bill of interpleader, wherein the petitioner does set up some claim or interest but wishes the aid of equity as to the part in which he does not make any claim.[38]

While the equitable remedy of interpleader continues to exist by reason of equitable principles and the equity powers of the courts, it may be noted that Congress and most of the state legislatures have enacted legislation making provision for interpleader.[39]

---

[37] Brown v. Marsh, 98 Fla. 253, 123 So. 762 (1929); Kelly, Shuttlesworth & McManus v. Central Nat. Bank & Trust Co., 217 Iowa 725, 248 N.W. 9, 250 N.W. 171 (1933). See also Merwin, *Principles of Equity* (1895) 501 ff.; Lawrence, *Equity Jurisprudence* (1929) Sec. 923 ff.; Walsh, *Treatise on Equity* (1930) Sec. 119; Chafee, *Cases on Equitable Remedies* (1939) Ch. I.

[38] 2 Story, *Equity Jurisprudence* (1st Ed.) Sec. 824; Groves v. Sentell, 153 U.S. 465, 14 S.Ct. 898, 38 L. Ed. 785 (1894).

[39] See, *e.g., Callaghan's Wis. Pl. & Pr.* (3d Ed.) de Funiak and Williams, Ch. 72; Chafee, "Modernizing Interpleader," 30 *Yale L.J.* 814 (1921).

Interpleader in federal courts, see Chafee, "Federal Interpleader Since the Act of 1936," 49 *Yale L.J.* 377 (1940); Cyc. Fed. Proc. (3d Ed.) Ch. 22.

Constitutionality, construction, and application of federal statutes regarding interpleader by insurance company, see annotation, 106 A.L.R. 626.

TABLE OF CASES

243

INDEX